15

THE RISE OF A VICTORIAN IRONOPOLIS

MIDDLESBROUGH AND REGIONAL INDUSTRIALIZATION

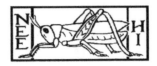

Regions and Regionalism in History

ISSN 1742-8254

This series, published in association with the AHRB Centre for North-East England History (NEEHI), aims to reflect and encourage the increasing academic and popular interest in regions and regionalism in historical perspective. It also seeks to explore the complex historical antecedents of regionalism as it appears in a wide range of international contexts.

Series Editor
Prof. Peter Rushton, Faculty of Education and Society, University of Sunderland

Editorial Board
Dr Joan Allen, School of Historical Studies, Newcastle University
Prof. Don MacRaild, School of Arts and Social Sciences, Northumbria University
Dr Christian Liddy, Department of History, Durham University
Dr Diana Newton, School of Arts and Media, Teesside University

Proposals for future volumes may be sent to the following address:

Prof. Peter Rushton
Department of Social Sciences
Faculty of Education and Society
University of Sunderland
Priestman Building
New Durham Road
Sunderland
SR1 3PZ, UK
Tel: 0191-515-2208
Fax: 0191-515-3415
Peter.rushton@sunderland.ac.uk

Previously published volumes are listed at the back of this book.

THE RISE OF A VICTORIAN IRONOPOLIS

MIDDLESBROUGH AND REGIONAL INDUSTRIALIZATION

MINORU YASUMOTO

THE BOYDELL PRESS

First published 2011
The Boydell Press, Woodbridge

ISBN 978-1-84383-633-9

The Boydell Press is an imprint of Boydell & Brewer Ltd
PO Box 9, Woodbridge, Suffolk IP12 3DF, UK
and of Boydell & Brewer Inc.
668 Mt Hope Avenue, Rochester, NY 14620, USA
website: www.boydellandbrewer.com

The publisher has no responsibility for the continued existence or accuracy
of URLs for external or third-party internet websites referred to in this book,
and does not guarantee that any content on such websites is, or will remain,
accurate or appropriate.

A CIP record for this book is available
from the British Library

Produced by Toynbee Editorial Services Ltd

Papers used by Boydell & Brewer Ltd are natural, recyclable products
made from wood grown in sustainable forests

Printed in Great Britain by
CPI Antony Rowe, Chippenham and Eastbourne

Contents

List of Illustrations   vi

Preface   xi

Acknowledgements   xv

1   Town Planning and the Birth of Middlesbrough   1

2   Industrial Agglomeration in the Cleveland Iron and Steel Industry   28

3   Demography and Urban Growth   61

4   The Labour Market in Cleveland Iron and Steel   110

5   Welfare Provision in Mid-Victorian Middlesbrough   157

6   Conclusion   188

Appendices   200

Sources and Bibliography   213

Index   227

List of Illustrations

Plates

1.1.	Middlesbrough in 1832	7
1.2.	The old Town Hall	23
1.3.	The new Town Hall	27
5.1.	North Ormesby Hospital, c.1900	158
5.2.	North Riding Infirmary	180

Maps

1.1.	Middlesbrough in 1845	8
1.2.	Middlesbrough in 1857	9
1.3.	Middlesbrough in 1882	15
2.1.	Cleveland Iron Store Yards, 1895	50
2.2.	Agglomeration and Product Specialization in Ironmaster's District	54

Figures and Tables

1.1.	General Balance Sheets of the Owners of the Middlesbrough Estate, 1845	5
1.2.	Occupations and Birthplaces of Middlesbrough Population, 1841	10
1.3.	Rateable Value of Middlesbrough, 1846–80	11
1.4.	Rateable Value and Estimated Rentals in Middlesbrough, 1865–86	12
1.5.	Growth of Houses and Shops in Middlesbrough, 1849–80	12
1.6.	Growth of Houses, Houses with Shops, Shops, Inns and Beerhouses etc. in Middlesbrough, 1849–80	13
1.7.	Private and Company-owned Houses in Middlesbrough, 1849–80	13
1.8.	Number of Houses in Middlesbrough Recorded in Census Returns, 1851–81	14
1.9.	Middlesbrough Improvement Acts, 1856–77	20
1.10.	Revenue of Middlesbrough, 1841–55	22
1.11.	Proportion of Rates to Total Revenue in Middlesbrough, 1841–74	24
1.12.	Revenue and Expenditure of Middlesbrough Borough Council, 1866–74	25
2.1.	Cleveland Ironstone Production, 1873–80	29
2.2.	Pig Iron Production in the North East, United Kingdom and the World, 1860–77	30
2.3.	Pig Iron Production in Cleveland, 1864–80	30
2.4.	Number of Blast Furnaces in the United Kingdom, 1874–77	32
2.5.	World Pig Iron Production, 1876	33
2.6.	Export of Cleveland Pig Iron, 1867–77	37
2.7.	Export of Cleveland Pig Iron from Middlesbrough, 1877–82	38

2.8.   Pig Iron Exports from the United Kingdom and Cleveland,
        1868–82   39
2.9.   Coastal Sales of Cleveland Pig Iron from Middlesbrough,
        1877–82   39
2.10.   Export of Pig Iron from North-east Ports, 1881–2   40
2.11.   Export and Coastal Sales of Cleveland Pig Iron from
        Middlesbrough, 1873–80   40
2.12.   Applications for Shares in the Middlesbrough Exchange, 1864–8 47
2.13.   Product Specialization in Cleveland Iron and Steel, 1870   55
2.14.   Wrought Iron Production in Middlesbrough, 1873   56
2.15.   Number of Blast Furnaces, Pig and Wrought Iron Production per
        Week in Middlesbrough, 1856–61   56
2.16.   Number of Blast Furnaces in Middlesbrough, 1873   57
2.17.   Number of Puddling Furnaces, Rolling Mills and Forges in
        Middlesbrough, 1873   57
2.18.   Industrial Agglomeration in Cleveland, Late-nineteenth and
        Early-twentieth Centuries   59
3.1.   Population of Middlesbrough and Linthorpe, 1801–81   62
3.2.   Age Structure of the Middlesbrough Population, 1851–81   64
3.3.   Migrants in Selected Industrial Towns in England, 1871,
        with Sex Ratio   65
3.4.   Sex Ratio of Middlesbrough, 1851–81   66
3.5.   Population of 15 Large Towns and Middlesbrough, 1881   68
3.6.   Causes of Death in 15 Large Towns and Middlesbrough, 1881   70
3.7.   Migration in Middlesbrough, 1851–61   74
3.8.   Migration in Middlesbrough, 1861–71   75
3.9.   Age-specific In-migration Rates in Middlesbrough, 1851–61   77
3.10.   Age-specific In-migration Rates in Middlesbrough, 1861–71   77
3.11.   Age Structure of In-migrants to Middlesbrough, 1851–61
        and 1861–71   78
3.12.   Age-specific Out-migration Rates from Middlesbrough, 1851–61 80
3.13.   Age-specific Out-migration Rates from Middlesbrough, 1861–71 81
3.14.   Age-specific Mortality in Middlesbrough, 1875–81   82
3.15.   Middlesbrough Out-migration Rates (Male) Adjusted
        to Reflect Deaths, 1851–61   83
3.16.   Middlesbrough Out-migration Rates (Male) Adjusted
        to Reflect Deaths, 1861–71   83
3.17.   Relationship to Heads of Households of In-migrant, Persistent and
        Out-migrant Population of Middlesbrough, 1851–61 and 1861–71 84
3.18.   Age-specific Proportion Ever Married of In-migrants and
        Persistent Population of Middlesbrough, 1851–61 and 1861–71 86
3.19.   Age-specific Net Migration in Middlebrough, 1851–61
        and 1861–71   88
3.20.   Age Structure of In-migrants, 1851–61, living in Middlesbrough
        in 1871   89

3.21. Male In-migrants to Middlesbrough, 1851–61, from Elsewhere
       in the United Kingdom, and Re-migration Rate, 1861–71   90
3.22. Male In-migrants from English Counties, 1851–61, and
       Re-migration Rate, 1861–71   91
3.23. Persistence by Occupation (Male), 1861–71   92
3.24. Persistence of Male In-migrants from the North East and Other
       Counties of England, 1861–71   96
3.25. Persistence of Native-born and In-migrants (Male) in
       Middlesbrough, 1851–71   97
3.26. Birth Countries of Wives of Irish-, Welsh- and Scottish-born
       Men in Middlesbrough in 1861   99
3.27. Birthplaces of the First to Seventh Surviving Co-resident
       Offspring of Irish, Welsh and Scottish Parents in 1861   100
3.28. Stepwise Migration to Middlesbrough: Birthplaces of
       In-migrating English Male Household Heads, 1861   101
3.29. Stepwise Migration to Middlesbrough: Birthplaces of Wives of
       In-migrating English Male Household Heads, 1861   102
3.30. Stepwise Migration to Middlesbrough: Birthplaces of Surviving
       Co-resident Children of English-born Household Heads, 1861   103
3.31. Crimes by Migrants According to Duration of Stay in
       Middlesbrough, 1860s–1880s   105
3.32. Urban Crimes, 1861   106
3.33. Urban Crimes: Arrest Rates for Drunkenness and Minor
       Offences, 1861   108
4.1.   Industrial Structure of Middlesbrough, 1851–81   112
4.2.   Iron and Steel Workers as a Proportion of Middlesbrough's
       Manufacturing Workforce, 1851–81   113
4.3.   Occupational Structure of In- and Out-migrants, 1851–61   116
4.4.   Occupational Structure of In- and Out-migrants, 1861–71   117
4.5.   Birthplaces of In-migrant Ironworkers, 1851–71   118
4.6.   Birthplaces of In-migrant Ironworkers from England, 1851–71 119
4.7.   Marital Status of In-migrant and Persistent Skilled and Semi-
       skilled Workers, 1861–71   120
4.8.   Marital Status and Relationship to Household Head of
       In-migrant Welsh and Irish Puddlers, 1851–71   121
4.9.   Age Structure of In-migrant Welsh and Irish Puddlers, 1851–71 122
4.10. Birthplaces of Offspring of In-migrant Welsh and Irish Puddlers,
       1851–71   123
4.11. Marital Status and Relationship to Household Head of
       Incoming Irish and Non-Irish Labourers, 1861–71   125
4.12. Middlesbrough-born Population Living in England and
       Wales, 1881   127
4.13. Places of Origin of In-migrants, 1861–71, and Residence of
       Middlesbrough-born People, 1881   128

4.14. Irish In-migrants, Persistent Population, and Out-migrants, 1851–71   129

4.15. Sex Ratio of Irish and Non-Irish In-migrants, 1851–71   130

4.16. Out-migration Rates of Irish and Non-Irish Populations in Middlesbrough, 1851–61   130

4.17. Households as Reception Space for Incoming Migrants, 1861–71   132

4.18. Relationship to Household Heads of Incoming Single Relatives, 1861–71   133

4.19. Household and Family Structure of In-migrant Irish and Non-Irish Populations in Middlesbrough, 1861–71   134

4.20. Out-migration Rates of Irish and Non-Irish Iron-workers from Middlesbrough, 1851–71   134

4.21. Out-migration Rates by Occupation of Irish and Non-Irish Populations from Middlesbrough, 1861–71   135

4.22. Life-course Changes in Occupation of Persistent Irish and Non-Irish Labourers, 1861–71   136

4.23. Origins and Destinations of Migrant Engineers, 1868   140

4.24. Migrant Engineers, 1868   141

4.25. Mobility Pattern of James Alexander, 1868   141

4.26. Mobility Pattern of Richard Schofield, 1868   143

4.27. Mobility Pattern of Charles Mordue, Middlesbrough Engine-smith, 1866–67   144

4.28. Origins and Destinations of Migrant Engineers of ASE Middlesbrough Branch, 1865–72   145

4.29. Wage Rates in Cleveland District, Staffordshire and Wales, 1866   147

4.30. Wage Rates in the North of England and Belgium in 1866   147

4.31. Formation of Indigenous Labour Market in Middlesbrough Persistent Skilled and Semi-skilled Workers, 1851–61   148

4.32. Formation of Indigenous Labour Market in Middlesbrough Persistent Skilled and Semi-skilled Workers, 1861–71   149

4.33. Indigenous and Exogenous Labour Market in Middlesbrough, 1861 and 1871   150

4.34. Indigenous Labour Market in Middlesbrough, 1851–1861–1871   150

4.35. Out-migration Rates of Skilled and Semi-skilled Workers, 1851–71   151

5.1. Number of Patients in North Ormesby Hospital   160

5.2. Age Distribution of Patients in North Ormesby Hospital   161

5.3. Morbidity Rates from Hospital Records, 1861–70 and 1883–1908   162

5.4. Age-specific Morbidity Rates, 1883–1908   163

5.5. Causes of Death in North Ormesby Hospital   164

5.6. Mortality in North Ormesby Hospital   165

5.7. Workers' Contributions to North Ormesby Hospital   166

5.8.   Hospital Fund-raising (North Ormesby Hospital and Leeds
       General Infirmary)   167
5.9.   Company and Employee Contributions to North Ormesby
       Hospital, 1860–81   168
5.10. Referrals by Companies to North Ormesby Hospital, 1860–71 170
5.11. Referrals to North Ormesby Hospital, 1883–1908   171
5.12. Fund-raising and Expenditure of Middlesbrough Associations,
       1876   176
5.13. Donations Promised to North Riding Infirmary, 1860   181
5.14. Subscriptions by the Borough of Middlesbrough to the North
       Riding Infirmary, 1866–74   183
5.15. Number of In- and Out-patients, 1873–94   183
5.16. North Riding Infirmary House Committee Members, 1872–5   186
6.1.   Dependency Ratio among the Middlesbrough Population,
       1851–81   196
6.2.   Age Distribution of Middlesbrough-born Males (Resident and
       Out-migrating) in 1881   197
6.3.   Age Distribution of Middlesbrough-born Females (Resident and
       Out-migrating) in 1881   197
6.4.   Labour Force Participation Rates of Three Different
       Middlesbrough Populations aged 15–64, 1881   198
6.5.   Age-specific Labour Force Participation Rates of
       Middlesbrough-born Population (Resident and Outgoing), 1881 199

Appendices

1.   Land Sales by the Owners of the Middlesbrough Estate,
       1848-91   201
2.   Wrought Iron Sales in the North of England, 1873–1917
       (% by Weight)   202
3.   Wrought Iron Sales in the North of England, 1863–1917   203
4.   Infant Deaths in Middlesbrough, 1854–99   206
5.   Crimes by Migrants According to Duration of Stay in
       Middlesbrough, 1860s–1880s   208
6.   Crimes by Income Levels in Middlesbrough, 1863–85   210
7.   Crimes by Literacy Levels in Middlesbrough, 1861–89   211
8.   Crimes by Nationality in Middlesbrough, 1861–89   212

Acknowledgements

Premission to reproduce plates and maps is gratefully acknowledged:
Teesside Archives: Plates 1.1 and 5.1, Maps 1.1, 1.2 and 1.3
Middlesbrough Reference Lib.: Plates 1.2, 1.3 and 5.2.
Ordnance Survey 25", Yorkshire VI (14): Map 2.1
Harrison, *John Gjers, Ironmaster*, p. 7, published by permission of John
Harrison.: Map 2.2

Preface

This book is based on an investigation undertaken since the early 2000s, into relationships between industrialization, urbanization and demographic change in England, with special reference to Victorian Middlesbrough and the surrounding Cleveland region of north-east England. It is the second work on this topic, following research on Leeds in the late-eighteenth and early-nineteenth centuries. In contrast with Leeds, an old-established and large-scale provincial town with a long history as a centre of the textile industry during the classical period of the Industrial Revolution, Middlesbrough was a newly-born, planted town which rose overnight to a Victorian 'Ironopolis'. Compared with Leeds, the development of Middlesbrough as a town and as a centre of industry demonstrates a range of unusual and individualistic characteristics.

Just as Frederick Jackson Turner described in *The Frontier in American History* about the historical development of the New World, Middlesbrough's historical trajectory may be one of the richest fields within which to study those forces operating and interplaying in the making of modern British urban society.[1] Its idiosyncrasies include the briefest period of urban development, a population of heterogeneous composition, a rapid industrial growth under the *laissez-faire* regime of the late-nineteenth century, the nature of various institutions established there, and its culture, social and human relations. There is an apparent inconsistency in holding up Middlesbrough, with all its uniqueness, as an indicator of general trends in how British urban centres developed during the period. Yet in its pattern of growth, and in its changing economic and social structure and institutions, Middlesbrough did indeed share some of the essential characteristics of nineteenth-century British urban communities.

From its late birth in the 1830s, Middlesbrough grew very rapidly to become one of the leading industrial towns in mid-Victorian Britain, an 'infant Hercules', with its staple industries of iron and steel.[2] This book pays close attention to Middlesbrough's unusual experience, its uniquely rapid pace in industrialization and urbanization. Yet the downturn began as early as the 1880s. From the beginning of that decade, the Cleveland iron and steel industry was beginning to ebb, measured in sales of pig iron and

---

[1] Turner, *Frontier in American History*, p. 334.
[2] *The Times*, 11 Oct. 1862; *Stockton and Hartlepool Mercury*, 11 Oct. 1862; *Stockton Gazette and Middlesbrough Times*, 9 Oct. 1862

malleable iron products for home and foreign markets. The transience of Middlesbrough's prosperity is another important theme in this book.

The community study contained in this book deals with a micro world, and aims to present a local account as minutely as possible. At the same time, it pursues a more universal relationship with larger historical processes, through examples and comparisons. Thus in this book, the history of Middlesbrough and Cleveland is contrasted as much as possible with counterparts in other countries. The term 'region' is used flexibly throughout the book, as a practical means of dealing with an historical district. As Jones has pointed out:

> [R]egions present almost insuperable problems of definition (someone once dismissed them as metaphysical units used by geographers). They need to be redefined continually according to the fortunes of the economic activities they contain and for which they are often rather clumsy proxies. This makes them uncertain vessels in which to pour history, which is necessarily about change through periods over which the regional assemblages may not be stable.[3]

The book is organized as follows. Chapter 1 is given to an analysis of the making of the town by the Owners of the Middlesbrough Estate and the Stockton and Darlington Railway Company, by the ironmasters, and later on by the local authority. Sections within this chapter are devoted to the spatial expansion of built-up areas, and to the development of municipal organization and finance. In Chapter 2, the creation of a Victorian ironopolis and the growing markets for its products are examined with reference to the development of an industrial agglomeration in the region. From the mid 1850s, Middlesbrough concentrated on producing pig iron, wrought (or malleable) iron and finished iron products such as rails, plates, bars and angles. In a decade or so, it came to dominate the world market, a position credited to the Cleveland Practice of ironmaking, a technique developed from the middle of the nineteenth century.

The Cleveland iron and steel industrial region forms a model case for research into industrial clustering and agglomeration. Recent studies of industrial clustering have enlightened our analysis of the fast-growing Cleveland industrial agglomeration from the late 1860s. Industrial location, product specialization among the iron companies, and the diffusion of technology, are investigated in this chapter. With respect to technological innovation, its diffusion and accumulation in the Cleveland industrial agglomeration, those institutions that maintained scientific discipline, besides collecting and sharing information on ironmaking technologies, the state of trade, and so on, are considered. The chapter also examines how three significant institutions, the chamber of commerce, the exchange and the Warrant Stores,

---

3   Jones, *European Miracle*, pp. xv-xvi

were formed, and how they worked to the benefit of ironmasters, improving merchandizing by reducing transaction costs.

Compared with the very comprehensive German population records, which have enabled researchers to trace an entire nation's migratory behaviour over the past 200 years with unparallelled precision, British migration studies are heavily handicapped. Given the shortcomings of British records for the study of historical demography, computer-aided record linkage from census enumerators' books has been used to analyse longitudinal migration profiles of individuals, between the censuses of 1851 and 1861, and those of 1861 and 1871. Based on this exercise, Chapter 3 illuminates not only patterns of in-migration and out-migration, but also the economic and demographic behaviour of those thought to have stayed in Middlesbrough throughout the period. Also considered are the changing age- and gender-specific patterns within the town's population structure, and the demographic implications of these findings.

Chapter 4 also uses record linkages from census enumerators' books to establish distinctive features of the labour market in the iron and steel industrial areas of mid-Victorian Middlesbrough and Cleveland. Skilled, semi-skilled and unskilled workers were recruited from around the United Kingdom, with skill-specific migration patterns observed among skilled and semi-skilled ironworkers from other English and Welsh ironmaking centres, short-distance migration seen in unskilled labour from neighbouring rural and urban areas, as well as large number of migrants arriving from Ireland. The demographic behaviour of Irish and non-Irish inhabitants, especially in their migration patterns and family types, is compared. These investigations reveal a mobile and unified labour market in the iron and steel industry of the North East during this period. Information on trade-union assisted short-term mobility all over the country, gathered by deploying linkage techniques on trade union records, suggests that skilled workers in Britain before the 1870s were highly mobile.

Chapter 5 presents a case study of medical facilities provided for the victims of industrial accidents by the voluntary North Ormesby Hospital. The chapter is concerned mainly with medical care provided by the institution, and with the complex welfare mechanisms through which the working population could ensure a safety net, at a time when the hospital was supported largely by worker subscriptions. The creation of this working-class dominated medical institution reflects the strong sense of solidarity within that class. Middlesbrough workers were closely involved in a range of self-help organizations, of which Middlesbrough Cottage Hospital, later re-named North Ormesby Hospital, was just one. Meanwhile, the local élite began to interest itself in a paternalistic type of social welfare, including medical care for industrial accident casualties. Cleveland ironmasters, railway companies, dynasties such as the Pease family, landlords, magistrates and influential local politicians, founded the North Riding Infirmary as a means of regional governance. This chapter is devoted to investigating the morbidity, hospital management and funding, in each of these mid-Victorian Middlesbrough medical institutions.

The Great Strike of 1866 prompted the launch of the Board of Arbitration and Conciliation for the North of England Manufactured Iron Trade, an attempt to head off class conflict and to secure sustained growth in the regional economy. This conciliation system, set up in 1869, and later the adoption of sliding scale rules in fixing wage-rates, were novel in the history of British industrial relations and contributed substantially to improving class relations. The conclusion of this book looks at Middlesbrough's changing fortunes within a context of self-sustainable urban centres in regional industrialization. The town, so distinct from other Victorian industrial centres, initially took full advantage of its serendipitous geographical endowments, its coal and ironstone, railway and river navigation facilities, and its proximity to the North Sea. Yet from the end of the nineteenth century, these turned out to be shackles inhibiting further sustainable development.

The statistical appendices present data previously unpublished, relating to the nineteenth-century economic and social history of Middlesbrough and the Cleveland region.

Acknowledgements

This book is the outcome of a research project that began almost 10 years ago when I finished my work on Leeds during the Industrial Revolution. I feel a special debt to Dr Gillian Cookson for her advice and support. She has read and made helpful comments and queries on the whole manuscript, though of course I am responsible for any errors or misunderstandings. Without her exhaustive and painstaking check, this book would not have been possible. I do not know how to thank her enough. Professor Peter Rushton recommended publication of this book in the series Regions and Regionalism in History, for which I am grateful to him. Professor David and Dr Lynda Rollason who accepted me as a visiting fellow to the Department of History at Durham University for the years 2005 and 2006, have encouraged me warmly to publish this book, and to them I am much indebted. They also arranged research facilities for me while I was based at Durham.

In the spring of 1997, while I was seeking a new research topic after the work on Leeds, Professor R.J. Morris advised me at his office in William Robertson Building in Edinburgh to work on Middlesbrough, about which I honestly knew little. Since then he has given important suggestions for which I am very grateful. Most of the primary source material used in this book has been collected at Teesside Archives. I should like to thank Dr David Tyrell, and especially Dr Janet Baker, who generously helped me in searching, identifying and copying documents in the archives. While I was based at the University of Essex from 1998 to 1999 as an exchange scholar under a reciprocal academic exchange agreement between the British Academy and the Japan Society for the Promotion of Science, Professor A.J. Pollard of the University of Teesside arranged seminars and facilitated my research.

A number of British and Japanese historians and economists have taken an interest in this work, and provided important advice and comments. In particular, Professor Barry Doyle, with his wealth of knowledge on the welfare history of Middlesbrough and its environs, helped me to widen the scope on the social history of the region. Professor Malcolm Chase of the University of Leeds has given important pointers on the labour history of the North East, for which I owe thanks. I am in debt to Professor Ray Hudson who has provided important suggestions on the history of Teesside in the nineteenth and twentieth centuries from a geographical point of view. I would like to thank Professor Ranald Michie for his many helpful hints concerning the theme of this book.

Dr Malcolm Smith has kindly let me use his programme to calculate step migration. I am grateful to Dr Anne Orde for providing me with useful information on the Quakers of north-east England. From discussions with Mr Stephen James of the University of Teesside, I have derived valuable suggestions on the business network in nineteenth-century Cleveland. I would also like to thank Dr Matthew Woollard of the University of Essex for his useful suggestions on the census returns. The late Professor Tony Hepburn provided me with important information and specialist insights into Irish migrants in the north- east, for which I am indebted.

My thanks are also due to Mr Peter Tilley, who kindly allowed me to use his program of record linkage with the census enumerators' books, and patiently guided me to manipulate the program. I am amazed to look back on how frequently we exchanged emails with enquiries and answers on methods of calculating results during the time I worked on analysing the record linkages. Mrs Robina Weeds inputted for me data from the Middlesbrough census enumerators' books for the years 1851, 1861 and 1871, according to the input-format of Peter Tilley's program. This amounted to 53,609 individuals, and I am deeply indebted to Mrs Weeds for her invaluable assistance.

From Mr Geoffrey and Mrs Jennifer Braddy, who are both from the old town of Middlesbrough, I have learnt much about Cleveland history. Their vivid recollections of people, landscape, customs, working life and culture in the town in the mid-twentieth century were a precious primary source of oral history. My thanks also go to Mr John Harrison, an industrial archaeologist in Guisborough, who showed me round the remains of sites of the Cleveland iron and steel industry in Middlesbrough, Eston and Redcar. He also instructed me in the technological details of ironmaking. The late Dr Geoffrey Stout, who had worked at North Ormesby Hospital, helped me to understand the public health of Middlesbrough in the late nineteenth century, as well as the history of the hospital.

It is a great pleasure to me to see that while I was working on Middlesbrough and Cleveland history, the British Steel Archive Collection Project was launched. This project is especially significant in that it is engaged in collecting systematically any documents relating to the north-east iron and steel industry from 1840 to 1970, hitherto held separately by record offices, universities or local archives. Collecting and restoring these documents, and producing an on-line list, are now proceeding under the auspices of the University of Teesside and Teesside Archives, aided by the Heritage Lottery Fund. This centrally controlled collection and storage of documents will in the near future achieve fruitful results.

This research has been financed by the following research funds: Japan Society for the Promotion of Science, Researcher Exchange Programme for 1998 (University of Essex, Department of History); Japan Society for the Promotion of Science, Grant-in-Aid for Scientific Research (B) for 1999–2001 and 2004–6; Komazawa University Subvention for Research for 2002; Komazawa University Subsidy for Study Leave Abroad for 2005–6

(Durham University, Department of History). I am pleased to offer thanks for the support of these institutions. Finally I should like to thank Komazawa University for awarding a grant for publication for the year 2010.

M.Y.
Komazawa University
August 2010

Town Planning and the Birth of Middlesbrough

Middlesbrough was not discovered – it was invented. It did not grow –
it was manufactured. America, which produces a town at three month's
notice, achieves no substantial product like Middlesbrough... Cincinnati
and Chicago are perhaps the best specimens of American-made towns
with which Middlesbrough can be compared; but these do not equal in
self-sustaining vigour or rapidity of growth the Pease-founded colony on
the banks of the Tees.[1]

Middlesbrough in a Cradle

In the early morning of 18 August 1828, Joseph Pease the younger, a
Darlington merchant and leading member of the north-east Quaker Pease
dynasty, 'took boat and entering the Tees mouth sailed up Middlesbro to
take a view of the proposed termination of the contemplated extension of
the railway'. As he wrote in his diary, he 'was much pleased with the place
altogether' and 'its adaptation to the purpose far exceeded any anticipations
I had formed'. He also recorded that 'imagination here had ample scope in
fancying a coming day when the bare fields we then were traversing will be
covered with a busy multitude and numerous vessels crowding to these banks
denote the busy seaport'.[2]

No account captures the trajectory of mid-Victorian Middlesbrough quite
as well as that of Asa Briggs in his *Victorian Cities*, where he concludes: 'The
real interest of Middlesbrough's nineteenth-century history lies, indeed, not
so much in the newness of the community which was created there as in the
speed with which an intricate and complex economic, social, and political
sequence was unfolded.'[3]

Middlesbrough, because of the speed of its industrialization and urbanization, and its multi-ethnic demographic structure derived from high levels of
in-migration from Ireland, Wales, Scotland and even the countries of conti-
nental Europe, displayed vividly many contemporary problems of social
cohesion and segmentation, in particular those relating to rootlessness and
alienation. The town also offers a test case through which to examine how a

---

[1] Praed, *Rise and Progress of Middlesbrough*, p. 3.
[2] Middlesbrough Central Lib., MM1942, diary of Joseph Pease, 1827–8, pp. 208–9.
[3] Briggs, *Victorian Cities*, p. 274.

newly built Victorian urban community matured into a fully fledged municipal corporation within a relatively short period.

It is well known that Middlesbrough was designed initially as a railway town to transport coal from south-west Durham via an extension of the Stockton and Darlington Railway. The town was developed through a collaboration between the Owners of the Middlesbrough Estate, the Stockton and Darlington Railway, the ironmasters and later the local authority. After the discovery of the Cleveland Main Seam in 1850 in nearby Eston, Middlesbrough grew swiftly into a production centre of Cleveland iron and steel. This chapter considers the making of a new urban community, the spatial expansion of built-up areas, and the development and financing of municipal government.[4]

Alone among the many railway towns planned in the early-nineteenth century, Middlesbrough had as its initial aim not only a railway depot for coal transport, but also the building of a harbour for export and for coastal sales of coal within Great Britain. Most such planned towns in this period continued to function mainly as transportation centres, but Middlesbrough was unusual – only Barrow-in-Furness is a comparable case – in transforming itself from the mid-nineteenth century into a production as well as distribution centre for heavy manufacturing.[5]

A further exceptional feature of mid-Victorian Middlesbrough was the way in which it was built. In most planned railway towns, as Crewe, Swindon and Wolverton show, houses, streets, waterworks and other public health facilities, schools, churches and hospitals, and other features of urban infrastructure, were almost wholly developed by the railway companies.[6] These towns were therefore company towns, with industrial facilities such as distribution centres, locomotive engine works and repair shops. Yet Middlesbrough was planned by the Owners of the Middlesbrough Estate, a partnership organization specifically founded to develop the area.

One reason to form a company apart from the Stockton and Darlington Railway was evidently to avoid the legal difficulties in holding land, managing the estate, and developing and selling property, which might have been encountered by a body not incorporated for those purposes. Middlesbrough followed the example of Barrow-in-Furness in setting up a town-planning body that was separate from the railway company.[7] The owners would also have been concerned about the feasibility of their project, and aware that construction of a harbour, railways and other urban infrastructure required large investment. Setting up a separate company to guide the new venture was a means of spreading risk, and of protecting their highly profitable railway business.

---

4   Durham R.O., D/PS 5/2; Bell, *City Fathers*, p. 173; Tomlinson, *North Eastern Railway*, p. 190; Kirby, *Men of Business and Politics*, pp. 22–5; Casson, *The World's First Railway System*, pp. 82, 121–8; Bullock, 'Origins of Economic Growth on Teesside', pp. 79–96 ; Evans, 'Two Paths to Economic Development', p. 203.
5   Bell, *City Fathers*, p. 173.
6   Bell, *City Fathers*, p. 171; Drummond, *Crewe*, pp. 9–34.
7   Pollard, 'Town Planning in the Nineteenth Century', p. 111.

In 1829, the Owners of the Middlesbrough Estate purchased from William Chilton for £35,000 the Middlesbrough property of 527 acres. The partnership then consisted of Joseph Pease the younger, merchant, of Darlington; Edward Pease the younger, brother of Joseph and a merchant in Stockton; Thomas Richardson, a London bill broker originally from Darlington and cousin of Joseph Pease; Henry Birkbeck, banker, of Norwich, brother-in-law of Joseph Pease; Simon Martin, a Norwich banker; and Francis Gibson of Saffron Walden in Essex, a brewer and brother-in-law of Joseph Pease. Their share holdings were Joseph Pease (2/10), Edward Pease the younger (1/10), Thomas Richardson (2/10), Henry Birkbeck (2/10), Simon Martin (2/10) and Francis Gibson (1/10). All these men were Quakers.[8]

Joseph Pease, a founder of the Stockton and Darlington Railway, and later known as the father of Middlesbrough, was the driving force in this town-planning exercise. The Stockton and Darlington Railway had opened up the previously inaccessible Auckland coalfield in the west of Co. Durham, where Pease had bought leases on a number of collieries including Bishop Auckland. The railway's extension to Middlesbrough is indication of Pease's vision, for in founding a coal-export harbour he greatly increased the potential of his Auckland coal investments. The Owners of the Middlesbrough Estate company was formed in 1829 with £7,000, loaned by the Norwich banker Joseph Gurney, father-in-law of Joseph Pease, a year after the passing of an Act of Parliament for the Middlesbrough Extension of the Stockton and Darlington Railway, and a year before the railway extension opened.[9]

Immediately after the Owners of the Middlesbrough Estate was formed, it required a loan for business expenses from the Alliance, British and Foreign Fire and Life Insurance Co. of London. This enterprise, established in 1824, had as its members the leading London merchant bankers Nathan Meyer Rothschild and Moses Montefiore; Francis Baring, of Baring Brothers; Samuel Gurney, a London bill broker; and John Irving. In 1830, Thomas Richardson, a member of the Owners of the Middlesbrough Estate partnership, and also by this time a director of the Alliance Insurance company, arranged a mortgage of the Middlesbrough property for the sum of £20,000, with interest at 4% per annum. The debtors were all the partners of the Owners of the Middlesbrough Estate, and the lenders all personal investors in the insurance company.[10]

The loan, which carried a £40,000 penalty for breach of contract, seems to have been to alleviate a lack of short-term operating funds. As security, 93% of the estate purchased in 1829 was offered, including 26 fields in Middlesbrough amounting to 264 acres, a property called Monkland consisting of 14 fields of 63 acres, and further lands previously owned by Warcop Consett, measuring 159 acres.[11]

---

[8] Teesside Archives, U/BSC 1/1; Kirby, *Men of Business and Politics*, pp. 22–5, 136.
[9] Kirby, *Men of Business and Politics*, pp. 5, 21; *Origin of Railway Enterprise*, pp. 77, 79.
[10] Teesside Archives, U/OME (2) 5/87, 88, 93, 95, 100; Guildhall Lib., MS 14075/1 from 231, 23 Sep. 1830; Schooling, *Alliance Assurance*, p.15. For Samuel Gurney, see Pressnell, *Country Banking*, pp. 114–15.
[11] Teesside Archives, U/OME (2) 5/88, 5/386.

Thomas Richardson's network of associates is illustration of the strong family and business links between Quaker merchants and financiers in Darlington, London, Norwich and elsewhere. Richardson had become wealthy through a bill-broking partnership that he founded with his brother-in-law, John Overend, in 1802. They were joined in 1807 by Samuel and John Gurney, of the Norwich banking family to which Joseph Pease's wife belonged. Samuel Gurney and Richardson became partners in the Alliance, British and Foreign Fire and Life Insurance Co. Richardson, Overend and other Darlington Quakers, who had enjoyed success in the City of London, invested heavily in the railway, its extension and the founding of Middlesbrough. Quaker precepts, mutual values and the commercial information that they shared, were bonds formed between them, as were the many inter-marriages between these Quaker dynasties, including the notable banking families of Gurney, Backhouse and Birkbeck. The Peases, though, were pre-eminent in North East England, with their far-flung interests in railways, iron, coal, textiles, and increasingly in local and national politics.[12]

The close religious ties among Quakers and their family relationships formed through inter-marriage were influential in establishing these business groupings, a network widespread across the country, which facilitated exchanges of business information, credit provision and finance. Hudson has pointed to similar experiences stemming from the insurance industry: 'On the basis of relationships initiated in the fire insurance sector, businessmen collectively shifted into joint-stock canal investment and banks, dock, water, gas, retail and property companies. They created institutions and conventions to increase mutual trust and cooperation.'[13]

Developing a town, and the whole of its industrial infrastructure, was a vast undertaking for the Owners of the Middlesbrough Estate. Their general balance sheets for 1845, reproduced in Table 1.1, show a business ranging from management of ballast wharves, brick-making, gas works, farming and breeding stock, to the purchase and sale of land as well as managing an estate of houses, cottages, wharves, warehouses, ferries and the railways that served Bolckow and Vaughan's ironworks and the Middlesbrough pottery. Their total assets of £170,881 represented 15 times the town's rateable value in 1846. Liabilities included the treasurer's balance of £32,415, money owed to the company proprietors (£27,500), and to Simon Martin's executors, to Gurney & Co., to Ann Graves and to the dock company.[14]

Joseph Pease's commitment to the development of Middlesbrough can be surmised from the general balance sheets of the Owners of the Middlesbrough Estate, which catalogue his many interventions under a heading 'Joseph Pease

---

12 Pressnell, *Country Banking*, pp. 114–15; Orde, *Religion, Business and Society*, pp. 19–61; Gilzean-Reid, Sir H. (ed.), *Middlesbrough and its Jubilee*, p. 146; Cookson, *Victoria History, iv, Darlington*, pp. 140–1.

13 Hudson, 'Industrial Organization and Structure', p. 51.

14 Teesside Archives, CB/M/T, Poor Rate books, 1846, 1849, 1856, 1858, 1861, 1862, 1871, 1872, 1876, 1880; U/OME (2) 4/15.

Table 1.1. General Balance Sheets of the Owners of the Middlesbrough Estate, 1845

Assets	£	s	d
Land in occupation of Tenants as per Valuation 31 Dec. 1844	45,543	15	1
Land in Owners hands	28,154	8	1
Land laid out for Building	35,602	19	6
Ballast Wharf Plant a/c	3,143	10	6
Brick Yard Plant a/c	2,102		
Brick yard Stock	4,473	6	8
Gas Works Plant a/c	5,242	18	3
Gas Works Stock	605	12	0
Farming Stock	771	4	9
House and Cottage Property, Wharf & Warehouse	9,884	11	10
Ferries over the river Tees	600		
Water Pipes & Ponds	3,879		
Railway to Bolckows, Pottery	1,287	15	0
Sundries on Loan	5,448	16	2
Roads, Streets & Sewers	815	18	0
Walls surrounding Building Land	1,275	6	7
Debts Receivable on a/c of Land & Interest	6,338	2	9
Arrears of Rent & Rental accruing	321	10	9
Stockton & Darlington Railway for Rent of Dock Land	7,997	10	5
Dock Company Balance as per their Balance Sheet	1,103	10	9
Ramsays Engine	150		
Building Society	176	9	2
Exchange Association	2,121	11	2
Increased Value of the Estate by Expenditure on a/c of Draining, Plantations, and Derelict Land	273	17	1
Increased Value of the Estate on a/c of Redcar Railway	2,500		
Graham (?) & Bill & Interest	45	15	3
Stockton & Darlington Railway Co. for New Road Repairs	115	12	9
Grand Total	170,881	8	9
Balance Forward	81,807		
Liabilities			
Treasurers Balance			
Balance of Capital Acc.	25,529	5	10
Balance of Current Acc.	6,886	1	6
Total	32,415	7	4
Proprietors of the Estate	27,500		
S. Martin's Executors	22,000		
Gurneys & Co.	2,000		
Ann Graves	700		
Interest on the above	279	15	10
Total	24,979	15	10
Due to the Dock Co. per Award of Cubitt & Donkin	4,178	13	7
Balance forward	81,807	13	0
Grand Total	170,881	8	9

Source: Teesside Archives, U/OME (2) 4/15.

Junior in account with the Middlesbrough Dock Company'. The building of Middlesbrough docks was undertaken in 1840 by the Owners of the Middlesbrough Estate under the auspices of the Stockton and Darlington Railway Co. The work was completed in 1842, on a nine-acre site where 10 coal drops were laid, each staith shipping 16 tons of coal per hour. In 1849, a consolidating Act of Parliament dissolved the dock company, which was absorbed into the Stockton and Darlington Railway.[15]

The balance sheet for 1845 shows that Pease and his partners had gathered capital for these major works from family members and Quaker business associates, the most significant amount, £109,401 of the total £137,732 owed at that point, having come from the Stockton and Darlington Railway. Other amounts on loan included £7,300 from Henry Birkbeck, £11,000 from Emma Pease and family, and £10,000 from Thomas Richardson. The cost of the dock works amounted at the end of 1842 to £124,673.[16]

Itemized under receipts and payments, liabilities and assets, these various sums illustrate the personal style of management, and the overlapping interests of companies controlled by Pease and his associates. Liabilities include 'sundries on loan as above' (£28,300 plus £398 6s 2d for interest to date); George Adamson (£30 10s 7d); and 'balance forward' (£1,105 10s 9d), amounting altogether to £29,382 7s 6d. On the other side are the assets: 'balance due from Joseph Pease Junior as above' (£9,446 18s 10d); 'Stockton and Darlington Railway Company as per account' (£16,206 15s 1d); 'Middlesbrough Estate per award of Cubitt and Donkin' (£4,178, 13s 7d.). A further £1,103 10s 9d was entered as 'balance in favour of the Dock Co., being the difference of interest paid by them and charged by them to the S. & D. Railway Co.'[17]

Joseph Pease's personal involvement in Middlesbrough's development seems to have ceased by the beginning of the 1860s. The process of his withdrawal may have begun before the dock company was wound up, for his name does not appear on balance sheets after that dated June 1846. His documented house and estate ownership in the town came to an end in 1858. From the mid-nineteenth century, the town's rapid growth, accompanied by possibly unforeseen levels of congestion and environmental disruption caused by the exceptional influx of migrants and resultant loss of open space, may not have matched his expectations of what a new port town would be. Pease was at the very least indifferent towards this lively but rough newcomer, and shifted his attention back to the older town of Darlington, his home. He and his relatives had never committed politically to Middlesbrough.[18]

---

[15] Lillie, *History of Middlesbrough*, pp. 55–6.
[16] Teesside Archives, U/OME (2) 4/15.
[17] Teesside Archives, U/OME (2) 4/15.
[18] Teesside Archives, CB/M/T, Poor Rate books, April 1846, pp. 3–4; 1861, p. 55; for the expansion of built-up areas in Middlesbrough at this time, see Glass, *Social Background of a Plan*, p. 196; Ranger, *Report to the General Board of Health*, pp. 14–15.

MIDDLESBROUGH IN 1832.

Plate 1.1. Middlesbrough in 1832

House-building and Spatial Expansion

As the Owners of the Middlesbrough Estate started to plan the town, Middlesbrough was still a hamlet surrounded by salt marshes near the mouth of the River Tees. The 1831 census returns recorded that the whole parish of Middlesbrough 'contains 383 inhabitants. The Stockton and Darlington railroad terminating near this place, has tended to increase the population (137 persons).' Middlesbrough township had only 30 families, 154 people in all, while 49 families, 229 people, lived in the adjacent township of Linthorpe in the south of the parish. Middlesbrough's 30 families included 15 mainly employed in agriculture, five in trade, manufacture or handicraft, and 10 'other'. Most of the adult population were agricultural labourers, 18 in all, with 15 'labourers employed in labour not agriculture', eight employed in the retail trade, or in handicraft as masters or workmen, three other men and seven female servants.[19]

Within a year of this, Middlesbrough began to swell. The Owners of the Middlesbrough Estate covenanted to sell 123 plots of land, to a range of buyers, many of them individuals engaged in constructing the railway or inland and export coal harbours. The buyers were a merchant; iron merchants (2); ironfounder (1); shipbuilder (1); housebuilders (2); coalfitters (2); innkeepers (4); joiners (2); shoemakers (3); butchers (2); bricklayers (2); blacksmith (1); yeomen (2); miller (1); land surveyor (1); common brewer (1); tailor (1); draper (1); farmer (1); cabinet maker (1); cartwright (1); coach

---

[19] PP, XXXVII, 1831 Census, enumeration abstract, p. 225.

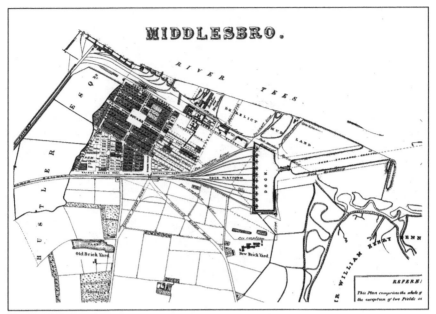

Map 1.1. Middlesbrough in 1845

painter (1); gentleman (1); and accountant (1). Thomas Richardson himself also purchased a plot of land.[20]

Joseph Pease's agreements in 1839 with prospective buyers of houses and land in two streets in the town show a similar range of occupations. Many had interests related to the harbour facilities developing for the transportation of Durham coal: ship-owners (2); master mariners (2); pilots (3); coal trimmer (1); sailmaker (1); bricklayers (3); stonemason (1); joiners (2); slater (1); breadmaker (1); accountant (1); druggist (1); carpenter (1); shopkeeper (1); solicitor's clerk (1); widows (3); and yeomen (4).[21]

As will be discussed in more detail in Chapter 3, population growth started to accelerate during the 1830s, between the time when a grid pattern plan was laid out for residential development by the Owners of the Middlesbrough Estate, and the taking of the 1841 census. During this decade, Middlesbrough's population increased by a factor of 35, an extraordinary rise from 154 in 1831 to 5,463 in 1841. Growth in subsequent decades was substantial, the population multiplying 1.4 times to 7,631 in 1851, and 2.5 times to 18,714 in 1861. Yet these rates were not conspicuously high by the standards of mid-Victorian industrial towns. The increase between 1831 and 1841, though, was exceptional, far beyond comparable places elsewhere in England and Wales.[22]

---

20   Teesside Archives, U/BSC 1/1, f. 11.
21   Lillie, *History of Middlesbrough*, p. 68.
22   Even compared with the exceptionally high population growth rate of Cardiff, centre of the Welsh coal industry, Middlesbrough's expansion was remarkable. For population increases in Cardiff

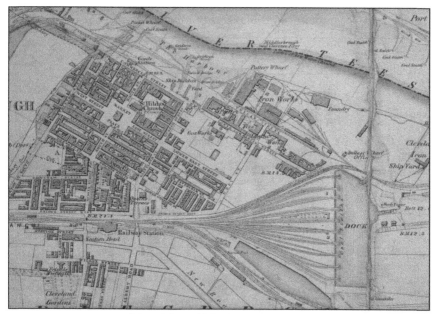

Map 1.2. Middlesbrough in 1857

Table 1.2 is illustration of those who made early Middlesbrough. The inhabitants in 1841 ranged in age from 9 to 90, 1,874 of them male and 242 female. The largest occupational group was 225 male labourers in unspecified industries, who made up 10.7% of all those employed. Of them, 61 were from Ireland. Joiners, 187 in all, were the second largest group, 8.8% of all employed people. Many of the joiners were from Scotland, and some would have been engaged in shipbuilding. As construction of railway sidings, docks and coal staiths was still underway, inhabitants in 1841 were likely to be involved in the building industry as well as engaged in occupations related to coal transportation, shipping, shipbuilding, or piloting. There was still a substantial number of agricultural labourers.[23]

Pottery workers, 138 in total, made up 6.2% of all employed people. They included 112 potters, male and female, as well as 18 pot makers, six transferers (women who applied designs by transfer) and two pot-ware keepers. Pottery had been the first manufacturing industry in the town, originating with the Middlesbrough Pottery Co., founded in 1834 by Richard Otley and Joseph Pease with a capital of £1,700. The company employed on average 100 workers before its closure in 1887.[24] Already there were recorded 55

and other industrial towns in the nineteenth century, see Daunton, *Coal Metropolis*, p. 11 and Welton, 'On the Distribution of Population', pp. 531, 547.

[23] National Archives, HO 1256/1-6. Regarding the reliability of 1841 census enumerators' books, see for example, Higgs, *Making Sense of the Census*, pp. 7–10, 27–31; for the heavy influx of joiners into newly built urban centres, see Smith, 'Influx of Population', pp. 96–7, 120–1, 141.

[24] Cockerill, 'Middlesbrough Pottery', pp. 23, 35; Williams, *Pottery that Began Middlesbrough*, p. 20.

Table 1.2. Occupations and Birthplaces of Middlesbrough Population, 1841

Male			Female		
Occupation	No.	%	Occupation	No.	%
Labourers	225	12.0	Servants	137	56.4
Joiners	187	10.0	Potters	23	9.5
Agricultural lab.	137	7.3	Dress makers	19	7.8
Potters	108	5.7	Independent	17	7.0
Brick makers	67	3.6	Charwomen	9	3.7
Mariners	62	3.3	Transferers	6	2.5
Coal trimmers	59	3.1	Spinsters	4	1.7
Engineers	57	3.0	Milliners	3	1.2
Seamen	46	2.5	Publicans	3	1.2
Shoemakers	46	2.5	School mistress	2	0.8
Others	880	47.0	Straw hat makers	2	0.8
			Others	18	7.4
Total	1,874	100.0	Total	243	100.0
Places of Birth	No	%		No	%
Yorkshire	967	51.6		135	55.6
Other England	723	38.6		104	42.8
Scotland	75	4.0		2	0.8
Ireland	108	5.7		1	0.4
Wales	1	0.1		0	0.0
Foreign Countries	0	0.0		1	0.4
Total	1,874	100.0		243	100.0

Source: National Archives (Public Record Office), Census Enumerators' Books, HO 107/1256/1-6.

residents who worked in the iron industry, as puddlers, founders, forgers, moulders and an iron turner. The real figure was higher, as it would include some of the unskilled labourers whose industry was not noted. In addition, 57 mechanical engineers were recorded, who made and fitted engines and machinery, along with millwrights, engine smiths and pattern makers.

More than one-half of adult inhabitants in 1841 had been born within Yorkshire, with 39% of men and 42.8% of women originating elsewhere in England. Smaller proportions came from Ireland and Scotland, 5.8% and 4.8% respectively. The electoral roll in 1841 showed 198 people qualifying to vote through their freehold property, houses, shops or land in Middlesbrough, of whom 155 lived in the town, 14 in Darlington, 3 in Stockton and 26 in other places.[25]

The discovery of the Cleveland main seam of iron ore in 1850, and subsequent upsurge in iron production in and around Middlesbrough, are reflected in estate valuations and in rentals of houses, factories and industrial premises,

[25] Middlesbrough Central Lib., MMI 324 56361.

Table 1.3. Rateable Value of Middlesbrough,
1846–80

Year	£	s
1846 (Apr.)	11,718	10
1849 (Jan.)	13,569	
1849 (Sep.)	14,149	10
1856 (Dec.)[a]	28,545	7
1858 (Jan.)	30,235	10
1861 (Jun.)	38,170	10
1861 (Oct.)	37,291	10
1862 (May)	47,932	10
1862 (Oct.)	48,347	10
1871 (Nov.)	93,079	10
1872 (Apr.)	93,878	10
1872 (Nov.)	97,166	10
1880 (Apr.)	182,191	10

Note: [a]In 1853, by incorporation, the borough boundary was extended. Also in 1858, 1866 and 1874 the boundaries were extended, which would have been reflected in the increase of the rateable values.

Source: Poor Rate Books, 1846, 1849, 1856, 1858, 1861,1862, 1871, 1872, 1876, 1880, Teesside Archives, CB/M/T

and land. Ignoring price changes during this period, the total rateable value of houses, factories, warehouses and other industrial buildings in the first half of the 1850s increased annually by an average 14.5%, by 26.7% in the early 1860s, and by 3.6% in the early 1870s, as illustrated in Tables 1.3 and 1.4. Gross estimated rentals also rose steadily in the 1870s, showing an especially sharp rise, 1.2 times, between 1877 and 1878. The middle of the 1880s also saw a steep rise in rentals.[26] These indices represent the Cleveland iron and steel industries becoming firmly established in the Middlesbrough area in the late-nineteenth century, with a concomitant increase in numbers of industrial buildings, and a rapid growth of population and houses as migrants flowed into the town.

This new prosperity from the mid 1860s and through the first half of the 1870s resulted in a massive physical expansion of Middlesbrough 'South of the Border', beyond the railway line that had served as southern boundary of the settlement. A plan drawn in 1877 shows, coloured yellow, those houses which had been built between the Christmases of 1861 and 1871, a vivid illustration of this outward growth. The extension of the built-up area can be deduced from Tables 1.5 to 1.7, which show how many new properties

---

[26] Teesside Archives, CB/M/T, Poor Rate books, 1846, 1849, 1856, 1858, 1861, 1862, 1871, 1872, 1876, 1880; North Yorks. R.O., QFR 1/49/16, 1/50/17, 1/51/10, 1/53/10, 1/54/10, 1/55/11, 1/56/10, 1/57/10, 1/58/10, 1/58/23, 1/43/18 (1865-84), QFR 1/43/18 (1859).

Table 1.4. Rateable Value and Estimated Rentals in Middlesbrough, 1865–86

Year	Gross Estimated Rental (£ s d)	Rateable Value (£)
1865	78,972	64,992
1869	103,903	84,920
1874	122,552	107,458
1877	131,178	
1878 (Apr.)	158,903 10s	136,203
1878 (Dec.)	158,730 16s 8d	136,055
1880	183,490	152,908
1884	187,458	156,215
1885	209,394	175,288
1886	210,293	175,263

Source: Assessment of the County Rates for the North Riding of the County of York, North Yorkshire County Record Office, QFR 1/49/16, 1/50/17, 1/51/10, 1/53/10, 1/54/10, 1/55/11, 1/56/10, 1/57/10, 1/58/10, 1/58/23, 1/43/18 (1865-1884), QFR 1/43/18 (1859).

Table 1.5. Growth of Houses and Shops in Middlesbrough, 1849–80

Year	Houses	Houses with Shops	Total
1849 (Jan.)	1,316	92	1,408
1856 (Dec.)	2,108 (8.6)[a]	316 (34.8)[a]	2,424 (10.3)[a]
1861 (Jun.)	2,940 (7.9)	418 (6.5)	3,358 (7.7)
1871 (Nov.)	4,528 (5.4)	558 (3.3)	5,083 (5.1)
1880 (Apr.)	6,384 (4.6)	873 (6.3)	7,257 (4.8)

Note: [a]Average growth rates per annum (%).
Source: Poor Rate Books, 1849, 1856, 1861, 1871, 1880, Teesside Archives, CB/M/T.

appeared between 1849 and 1880. The figures are based on investigation of the Poor Rate books, which differentiate between houses built by private builders, those erected by the Owners of the Middlesbrough Estate, and some which were constructed by ironmasters.[27]

In Tables 1.5 to 1.7 the numbers of houses, and houses with shops, are given for the period of most rapid growth from the 1840s, until that time in the 1880s when a cloud hung over the Cleveland iron and steel industries and the rate of increase tailed off. The town's most rapid residential expansion occurred during the 1850s, with average annual growth rates in numbers of houses 8.6% in the first part of the decade and 7.9% in the latter half. Throughout the period, more than 90% of houses, including those owned by companies, were rented. The number of owner-occupied houses stood at a consistent level of around 10%. The growth in residential houses and those with shops attached, taken together, reached a high point in the latter half of the 1850s, increasing from 2,424 to 3,358 between 1856 and 1861. The

---

27 Teesside Archives, CB/M/E (5) 7/2; CB/M/T, Poor Rate books, 1849, 1856, 1861, 1871, 1880.

Table 1.6. Growth of Houses, Houses with Shops, Shops, Inns and Beerhouses etc. in Middlesbrough, 1849–80

Year	Houses	Houses with Shops	Inns	Beerhouses	Shops	Stores	Total
1849 (Jan.)	1,316	92			2		1,410
1856 (Dec.)	2,108 (8.6)[a]	316(34.8)[a]	17	27			2,481(10.9)[a]
1861 (Jun.)	2,940 (7.9)	418 (6.5)		5	5	7	3,375 (7.2)
1871 (Nov.)	4,528 (5.4)	558 (3.3)	52	62	49	5	5,254 (5.6)
1880 (Apr.)	6,384 (4.6)	873 (6.3)	53	43	114	3	7,470 (4.7)

Note: [a]Average growth rates per annum (%)
Source: Poor Rate Books, 1849, 1856, 1861, 1871, 1880, Teesside Archives, CB/M/T.

Table 1.7. Private and Company-owned Houses in Middlesbrough, 1849–80

Year	Owner-occupiers	Occupiers	Company-owned Houses	Total
1849	164 (11.6)	1,098 (78.0)	146 (10.4)	1,408 (100.0)
1856	246 (10.1)	1,924 (79.4)	254 (10.5)	2,424 (100.0)
1861	337 (10.0)	2,733 (81.4)	288 (8.6)	3,358 (100.0)
1871	455 (9.0)	4,365 (85.8)	263 (5.2)	5,083 (100.0)
1880	646 (8.9)	6,161 (84.9)	450 (6.2)	7,257 (100.0)

Source: Poor Rate Books, 1849, 1856, 1861, 1871, 1880, Teesside Archives, CB/M/T.

censuses from 1851 to 1881 counted total numbers of houses in the township of Middlesbrough, shown in Table 1.8, which are consistent with the numbers calculated from Poor Rate records, with the exception of 1880.

Poor Rate records show numbers of company-owned houses standing at about 10% of total housing stock until the beginning of the 1860s, after which there was a relative decline. The figures are given in Table 1.7. How this proportion of company-owned dwellings, averaging 7.2% in Middlesbrough from 1849 to 1880, compares with other industrial towns, is difficult to assess, as data is lacking. The level of owner-occupation of houses, irrespective of social class, was slightly lower in Middlesbrough, at 8.9%, than in the town of Bochum in the Ruhr, a German town of similar industrial structure, with which Middlesbrough is sometimes compared and where there were 9.7% of owner-occupiers in 1880.[28]

Most of Middlesbrough's company-owned houses seem to have been built for the purpose of attracting labour to the town. Workers would have been drawn by the accommodation available at fairly reasonable rents. Some ironworkers rented company-owned houses, which were tied to their employment, as shown in the work rules of the Cleveland wrought iron manufacturers in 1871: 'Any workman occupying a house belonging to the firm must quit the house not later than the

---

28 Crew, *Town in the Ruhr*, p. 97.

Table 1.8. Number of Houses in Middlesbrough Recorded in
Census Returns, 1851–81

Year	Inhabited	Uninhabited	Building	Total
1851	1,304	42	21	1,367
1861	3,070	157	90	3,317
1871	4,940	80	37	5,057
1881	6,894	704	5	7,603

Source: *British Parliamentary Papers, Census of England and Wales for the Year 1861*,
Population Tables, Vol. I, Numbers and Distribution of the People, 1862 (3056), L, 1., p.696;
British Parliamentary Papers, Census of England and Wales, 1881, Vol. II, Area, Houses,
and Population, 1883 (C.3563) lxxix, 1, p.558.

Monday week following the expiration of the notice under which he leaves his
service, a sufficient amount being retained from the wages due to guarantee the
rent.' Rent for company-owned housing might be deducted from pay, for instance
in the case of John Dixon, an employee of Bell Brothers, from whose fortnightly
wages 7s rent was taken during 1867. Dixon's fortnightly income amounted to
£4 7s 8d, so that about 8% was expended on house rent.[29]

The majority of company-owned housing was the property of Bolckow
and Vaughan or Cochrane & Co. iron works. From 1849 to 1880, Bolckow
and Vaughan owned 68 houses on average, amounting to more than one-
half the company housing in the town in 1849, but declining to about 14%
by 1880. The percentages of Bolckow and Vaughan's holding, in relation
to total company housing, were 54.1% in 1849, 28.9% in 1856, 38.8% in
1861, 39.5% in 1871 and 13.7% in 1880. It seems that they also organized
among their workforce a self-help savings club to provide houses for their
members. In 1853, 4,200 square yards of land were purchased for £1,323
by the Middlesbrough Iron Works Building Society, of which Henry W.F.
Bolckow, John Vaughan and William Evans were trustees.[30]

In addition to houses built by private builders and ironmasters, the Owners
of the Middlesbrough Estate developed some workers' housing. Even in the
early 1840s, they built and owned cottages valued at £430. They owned 19
houses in 1849 and 34 houses in 1856, all assessed as being of low value. In
1855, the rate books show houses worth £540 in their ownership. Sometime
around 1860 they built 70 further houses, and a house with a shop. In 1871,
they owned 94 houses and seven houses with shops, and, in 1880, 55 houses
and eight houses with shops.[31]

The number of houses with shops grew rapidly between 1849 and 1856,
as shown in Table 1.5. As fast as the increase was in houses without shops at

---

[29] Modern Records Centre, Univ. of Warwick, MSS 365/NEI, 5 Jan. 1871; British Lib. of Political
and Economic Science, Coll. Misc. 0003.

[30] Teesside Archives, U/OME (2) 5/1–5/4.

[31] Teesside Archives, U/OME (2) 4/34; CB/M/T, Poor Rate books, 1849, pp. 135–6; 1856, pp. 41–2;
1861, 1871, 1880.

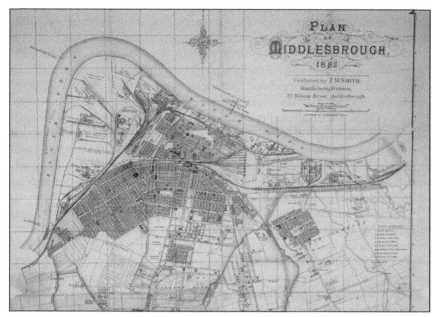

Map 1.3. Middlesbrough in 1882

this time, the annual growth rate, 34.8% on average, of houses with shops was remarkable, four times higher than houses alone. So besides the huge numbers of in-migrating industrial workers, there was a substantial growth from 1850 in the service sector, as Table 1.6 suggests: shopkeepers, especially small-scale retail traders; inn and beer-house keepers, and other providers of entertainment.

These groups supplied the mass of working-class people, in-migrating in large numbers during the 1850s and 1860s, with necessities of life such as food, drink and clothing, as well as inns, boarding and lodging facilities for short- and long-term residents. Given how quickly the urban centre had to absorb so many skilled and unskilled workers, the growth in demand for small-scale retail shops and lodging houses must have been immense. The attitudes and political behaviour of the new 'shopocracy' differed markedly from those of other middle-class inhabitants. This conservative and regressive shopocracy brought considerable influence to bear on the form of Middlesbrough's urban infrastructure, to be further discussed below.

Municipal Organization and Finance

Middlesbrough has sometimes been compared with Ballarat in Australia, the Klondike in Canada or the gold rush districts of California, where boom towns appeared after the discovery of gold in the mid-nineteenth century. Other urban histories have categorized it as an industrial complex with a belatedly developing urban infrastructure, backward in gaining self-government, a municipal corporation or civic pride. Yet closer inspection of the town's nineteenth-century trajectory suggests that Middlesbrough actually acquired an urban identity in an exceptionally short period of time.[32]

At the dawn of the town's existence, in 1831, the deed of covenant between the Owners of the Middlesbrough Estate and the 36 original purchasers of 123 plots of land in the town stipulated that a self-governing body should be formed among the residents, with an annual general meeting and other special meetings. These would consider all matters relating to the estate: standards of housing, maintenance and repair of streets and sewers, levying of rates to pay for works, highways and nuisances, and so on. These various meetings could enact by-laws, ordinances and so on, binding on all residents. Owners of property in the township rated at over £5 were entitled to attend meetings and had one vote, with an additional vote for every additional £5 in value.

The town surveyors were the most influential of the various officials employed to implement decisions of the general and special meetings. These men were responsible for surveying streets, highways and sewers, and reported back to committees subordinate to the general meetings. The surveyors also had powers to assess rates and allocate the revenue to pay for repairs, to inspect building standards, to permit constructions, to enforce various by-laws against obstructions, nuisances and annoyances, and to collect and administer rates, selecting and making agreements with contractors.

For their part, the surveyors had to pay a security of £500 on taking office, and were required to have two or more committee members stand surety on their behalf. In their practical responsibilities, the surveyors took overall charge of town administration, yet by the terms of the deed of covenant, their functions were not precisely defined, though they seem to have embraced the roles of treasurer, keeper of the peace and promoter of public health.[33]

The organization stipulated in the 1831 covenant might be described as an embryonic grassroots self-governing body based on a private contract between the residents and the owners of the estate. Without doubt it was forerunner of the later improvement commissioners, that is, 'free associations of their own to obtain from Parliament, by means of a petition or local bill, powers to levy a local rate to provide urban areas with street-lighting, stone paving, watchmen, refuse removal and much else'.[34]

The Owners of the Middlesbrough Estate entered into this contract with prospective residents, covering a wide range of housing and environmental matters, for obvious reasons: because physical conditions presented urgent problems in a congested urban community, and some kind of governing body with the finance-raising powers to maintain and improve the town, was indispensable.

In England before the Restoration, 'neither the court leet nor the municipal corporation, neither the parish nor the Justices of the Peace, possessed the necessary coercive or regulative powers' to pave and maintain the town streets.

[32] Briggs, *Victorian Cities*, p. 250.
[33] Teesside Archives, U/BSC 1/1, f. 8.
[34] Thane, 'Government and Society', pp. 6–7.

After the Restoration, there emerged in almost every urban centre a statutory body called the Improvement Commission, endowed by means of a local Act of Parliament with various powers over urban sanitation and improvement. It was, as the Webbs suggested, 'the starting-point of the great modern development of town government. And it is these improvement commissioners, not the mayor, aldermen and councillors of the old corporation, who were the progenitors of nearly all the activities of our present municipalities'. The Improvement Commission was a prototype of the 'specialized organ of collective administration acting by salaried officials and hired labour, and maintained by uniform poundage rates on all occupiers'. [35]

Although most urban centres in Britain were already provided with improvement commissioners, other statutory bodies or charters of incorporation, it was not possible for Middlesbrough, as a newly planned town constructed as late as the 1830s, to obtain at that stage a local Act of Parliament awarding the powers of an Improvement Commission over paving, cleansing, lighting and policing the streets. The Owners of the Middlesbrough Estate, a partnership of six individuals, therefore dealt with its responsibilities as founder of a new urban community by covenanting privately with 36 purchasers of plots of land in the town, to conduct 'municipal' affairs using regulations and provisions modelled on those employed by improvement commissioners in other urban centres. Compared with the first Improvement Commission established in Middlesbrough 10 years later, the contents of the 1831 covenant were simple and unsophisticated. Yet that agreement symbolizes the starting point of a municipal community before any statutory recognition of the municipality.

In 1841, in response to the rapid growth of population and houses in the 1830s, Middlesbrough obtained a local Act 'for paving, lighting, watching, cleansing, and otherwise improving the town of Middlesbrough and the neighbourhood thereof in the North Riding of the County of York, and for establishing a market therein', an elaborate piece of legislation with 288 clauses and eight schedules. It established the first Improvement Commission, and came to pass through the inhabitants' earnest desire to obtain government sanction. Urban government was thus entrusted to a statutory authority consisting of seven commissioners, many of them influential ironmasters and merchants.[36]

Later, the Commission was increased to 12 members, whose essential qualifications were that they were 'either a resident inhabitant of the said town, rated to the rates made for the relief of the poor of the township of Middlesbrough or of the township of Linthorpe in the annual Sum of £25 or upwards, or shall be seized or possessed or in the enjoyment of rents and profits of lands and hereditaments within the limits of this Act of the clear annual value of £20'. The first 12 commissioners were William Blenkinsop (innkeeper), H.F. Bolckow (ironmaster), George Chapman (joiner), William Fairbridge (butcher), William Fallows (ship owner and agent for the Stockton

[35] Webb, *English Local Government*, pp. 274, 235–6, 276.
[36] 4 & 5 Vict., c. lxviii, pp. 1425–1500.

and Darlington Railway), John Gribbin (draper of woollen and flax clothes), John Gilbert Holmes (shipbuilder), William Laws (builder), Richard Otley (land surveyor and pottery company manager), Isaac Sharp (accountant and agent for the Owners of the Middlesbrough Estate), Robert Ramsey (occupation unknown) and Henry Sidney (occupation unknown).[37]

Joseph Pease and other members of his family did not join the commissioners. Pease himself, however, besides taking a leading role in planning the town and building its industrial base, also paid the £552 9s 8d required to procure the first Improvement Act. As well, he offered funds to erect schools and churches in the town. Yet he never resided in Middlesbrough, and apart from his financial support to provide a physical infrastructure for the town, he did not channel the same enthusiasm into Middlesbrough politics as he displayed within his own community in the old-established, fashionable town of Darlington in the same region.[38]

The clauses of the Improvement Act 1841 range from administrative matters – the qualifications of commissioners, terms of office, eligibility and the right to vote, suffrage, general meetings, standing committees, auditing accounts, finance – to the powers of commissioners relating to paving, lighting, watching, cleansing the streets, housing, policing, nuisances and so on. There are 30 clauses regulating markets, including rules about cattle, food, weights and measures, tolls and stalls, and 44 regarding local rates.

It was noted towards the end, in clause 283, that any power and authority vested by this Act in the 1841 Improvement Commission would transfer to a new council if the town were in future granted a charter of incorporation. In any case the 1841 Act marks a considerable advance, much more consistent, self-contained, specific and detailed, than the provisions of the covenant 10 years earlier. All in all, its clauses represent the evolution of a self-governing body, moving from arrangements which were essentially personal, towards a distinct organ of collective administration.[39]

In 1853, Middlesbrough gained its long-awaited status of incorporated borough when granted a charter of incorporation. In the dozen years since the first Improvement Act, the town had grown up rapidly, becoming export base for the whole industrial agglomeration of Cleveland iron.[40] Its remarkable rise was greatly indebted to the discovery of the Cleveland Main Seam in 1850, bringing an abundant supply of iron ore from nearby Eston. The Middlesbrough district was able to build an unrivalled comparative advantage, for in addition to the rich vein of iron, it had access to plentiful supplies of high-quality South Durham coal, and the transportation facilities of the Stockton and Darlington Railway as well as river navigation on the Tees, its

37 Teesside Archives, CB/M/C 1/1, f. 1; 4 & 5 Vict., c. lxviii, pp. 1425–6; Lillie, *History of Middlesbrough*, pp. 58–60, 68; Ward's *North of England Dir.* (1851), pp. 46–7.

38 Lillie, *History of Middlesbrough*, p. 80; Orde, *Religion, Business and Society*, pp. 28–9.

39 4 & 5 Vict., c. lxviii, p. 1493; Webb, *English Local Government*, p.276.

40 For discussion of the concept of export base, see Chapter 2, pp. 33–51.

harbour exporting fuel, materials and finished products home and abroad. The development of a flourishing and diverse local economy was one factor that bred a municipal consciousness among Middlesbrough inhabitants.

Borough status was granted by the Privy Council in response to petitions from inhabitants, in line with the powers and provisions of the Municipal Corporations Act 1835, creating 'one body politic and corporate' called the Mayor, Aldermen and Burgesses of the Borough of Middlesbrough. Thereafter the town as an incorporated borough was entitled to have a common seal and to use armorial bearings and devices, could purchase land of any value within the town, and property outside the town worth up to £10,000 a year. The common council consisted of a mayor, four aldermen and 12 councillors. Councillors, assessors and auditors were elected by electors on the burgess roll, aldermen from among the councillors and the mayor from the councillors and aldermen. As Thane has pointed out, although the Improvement Commission was legally distinct (and in fact Middlesbrough gained five further Improvement Acts after 1853), it had members in common with the corporation, and in practice merged into the town council so that Middlesbrough became an independent municipal corporation in name and reality.[41]

The first mayor of Middlesbrough was Henry Ferdinand Bolckow, originally from Mecklenburg in Prussia, builder of the town's staple iron industry. Subsequently a Bench of Justices of the Peace was established, bringing an autonomous jurisdiction independent from that of the North Riding of Yorkshire. Two years later, in 1855, a public inquiry by an inspector of the General Board of Health under the Public Health Act 1848, into sewerage, drainage, water supply, the state of burial grounds, numbers and sanitary condition of inhabitants as well as paving, lighting, cleansing and watching, led to the formation of the Middlesbrough Local Board of Health.[42]

Even after Middlesbrough became a municipal borough, there were a further five Improvement Acts. Their provisions are shown in Table 1.9. Immediately after incorporation, the borough council established a committee to lobby for representation in parliament. In 1867, Disraeli offered to create a parliamentary constituency jointly with the rival town of Stockton, but the following year Middlesbrough acquired its own constituency, which included the suburbs of Ormesby, Linthorpe, Marton, South Bank and Normanby. Almost three-quarters of the electorate, 4,013 of the 5,456 registered to vote, lived in Middlesbrough. Middlesbrough's first mayor, Henry Ferdinand Bolckow, was also its first member of parliament. In 1888, the town became a county borough.[43]

The Improvement Commission's finances fluctuated sharply throughout the period of the authority's existence. There were wide variations in levels

[41] Teesside Archives, CB/M/C (2) 14/5b, pp. 1–8; Thane, 'Government and Society', p. 7.
[42] Lillie, *History of Middlesbrough*, pp. 162–3; Gott, *Henry Bolckow*, p. 69; 18 & 19 Vict., c. cxxv, pp. 1217–21.
[43] Gott, *Henry Bolckow*, pp. 71, 72, 74, 78; 29 & 30 Vict., c. cxliii, pp. 1845–99; 51 & 52 Vict., c. 41, pp. 257–355.

Table 1.9. Middlesbrough Improvement Acts, 1856–77

Year	Provisions	Clauses	Reference
1856	Divide borough into wards; purchase gasworks & light the district; enlarge the market place; establish a public wharf & passage over the River Tees	130	19 & 20 Vict., c. lxxvii
1858	Alter and improve boundaries of the municipal borough & district; enlarge the market place; construct landing places on the north side of the River Tees; establish a public passage up and over the River Tees; transfer the powers of the Burial Board to the Local Board; confer other powers on the Local Board & Corporation	86	21 & 22 Vict., c. cxl
1866	Extend and alter boundaries of the municipal borough and district; extend time for completion of the market place; construct additional gasworks and light adjoining townships; authorize compulsory purchase of the rights of the North-eastern Railway Co. in the Port Clarence landing place; construct a landing place at Newport; purchase lands for the same; extend powers of the Burial Board; provide a public park, an additional burial ground, a town hall and police station; improve certain streets and roads, and divert a public footpath; raise further monies; alter and amend existing Acts relating to the borough and district	123	29 & 30 Vict., c. cxliii
1874	Extend boundaries of the municipal borough; purchase a private road; raise further monies; alter, amend and in part repeal existing Acts relating to the borough and district	49	37 & 38 Vict., c. cviii
1877	Extend powers of the Corporation with respect to works for the storage of gas, markets, ferries and local government and improvement of the borough	42	40 Vict., c. xxx

of revenue throughout the 1840s. Spending also rose and fell, according to the particular projects then underway. Expenditure in 1841 included a large payment, £879, to parliamentary agents for procuring the first Improvement Act. Building a town hall and market house pushed up spending between 1845 and 1847, with £833 in 1845–6, and £1,536 in 1846–7, paid direct to builders, painters and joiners (see Table 1.10).[44]

Revenue from rates in 1841 amounted to as little as £144, an annual levy of only 4d in the pound on a total rateable value of £10,467 10s. At this

---

[44] Teesside Archives, CB/M/T, Income and Expenditure, Middlesbrough Improvement Act, 1841–50.

early stage in the making of Middlesbrough, the public authority often relied financially on the Owners of the Middlesbrough Estate. Yet gradually in the latter half of the 1840s, as the population and numbers of houses grew, the rateable value rose to more than £12,000 and the rate was increased from 4d to 9d in the pound, so that revenue from rates went up to £772 in 1847–8, and averaged £500 in the latter half of the 1840s.

To be blunt, however, immediately after the first Improvement Act very few tangible assets had accumulated in the town, so that little could be expected from regular revenue. In the lean years of the 1840s, town finances were unstable and the improvement commissioners had recourse to loans from members of the Owners of the Middlesbrough Estate, and other individuals. These loans seem to have been something like municipal bonds. A particular cause of the commissioners' financial problems during the first half of the 1840s was that the town had to repay the large sum borrowed to procure the Improvement Act 1841. In 1841, the town had taken a loan of £558 from Joseph Pease to settle other debts incurred in procuring the Act. That same year, to cover a deficit in revenue, further sums were sought, with another £300 borrowed from Joseph Pease, £266 from Thomas Richardson and £440 recorded as a loan from Mr R. Addison on the market tolls.[45]

In the first half of the 1840s, the town had to be supported many times to cover revenue deficits, loans coming mainly from the Owners of the Middlesbrough Estate. At least until the middle of the 1850s, the company continued to underpin the town's finances and promote its autonomy. From the outset, the town itself had not needed to spend much money on utilities and capital projects, since most of the urban infrastructure had been provided by the company. Moreover the Improvement Commission could rely on the Owners of the Middlesbrough Estate for loans whenever it was not possible to finance urban improvement from other sources. In addition to these sums lent to the Commission, the Owners of the Middlesbrough Estate donated the land on which the first town hall was built in 1846. Thus it could be said that the company was in fact another arm of town government.

While Middlesbrough's finances in the 1840s were small-scale compared with, for example, a total annual revenue and expenditure amounting to £17,000 in Birmingham in 1831, a stable rise in rateable value of property in the town and in revenue from rates indicates that Middlesbrough was moving steadily towards maturity as an urban community.[46]

Towards the end of the 1840s, financial reports received by the improvement commissioners show more balanced budgets, with a surplus of £116 in 1848–9. From this time, the local authority did not routinely borrow money to meet revenue needs. Discovery of the new iron measures in 1850, the subsequent burgeoning of the local iron and steel industries, and the grant of

[45] Teesside Archives, CB/M/C 1/1, pp. 12–13; CB/M/T, Income and Expenditure, Middlesbrough Improvement Act, 1841–2.
[46] Webb, *English Local Government*, p. 256.

Table 1.10. Revenue of Middlesbrough, 1841–55

Year	Revenue			Debts[b]			Debts[c]		
1841–42	£1,198	15s	0d	£1,128	9s	1d			
1842–43	£512	10s	11.5d	£1,008	7s	10d			
1843–44	£1,524	11s	8d	£1,000	0s	0d			
1844–45	£516	19s	7d	£900	0s	0d			
1845–46	£2,139	4s	11d	£2,300	0s	0d			
1846–47	£2,003	12s	11.5d	£2,783	9s	8d			
1847–48	£982	18s	0d	£2,759	5s	0d			
1848–49	£852	15s	0d	£2,794	4s	3s	£30	3s	7d
1849–50	£899	7s	6d	£2,722	11s	0d	£4	16s	0d
1850–51	£970	6s	10.5d	£2,700	0s	0d	£9	10s	0d
1851–52	£1,317	4s	9d	£2,700	0s	0d	£6	18s	6d
1852–53[a]	£1,805	7s	3d	£3,072	16s	3d			
1853–54	£4,207	0s	2d	£4,089	3s	6d			
1854–55									
General Account	£6,903	2s	7d						
Watch Rate & Police Acc.	£385	19s	10d						
Borough Fund Acc.	£4,271	12s	1d						
Total	£11,560	14s	6d	£5,268	2s	3d			

Notes: [a]In 1853, by incorporation, the borough boundary was extended. [b]Debts owing by the Commissioners. [c]Debts owing to the Commissioners.

Source: Teesside Archives, CB/M/T, 1841–1853, Statement and Account of Income and Expenditure, The Commissioners under the Middlesbro' Improvement Act, 1854–1855, Statement of Income and Expenditure, Town Council of the Borough of Middlesbrough, Acting in the Capacity of Commissioners under the Middlesbrough Improvement Act.

incorporation as a borough in 1853, undoubtedly stabilized Middlesbrough's finances. In 1853 and 1854, total annual revenue reached £4,207, that is, 2.3 times that of the previous year, which was mainly due to the change in urban boundary resulting from incorporation. In 1854 and 1855, a further advance was made, with revenue growing to 2.7 times that of 1853 and 1854.[47]

Table 1.11 shows changes in the proportion of the general rates in relation to total revenues. In the 1840s, revenue from rates never reached £1,000, while total revenues fluctuated wildly between £500 and £2,000, so that the proportion was extremely inconsistent. From the middle of the 1860s, revenue from rates never fell below £8,000 and began to top £10,000, and the proportion stabilized at somewhere around 40%. As well as the increase in revenue, which flowed from the town's expansion and a consequent rise in rateable value, new sources of income presented themselves. In the later 1860s, the council raised money from sales of manure, from profits of the gas works, markets, horses and carts, rents from various town properties including houses, shops, stables, industrial buildings and warehouses, and

---

[47] Teesside Archives, CB/M/C 1/2, p. 94; CB/M/T, Income and Expenditure, 1841–53.

Plate 1.2. The old Town Hall

from the police. Through this diversification, the town became less dependent on the general district and borough rates.

The revenue generated by the police force became substantial, in the late 1860s the second largest source of income after the borough rates themselves. These proceeds made up 8.9% of total revenue in 1867, 10.1% in 1868, 9.8% in 1869 and 7.6% in 1870. Financial records in 1855 show that the watch rate and police account included amounts allowed by the county authorities for the rent of cells and for the superintendent's salary; a sum paid by Bolckow and Vaughan for the salary of a police officer for nine months; and the watch rate, at 4d amounting to £385 19s 10d. The improvement commissioners' minutes in 1850 record a request from Bolckow and Vaughan's ironworks to dispatch private police and a private watchman. This suggests a system whereby private enterprises could ask the local authority to supply public officials.[48]

In 1854–5, the method of recording income and expenditure changed. To the general district revenue were added a borough fund account, and watch and police account. Between 1855 and 1866, an accounting system emerged that recorded estimated as well as actual figures. At the outset, differences between estimates and actual tended to be considerable. Later, the differences narrowed, perhaps indicating an improvement on the part of the administrators to make realistic estimates of revenue and spending. From 1872, a general district revenue fund was separately recorded from the borough revenue fund, and in 1873 the adoption of a half-yearly accounting system made budget administration more sophisticated still (see Table 1.12).[49]

---

[48] Teesside Archives, CB/M/T, General District Revenue, etc., 1850/1–1854/5; CB/M/C 1/2, p. 183.
[49] Teesside Archives, CB/M/T, General District Revenue, etc., 1866–74.

Table 1.11. Proportion of Rates to Total Revenue in Middlesbrough, 1841–74

Year	Rates			Total Revenue			Rates/Revenue (%)
1841–42	£144	6s	11	£1,198	15s	0	12.0
1842–43	£450	4s	1d	£512	10s	11.5d	87.8
1843–44	£420	16s	11d	£1,524	11s	8d	27.6
1844–45	£350	15s	11d	£516	19s	7d	67.9
1845–46	£510	16s	0d	£2,139	4s	11d	23.9
1846–47	£563	14s	1.5d	£2,003	12s	11.5d	28.1
1847–48	£772	17s	6d	£982	18s	0d	78.6
1848–49	£654	15s	8d	£852	15s	0d	76.8
1849–50	£597	12s	1d	£899	7s	6d	66.4
1850–51	£727	13s	8.5d	£970	6s	10.5d	75.0
1851–52	£935	3s	10.5d	£1,317	4s	9d	71.0
1852–53[a]	£1,090	17s	0d	£1,805	7s	3d	60.4
1853–54	£1,477	16s	8d	£4,207	0s	2d	35.1
1854–55	£1,937	7s	5d	£11,560	14s	6d	16.8
1866–67	£8,396	9s	6d	£21,650	17s	1d	38.8
1867–68	£8,723	18s	4d	£18,902	2s	5d	46.2
1868–69	£10,639	19s	2d	£20,777	3s	5d	51.2
1869–70	£8,660	1s	3d	£25,957	3s	2d	33.4
1870–71	£19,348	11s	1d	£29,408	18s	10d	65.8
1872–73	£19,578	17s	4d	£36,649	10s	7d	53.4
1873–74	£35,346	11s	11d	£46,068	7s	9d	76.7

Note: [a]In 1853, by incorporation, the town became borough and its boundary was extended. Also in 1856, 1866 and 1874, the boundaries of the borough were extended which would have been reflected in the increase in the rates.

Source: Teesside Archives, CB/M/T, 1841–1853, Statement and Account of Income and Expenditure, The Commissioners under the Middlesbro' Improvement Act, 1854–1855, Statement of Income and Expenditure, Town Council of the Borough of Middlesbrough, Acting in the Capacity of Commissioners under the Middlesbrough Improvement Act; Teesside Archives, CB/M/T, Borough of Middlesbrough, General District Revenue, etc., 1866–1874.

From 1876, the financial records were presented in a new style, entitled 'An Abstract and Statement of the Mayor, Aldermen and Burgesses of the Borough of Middlesbrough, *Under the Municipal Corporation Acts; The Middlesbrough Improvement Act, 1845, 1856, 1866 and 1874; the Local Government Act, 1858 and the Burial Board Acts, and so on*'.[50] The intention of this change seems to have been to specify the authority and responsibility for auditing. Furthermore, from this time, capital accounts were added. These amendments to the borough's financial system are a further reflection of the fact that the town was reaching maturity, not just in size and financial worth, but in the way it carried out its administrative business.

In summary, the substantial financial deficits following immediately after the first Improvement Act were mainly a result of the costs of procuring

[50] Middlesbrough Central Lib., MMI 352.17, 73483.

Table 1.12. Revenue and Expenditure of Middlesbrough Borough
Council, 1866–74

Year	Estimated	Actual	
	Receipts	Receipts	Expenditure
1866–67	£16,249 12s 0d	£21,650 17s 1d	£22,526 14s 7d
1867–68	£18,032 15s 11d	£18,902 2s 5d	£20,018 18s10d
1868–69	£20,603 16s 5d	£20,777 3s 5d	£22,424 19s11d
1869–70	£21,277 12s 8d	£25,957 3s 2d	£28,226 14s10d
1870–71	£29,660 16s 7d	£29,408 18s10d	£30,697 9s 1d
1872–73	General Distric Revenue Fund		
	£27,865 16s 3d	£30,377 11s 2d	£36,989 13s 1d
	Borough Fund Revenue		
	£5,276 6s 0d	£6,271 19s 5d	£10,514 17s 4d
Total	£33,142 2s 3d	£36,649 10s 7d	£47,504 10s 5d
1873 (1/2 year)	District Fund Revenue		
	£20,828 6s 1d	£22,264 12s10d	£23,322 18s 2d
	Borough Fund Revenue		
	£4,818 18s 8d	£1,661 10s 6d	£7,708 4s 6d
1874 (1/2 year)	District Fund Revenue		
	£16,930 14s 10d	£15,407 4s 2d	£16,920 0s 2d
	Borough Fund Revenue		
	£9,523 0s 1d	£6,735 0s 3d	£8,233 7s 0d
1873–74	District Fund Revenue		
	£37,759 0s 11d	£37,671 17s 0d	£40,242 18s 4d
	Borough Fund Revenue		
	£14,341 18s 9d	£8,396 10s 9d	£15,941 11s 6d
Total	£52,100 19s 8d	£46,068 7s 9d	£56,184 9s 10

Source: Borough of Middlesbrough, General District Revenue, etc., 1866–1874,Teesside
Archives, CB/M/T.

the Act, as well as meeting the costs of developing and maintaining urban
infrastructure to serve a rapidly increasing population. As the numbers of
people, and consequently the rateable value of the town, rose, income from
rates increased proportionately. All in all the financial records from the first
Improvement Act in 1841, into the 1870s, suggest that the municipality was
making substantial progress in breaking away from its financial dependence
on the Owners of the Middlesbrough Estate.

The early dominance of the Owners of the Middlesbrough Estate also had
consequences for local politics, as well as for urban development. Generally in the nineteenth and early-twentieth centuries, local government was
a partnership between municipality, private sector and voluntary providers
to serve the needs of residents. In Middlesbrough, the fabric of local politics was tripartite governance by the Owners of the Middlesbrough Estate,
the municipality and the ironmasters. Usually they collaborated, but at times

they would turn against each other. All improvement, civic development and reform had to depend on this multiplex governance.[51]

One remarkable change in the borough council's composition over the period was a decline in the dominance of substantial manufacturers and merchants. Instead, *petit bourgeois*, such as small producers, retailers, publicans and other shopkeepers, gradually came to predominate on the council. As will be analysed in detail in Chapter 3, the burgeoning population presented new markets for small tradesmen offering foodstuffs, clothes and accommodation, for those engaged in building and construction, and for other service industries. These traders added an important element of stability to the town, as they tended to be much more settled than other groups of in-migrants.

In the late-nineteenth century, the hegemony of merchants and manufacturers on the town council gradually weakened, with 'intermediate social classes', particularly local shopkeepers, coming into greater prominence. The first town councillors after incorporation in 1853 included four ironmasters, a merchant, a shipbuilder, a miller and six others. The rise of the 'shopocracy' was evident in 1872, with 10 ironmasters and seven shopkeepers on the council. By 1912, there were 15 shopkeepers and only one ironmaster.[52]

Of the four sources for urban finance in the late-nineteenth and early-twentieth centuries – rates, central government grants, income from estates, dues and services, and loans – Middlesbrough could rely only on rates and municipal trading. In the beginning, a basic urban infrastructure was provided by the Owners of the Middlesbrough Estate, which was institutionally distinct from the municipality, but the additional infrastructure demanded by a rapidly growing town later in the nineteenth century was dependent on funds raised mainly from the rates.[53]

As the presence of large manufacturers on the town council declined, ideas of constructive improvements in the urban environment retreated, for the lower middle-class group in control of municipal affairs would avoid at all costs any increase in the rates, their main aim being to keep the cost of local public services to a minimum.[54] For example, when the first mayor, Henry Bolckow, with his keen interest in public health, advocated a better drainage system and the introduction of water closets in the middle of the 1850s, he encountered two sources of opposition. One was the Owners of the Middlesbrough Estate, which as owners of the majority of land had a powerful voice in any discussion of proposed reform of the urban environment. The other seat of resistance was the town council, reluctant to undertake a project that necessitated a rate increase. They consented, but unwillingly. Indeed, Buchanan's report in 1871 noted that the scheme had not been completed, and that by-laws setting minimum standards for new houses were not enforced.[55]

51 Doyle, 'Changing Functions of Government', p. 313.
52 Briggs, *Victorian Cities*, pp. 258–9; Doyle, 'Changing Functions of Government', p. 298.
53 Doyle, 'Changing Functions of Government', pp. 294–5.
54 Gott, *Henry Bolckow*, p. 69; Thane, 'Government and Society', p. 23; Nossiter, *Influence, Opinion and Political Idioms*, pp. 144–5; Day, 'A Spirit of Improvement', pp. 105, 111.
55 Gott, *Henry Bolckow*, p. 69; National Archives, MH/113/4, pp. 6–7.

By the late 1860s, Middlesbrough had become a self-contained administrative unit, with an autonomous town government, its own courts and local
board of health, as well as an institutional framework serving the industrial
agglomeration: a chamber of commerce, Royal Exchange, the Cleveland
Warrant Store system for the local pig-iron trade, ironmasters' organizations
such as the Cleveland Ironmasters' Association and the North of England
Iron Manufacturers' Association, ironworkers' trade unions, and the Board
of Arbitration and Conciliation for the North of England Manufactured Iron
Trade. Yet the town was unfortunate in that the 'shopocracy' which had risen
to power in the late-nineteenth century was indifferent, as were its equivalents in other Victorian towns, to the urban improvements so urgently needed.

Plate 1.3. The new Town Hall

2

Industrial Agglomeration in the Cleveland Iron and Steel Industry

Many various causes have led to the localization of industries; but the chief causes have been physical conditions, such as the character of the climate and the soil, the existence of mines and quarries in the neighbourhood, or within easy access by land or water. Thus metallic industries have generally been either near mines or in places where fuel was cheap. The iron industries in England first sought those districts in which charcoal was plentiful, and afterwards they went to the neighbourhood of collieries.[1]

Industrial Development

The development of Cleveland iron and steel through the second half of the nineteenth century, it can be argued, offers a classic example of industrial agglomeration building in a region that had made the most of its early historical and geographical endowments. In this model, factors favour early industrialization, and once that process is underway, the benefits become cumulative. Scale economies and low transport costs consolidate an initial advantage, and industrial concentration results.[2] This chapter examines, first, the background to industrial agglomeration in the region, and the historical development of the Cleveland iron and steel industry. Second, it considers the productivity and markets that sustained the industry and, finally, attempts to consider how industrial agglomeration advanced in this region.

From the mid-nineteenth century, Middlesbrough concentrated upon manufacturing pig iron, wrought or malleable iron, and finished products including rails, plates, bars and angles. Production of ironstone, pig and wrought iron, as well as rail and other finished products, grew spectacularly during the period.[3] The level of ironstone produced, 188,000 tons in 1851, had increased five times by 1861, and in the next decade grew to four

---

1 Marshall, *Principles of Economics*, Vol. I, pp. 329–30.
2 For Catalan industrialization in Spain in the same period, see Tirado *et al.*, 'Economic Integration and Industrial Location', p. 350.
3 Bullock, 'Origins of Economic Growth on Teesside', pp. 85–7; Harrison, 'Development of a Distinctive Cleveland Blast Furnace Practice', pp. 57–64, 74–9, 84–94; Isard, 'Some Locational Factors in the Iron and Steel Industry', p. 208; Taylor, 'The Infant Hercules and the Augean Stables', pp. 54–5; for technical aspects of pig and wrought iron- and steel-making processes during the period, see Burnham and Hoskins, *Iron and Steel in Britain, 1870–1930*, p. 19.

Table 2.1. Cleveland Ironstone Production, 1873–80

Year	Output (tons)
1873	5,435,233
1874	5,428,497
1875	6,085,541
1876	6,571,968
1877	6,289,745
1878	5,327,663
1879	4,721,395
1880	6,500,000 (estimated)

Note: average annual output from 1873 to 1879: 5,694,291 tons.

Source: Modern Records Centre, Univ. of Warwick, MSS 365/CIA, Minute Book, Vol. 2; Secretary's Report, 1880.

million tons, its value then being approximately £1 million. In 1881, production reached a maximum of 6.5 million tons, as shown in Table 2.1. While a proportion of Cleveland ironstone was sent for processing in Co. Durham and Northumberland, most stayed within the Middlesbrough district where it was made into pig iron.

According to some estimates, Cleveland pig iron production increased from 24,300 tons in 1851, growing 20 times to 543,000 tons in 1861. From the middle of the 1870s it reached over 2 million tons annually, one-third of national output. In a decade or so from 1850, Cleveland came to control the world pig iron market. In the boom period of the 1870s, Middlesbrough and district produced approximately 30% of the total pig iron made in the United Kingdom, roughly 14–15% of world production, as shown in Table 2.2.[4] This rapid rise to international importance, within a period of less than 20 years after the discovery of the Cleveland Main Seam at Eston, was made clear in 1867 when Middlesbrough was added to the list of Britain's main industrial centres in *The Times*' 'State of Trade' reports, one of 15 hubs of manufacturing, including five old-established centres of the iron industry.[5]

During this period, the principal domestic market for pig iron was in inland areas, where the demand was largely for a higher quality pig iron than that produced in Middlesbrough. Consequently, almost half of Cleveland pig iron was exported abroad or transported by sea for domestic sale around coastal areas. Before the 1880s, the remaining half was consumed in or around Middlesbrough, used to make wrought iron and finished iron products. Table 2.3 illustrates in detail the destination of pig iron output: total production, ironmasters' stocks, holdings in Warrant Stores (to be further

---

[4] Bell, *Notes on the Progress of the Iron Trade*, p. 14; Bell, *Trade of the United Kingdom*, p. 11; Isard, 'Some Locational Factors in the Iron and Steel Industry', p. 208; Birch, *Economic History of the British Iron and Steel Industry*, p. 336; Bullock, 'Origins of Economic Growth on Teesside', pp. 85–6; Briggs, *Victorian Cities*, p. 250.

[5] *The Times*, 28 Feb. 1826; 11 Apr. 1826; 18 Nov. 1867.

Table 2.2. Pig Iron Production in the North East, United Kingdom
and the World, 1860–77

Year	North East	United Kingdom	World Total	% North East UK	% North East World
1860	543,000	3,889,750	7,243,209	14.0	7.5
1865	1,012,478	4,819,254	9,292,777	21.0	10.9
1870	1,627,557	5,963,515	11,616,726	27.3	14.1
1871	1,823,294	6,627,179	12,565,337	27.5	14.5
1872	1,921,052	6,741,929	14,445,351	28.5	13.3
1873	2,000,811	6,566,451	14,693,129	30.5	13.6
1874	2,020,848	5,991,408	13,407,053	33.7	15.1
1875	2,049,000	6,365,462	13,708,338	32.2	14.9
1876	2,069,185	6,555,997	13,671,540	31.6	15.1
1877	2,094,020	6,608,664	13,627,793	31.7	15.4

Note: Measured in tons.

Source: Gjers, 'President's Address', app. Tables B, C; Burton, 'Some Notes on Early History of Cleveland Iron Trade', p. 132.

Table 2.3. Pig Iron Production in Cleveland, 1864–80

Year	Output	Makers' Stocks	Warrant Stores	Total Stocks (%)	Export (%)
1864	926,054	42,385	39,955	82,340 (8.9)[a]	?
1865	975,311	34,305	42,600	76,905 (7.9)	?
1866	1,043,527	101,521	64,164	165,685 (15.9)	?
1867	1,147,900	102,519	71,826	174,345 (15.2)	136,378 (11.9)[a]
1868	1,233,418	80,898	72,029	152,927 (12.4)	136,806 (11.1)
1869	1,459,508	84,243	31,364	115,607 (7.9)	185,777 (12.7)
1870	1,695,377	104,606	12,739	117,345 (6.9)	216,908 (12.8)
1871	1,884,239	65,601	2,730	68,331 (3.6)	330,646 (17.5)
1872	1,968,972	40,697	931	41,628 (2.1)	386,624 (19.6)
1873	1,999,491	80,328	0	80,328 (4.0)	397,077 (19.8)
1874	2,001,233	89,737	0	89,737 (4.5)	275,721 (13.7)
1875	2,047,763	74,258	0	74,258 (3.6)	367,907 (18.0)
1876	2,075,565	161,041	21,500	182,541 (8.8)	357,333 (17.0)
1877	2,124,831	262,067	42,730	304,797 (14.3)	364,899 (18.0)
1878	2,023,177	248,139	89,198	337,337 (16.7)	397,316 (19.5)
1879	1,781,443	–	–	–	469,739 (26.0)
1880	2,510,853	–	–	–	614,564 (24.4)

Notes: Measured in tons. [a] Percentage proportions of total output.

Source: *Iron, Steel, and Allied Trades, Annual Report to Members* (1878), pp. 18–19; (1879), pp. 9–10; (1881), p. 10; Green, 'Royal Exchange', pp. 122, 127.

discussed below), and exports. It also shows the percentage of all locally manufactured pig iron which was held in stock or exported. In the decade after 1864, Cleveland pig iron manufacture increased in quantity more than 2.3 times, and exports grew 2.7 times, reaching 20% of production.

Although the financial crisis of 1866 brought a fall in growth rates, which led to a doubling in quantity of stockpiles both by ironmasters and in the Warrant Stores to 15%, the industry recovered in 1869. Afterwards it continued a steady growth until 1876, when a severe depression struck. Between 1867 and 1876, stocks continued on average as low as 4.7%. Compared to its Scottish counterpart during the same period, Cleveland showed conspicuous progress, its total production of 1,999,491 tons more than twice that of the whole of Scotland (993,000 tons) in 1873. In the proportion of stocks carried, Cleveland generally returned lower rates than Scotland, holding between 2% and 9% except during the financial crisis and the period of the Great Strike in the North East iron industry. In the same period, the average proportion of stock in Scotland was 53% before 1871.[6]

Even years of depression after 1873 did not bring any radical decline and failure in Cleveland iron and steel. At the beginning of the depression, in 1874, the United Kingdom's total production dropped to 5,991,408 tons, but it recovered to previous levels in 1876, although British ironmasters continued to complain about the depth and prolongation of price cuts. In Cleveland as in British iron and steel overall, the worst years were 1877, 1878 and 1879, coinciding with the world recession.[7] After 1879, the Cleveland iron industry exhibited considerable resilience in pig- and wrought-iron manufacture, as well as in exporting. In 1880, the quantity of Cleveland pig iron produced was 1.4 times that of 1879, while wrought iron production more than doubled. That same year, exports of Cleveland pig iron grew 1.3 times, matching the rise in pig iron and steel export from the whole of the United Kingdom.[8]

In 1877, there were no fewer than 265 pig iron producers dispersed around the United Kingdom, 39 of them in Cleveland and 27 in Scotland.[9] As Table 2.4 shows, during the difficult years of pig iron production between 1874 and 1877, the number of blast furnaces in the United Kingdom averaged 986, of which only 58%, on average 568 furnaces, were in blast. Cleveland accounted for 11% of the total United Kingdom blast furnaces, but made up 16% of the total in blast. Net working rates in Cleveland iron and steel at this time ranged between 70% and 80%, higher than those for Scotland. Although in 1877 Cleveland iron and steel experienced a downturn in working rate, to 74%, it remained much higher than the rates in Staffordshire, Scotland and other North East counties, which registered 30%, 57% and 63%, respectively.

6   *Iron, Steel, and Allied Trades, Annual Reports*, 1878, pp. 18–19; 1879, pp. 9–10; 1881, p. 10; Green, 'Royal Exchange', pp. 122, 127–8.

7   For the recession in Germany's heavy industries in these years, see Jackson, *Migration and Urbanization in the Ruhr Valley*, p. 193.

8   *Iron, Steel, and Allied Trades, Annual Reports*, 1878, pp. 18–19; 1879, pp. 9–10, 39; 1881, p. 10; Green, 'Royal Exchange', pp. 122, 127; Modern Records Centre, Univ. of Warwick, MSS 365/CIA, Secretary's Report for 1880; Minute Book, vol. 2; MSS.365/BAC, Mr. Waterhouse's Returns (Sale of Manufactured Iron), 3 vols, 1869–1919.

9   *Iron, Steel, and Allied Trades, Annual Report*, 1878, p. 16.

Table 2.4. Number of Blast Furnaces in the United Kingdom, 1874–77

Region	1874		1875		1876		1877	
	Total	In blast	Total	In blast	Total	In blast	Total	In blast
Cleveland	112 (8)[a]	91	116 (4)	90	116 (3)	88	119 (1)	88
North East	44 (5)	35	45 (2)	24	47 (1)	23	45 (2)	19
North West	91 (10)	57	95 (8)	55	92 (7)	51	97 (3)	59
South Staffordshire	169	86	163	74	147	55	147	42
North Staffordshire	45 (2)	29	43 (1)	24	40 (3)	26	40 (4)	25
Shropshire	25 (1)	17	24 (2)	19	23 (2)	15	25	13
West Riding	52	43	54	33	49 (1)	28	50	27
Derbyshire	54	44	54 (4)	35	57 (1)	35	58 (2)	38
Northampton	16 (1)	13	16 (3)	10	20	11	20 (2)	14
Lincolnshire	13 (6)	12	19	14	20 (3)	9	21 (2)	9
Gloucestershire ⎱ Wiltshire ⎰ Somerset	18	11	18	11	18	7	18 (1)	5
North Wales	13	7	13	6	12	3	11	2
South Wales & Monmouth	196	102	176 (1)	70	165	62	163	58
Scotland	157	121	154 (3)	114	157	116	155	88
Charcoal Furnaces	5	3	5	3	5	2	5	2
Total	1,010	671	993	582	968	531	974	489

Note: [a]Number of blast furnaces being built.

Source: Iron, Steel, and Allied Trades, Annual Report to Members (1878), pp. 27–8.

In a worldwide context, Cleveland, as mentioned already, accounted for 14% to 15% of total pig-iron production during the 1870s. As seen from Table 2.5, the United Kingdom produced approximately 47.3% of pig iron in the world in 1876. It also led the world in production related to size of population, with 3.8 hundredweight (cwt) per head. Cleveland, as the main pig iron making region of the United Kingdom, was in a paramount position. The United States of America, with 2,093,236 tons, came second after the United Kingdom. The United States figure was 15% of world production, and 1.08 cwt per head of population. During the recession which began in 1873, America experienced a fall from 2,868,278 to somewhere around 2 million tons, whereas the United Kingdom saw a smaller decrease, to 6 million tons in 1874, and recovering soon afterwards to 6.5 million tons. With levels of production continuing at three times those of the United States, the United Kingdom's supremacy persisted into the 1870s.

As we will see in more detail below, America and Germany were the two main overseas markets, taking nearly half of total British exports. In the early 1870s, almost half of British pig iron was sold abroad, with 25% of total exports, some 270,000 tons, coming from Middlesbrough. In 1871, 38% of

Table 2.5. World Pig Iron Production, 1876

Countries	Output in tons (%)	Estimated output per head (cwt)[a]
Great Britain	6,555,997 (47.3)	3.80
USA	2,093,236 (15.1)	1.08
France	1,449,536 (10.5)	0.80
Germany	1,862,500 (13.5)	0.96
Belgium	440,958 (3.2)	2.01
Russia	397,500[b] (2.9)	0.12
Sweden	339,486[b] (2.5)	0.58
Austria	480,000 (3.4)	0.28
Other Countries	228,000 (1.6)	
Total	13,847,213 (100.0)	

Notes: [a]Hundredweight (50.8 kg) per head of estimated population. [b]Output in 1875.

Source: Iron, Steel, and Allied Trades, Annual Report to Members (1878), pp. 28–9.

the 1.8 million tons of pig iron produced on Teesside, and 43% of the region's production in 1881, was sent overseas via the port of Middlesbrough. By the 1860s the town was 'export base' for the Cleveland industrial region.[10]

As for wrought iron, in 1861, production on Teesside was 600,000 tons, amounting to 20% to 25% of total British wrought-iron production. At that time there were 197 puddling furnaces and 35 rolling mills in this region. A decade later, 24 wrought-iron manufacturers were recorded, operating altogether 1,178 puddling furnaces. As ironstone-mining and pig-iron manufacture developed, there followed an expansion in production of wrought iron, and further diversification in finished-iron products. It has been estimated that, just as pig iron increased by 4.4 times from 8,590 tons of production in 1856 to 37,865 tons in 1872, so in that same period wrought-iron and finished-iron products grew at exactly the same rate, by a factor of 4.4, from 2,660 tons to 11,736 tons.[11]

Production of rails, plates, bars and angles in Cleveland were also undergoing rapid expansion. All finished-iron products saw a high growth rate between 1864 and 1865, from 84,863 to 138,216 tons. Rails accounted for a particularly high proportion of this growth, making up over 40% of total tonnage of finished wrought-iron products until 1876. Between 1866 and 1874, rail production increased by 3.6 times, from 96,275 tons in 1866 to

---

[10] Bullock, 'Origins of Economic Growth on Teesside', pp. 86–7. Regarding the concept of *export base*, we have drawn on North: 'The use of the term "base" has become popular among urban economists and city planners in the concept of an urban economic base, which refers to those activities of a metropolitan community that export goods and services to other areas'. See North, 'Location Theory and Regional Economic Growth', p. 247, footnotes; with respect to the concept of export base, see also Andrews, 'Mechanics of the Urban Economic Base', p. 161; Hudson, 'The Regional Perspective', p. 22; *The Industrial Revolution*, p. 102; Pollard, *Peaceful Conquest*, p. 39.

[11] Bullock, 'Origins of Economic Growth on Teesside', p. 89; Odber, 'Origins of Industrial Peace', p. 204.

343,242 tons in 1874. Thereafter, rail production in Cleveland fell dramatically, plunging from 107,830 tons in 1876 to 36,750 tons in 1877. This coincides with the shift in 1877 into producing plates for the shipbuilding industry already established on the Tees, which was at that time changing over from wooden to iron ships. From then until 1892, plates were the most significant of the finished-iron products. Puddle bars were the next most important item among finished-iron products. As a proportion of total finished wrought-iron products in Cleveland, bars rose from 15.6% in 1874 to 34.8% in 1892, and from 1893 surpassed production of plates. Puddle-bar production in Cleveland reached 852,199 tons in 1882, accounting for almost 30% of the UK's total of 2,841,834 tons.[12]

Productivity and Markets

The Cleveland iron and steel industries owed their domestic and international predominance from the mid-nineteenth century to a large extent to the so-called 'Cleveland practice' of iron making. This technique, standard procedure in the Ironmasters' District on the banks of the river Tees, is explained by Harrison:

> The Cleveland blast furnace was developed specifically to smelt large quantities of relatively low grade ironstone as cheaply as possible and to achieve this, reliance was placed on obtaining maximum thermal efficiency by increasing the height of the furnace stack in order to utilize the heat generated at the base of the furnace to heat the materials being charged in at the top.[13]

This system was made possible by the very high load-bearing qualities of Durham coke. Thus the Cleveland ironmasters were fortunate in that the disadvantage of relatively poor quality Cleveland ironstone was largely offset by the excellent quality of Durham coke.

When the region's iron and steel industries were at their zenith in the late 1860s and through the 1870s, the 'Cleveland practice' had a number of distinctive features:

1. To improve the quality of charge in the blast furnace, Cleveland ironstone was always *calcined*, that is, roasted in a kiln.
2. Blast furnaces were large, rising to a height of 80 feet and with an average capacity of 25,000 to 30,000 cubic feet.
3. Furnaces were worked with a closed top system.
4. Furnaces were worked with hot blast.

---

12 Modern Records Centre, Univ. of Warwick, MSS 365/BAC, Mr. Waterhouse's Returns (Sale of Manufactured Iron), vols 1–3; Bullock, 'Origins of Economic Growth on Teesside', pp. 89–91; Burton, 'Some Notes on the Early History of the Cleveland Iron Trade', p. 135.

13 Harrison, *John Gjers, Ironmaster*, p. 10.

5. The size of furnace called for an exceptional range of material-handling techniques, including water-balance, pneumatic, hydraulic or direct winding hoists.

6. Instead of beam blowing engines, direct-acting engines were used.

The enormous Cleveland furnaces towered above the flat marshy land on the river banks, and usually materials were lifted vertically with a variety of mechanized hoists. The older and smaller blast furnaces built between 1851 and 1859 were demolished and replaced by ones of the larger variety. One of the developers of the new furnaces, John Gjers, originally from Sweden and an engineer and ironmaster in Cleveland, argued that larger blast furnaces increased output, were economical on fuel and improved the quality of pig iron. It was thanks to the prevalence of the capital-intensive Cleveland practice during this period that the region's iron-making industry gained the potential to compete in domestic and international markets.[14]

Landes has pointed out that, at least until the end of the nineteenth and the beginning of the twentieth centuries, productivity and competitiveness in the British iron industry were certainly ahead of those of her nearest competitors, America and Germany:

> The *most powerful* furnaces in the Ruhr yielded around 250 tons of pig iron a week in 1870; the *average* British unit did almost as much (183 tons), and the new eighty-foot 'monsters' (the expression is Clapham) of the Cleveland district, with gas recovery and superheated blast, were turning out 450 to 550 tons a week in 1865.[15]

Sir Isaac Lowthian Bell, the Cleveland metallurgist and ironmaster, also noticed how the productivity of the British iron industry compared favourably with its equivalents in America, Germany, France, Belgium and Luxemburg. The number of ironworkers per furnace in America was 17% greater, while 50% less pig iron was produced from each furnace than in Cleveland. In America, nine blast furnace men made 260 tons a week on average, while in the United Kingdom six blast furnace men produced 460 tons a week. By Bell's calculation, American blast furnace men therefore produced an average 28.9 tons per head, while their British counterparts made 76.7 tons, a difference in productivity of about 2.7 times. It was, as Bell remarked, because labour-saving machinery had not then been introduced in America. As there were fewer skilled wrought-iron workers in America, it was also the case that wage rates there were double those of the United Kingdom.[16] Until

---

[14] Harrison, *John Gjers, Ironmaster*, pp. 10–11; Jeans, *Notes on Northern Industries*, p. 65; Gjers, 'President's Address', pp. 30–54, app. Tables B, C.; Gjers, 'Description of the Ayresome Ironworks', pp. 202–17.

[15] Landes, *The Unbound Prometheus*, p. 219, original emphasis.

[16] Bell, *Manufacture of Iron and Steel*, pp. 562–7.

the end of the nineteenth century, therefore, Britain maintained a lead in both pig and wrought iron.

British predominance over its European counterparts was also strongly evident. For example, although wage levels of blast furnace men in the United Kingdom were 50% higher than in Germany, France, Belgium and Luxemburg, the number of workers per ton engaged in furnace process in these countries was larger than in the United Kingdom. Consequently wage levels per ton in these countries, with the exception of Luxemburg, were 25% higher than in Cleveland.[17]

Crew has compared labour productivity in 1878 in a German iron works, Bochum Verein, with that of the Clarence Iron Works in Cleveland. Louis Baare, a director of Bochumer Verein, testified before the Iron Inquiry Commission that a German blast furnace required 75.5 workers at a cost per shift of 221.005 marks, whereas a comparable English furnace needed only 24.37 workers at a cost of 90.046 marks. Baare concluded: 'The difference in price is therefore to be ascribed to the higher working capacity of the English... [and] indicates clearly the superiority of the English worker and the lower working costs of the same.'[18] While Britain and Germany fought fiercely in the European markets, British iron and steel maintained advantages in terms of labour, transport and iron ore costs into the 1880s.

The domestic and export markets for Cleveland iron are shown in more detail in Tables 2.6 and 2.7, which analyse export markets for Cleveland pig iron from 1867 to 1877, and exports from Middlesbrough from 1877 to 1882. In the decade from 1867, Cleveland achieved a 2.7 times growth in pig iron export, from 136,378 to 364,899 tons. After a 30% fall during the 1874 recession, sales abroad recovered immediately afterwards, rising from 357,333 tons in 1876 to 364,899 tons in 1877. A worldwide reduction in freight rates, together with liberal trade reforms in the European continent from the 1870s onwards, generated a new upsurge in international trade.[19] The most important market in 1867 was Belgium, which received as much as 32% of total Cleveland pig-iron exports, though in the 1870s it lost its leading role, the Belgian share of Cleveland exports reducing to 12%. France was the next most significant, taking 29% of Cleveland's total export.

Early in the 1880s, the main export market consisted of Germany, the Netherlands (chiefly in transit for Germany), France, the Scandinavian countries, Italy, Japan, Austria and America. Exports to America declined sharply from 90,087 tons in 1880, to 6,150 tons in 1881, reviving slightly to 8,650 tons in 1882. Among Asian countries, Japan was the most important purchaser, taking increasing quantities of Cleveland pig iron from the latter half of the 1870s and importing almost 4,000 tons from Middlesbrough in 1882.

During this time, however, there came shifts in the structure of the

---

17 Bell, *Manufacture of Iron and Steel*, pp. 562–7.
18 Crew, *Town in the Ruhr*, pp. 39–40.
19 Tirado *et al.*, 'Economic Integration and Industrial Location', p. 348.

Table 2.6. Export of Cleveland Pig Iron, 1867–77

Destination	1867	1868	1869	1870	1871	1872	1873	1874	1875	1876	1877
Germany[a]	15,810	29,880	43,402	38,639	91,195	122,535	100,744	83,298	117,235	116,588	109,200
Holland[a]	12,514	13,990	22,563	36,003	89,832	117,729	116,355	61,622	77,832	77,675	70,204
Belgium	43,886	30,670	47,714	64,776	69,037	75,396	98,773	42,502	58,574	54,825	43,255
France	39,442	34,540	48,041	50,062	38,032	44,853	53,178	40,418	56,764	59,143	71,285
Spain	5,138	5,260	3,988	8,655	8,453	4,607	4,767	7,875	8,833	7,749	25,819
Italy	1,364	2,020	3,020	760	1,239	706	560	2,131	3,095	2,129	4,665
Sweden[b]	8,844	8,770	1,345	9,779	12,763	12,581	17,353	25,164	24,787	27,771	30,057
Russia	5,338	6,830	6,788	6,037	8,857	1,240	2,809	10,979	18,361	9,509	9,112
America	2,655	1,420	1,224	400	10,554	3,984	1,198	485	120	130	0
Others	1,387	3,426	1,758	1,797	684	2,989	1,340	1,247	2,306	1,824	1,302
Total	136,378	136,806	185,777	216,908	330,646	386,624	397,077	275,721	367,907	357,333	364,899

Notes: Measured in tons. [a]Chiefly in transit for Germany. [b]Includes Norway and Denmark.

Source: Iron, Steel, and Allied Trades, Annual Report to Members (1878), p. 19.

Table 2.7. Export of Cleveland Pig Iron from Middlesbrough, 1877–82

Destination	1877	1878	1879	1880	1881	1882
Germany	90,368	96,801	106,681	110,611	115,654	144,356
Holland	67,660	72,930	68,732	69,684	72,304	90,772
France	68,946	61,297	53,809	68,085	94,402	125,787
Belgium	41,620	50,270	44,565	73,144	46,919	39,188
Sweden	11,290	10,162	8,776	12,487	13,365	16,109
Norway	12,753	6,763	7,758	5,385	5,927	7,239
Spain	9,377	12,311	23,223	18,695	23,571	20,616
Portugal	4,901	11,592	10,250	6,328	11,437	6,730
Russia	7,199	9,000	22,060	33,454	26,710	19,235
Denmark	3,720	1,833	3,162	4,243	4,239	5,092
Italy	3,987	3,495	2,967	1,645	6,730	15,185
Jersey	–	80	75	–	25	25
India	125	270	–	250	250	250
Japan	–	550	–	900	1,753	3,932
China	–	–	–	300	550	270
Austria	–	–	600	140	–	3,100
British North America	–	205	1,000	–	275	–
USA	–	–	42,000	90,087	6,150	8,650
Egypt	–	–	–	200	–	–
Australia	–	–	–	–	–	100
Total	321,946	337,559	395,658	495,638	430,261	506,636

Note: Measured in tons.

Source: Iron, Steel, and Allied Trades, Annual Report to Members (1883), p. 19.

European export market for Cleveland pig iron. Belgium, Spain, Portugal and China lost ground, and the fall in the Belgian market was most conspicuous. Meanwhile, Germany was increasing in importance as a purchaser, enlarging its share so that it accounted for almost 30% of the total export from Cleveland in 1877. When the Cleveland iron industry began to decline in the 1880s, German and French markets still remained important, with shares of 28.5% and 25%, respectively. Between 1868 and 1877, a period for which data are available of total pig-iron export from Cleveland and from the United Kingdom overall, the contribution of Cleveland pig iron to total British exports was quite outstanding. As Table 2.8 reveals, Cleveland contributed on average 33% of total British pig-iron exports in that decade. In 1877, its share was over 40%. Significantly, the Cleveland share of total British exports rose after the recession of 1873.

The main domestic markets for Cleveland pig iron were Scotland, Wales and Newcastle (see Table 2.9). Of these, Scotland was foremost, accounting for nearly 70% of total coastwise domestic trade in 1877. As this trade in 1873 had amounted to 182,565 tons, this sector of the domestic market had increased by more than 2.5 times over the period. Besides the pig iron taken out by sea, about 500,000 tons were carried overland by rail to Manchester,

Table 2.8. Pig Iron Exports from the United Kingdom and Cleveland, 1868–82

Year	UK Pig Iron	UK Pig Iron & Steel	Value of Export (£)	Cleveland Pig Iron Tons (%)ᵃ
1868	552,999	2,041,852		136,806 (24.7)
1869	710,656	2,675,331		185,777 (26.1)
1870	758,339	2,825,575	24,038,090	216,908 (28.6)
1871	1,057,458	3,169,219	26,124,134	330,646 (31.2)
1872	1,331,143	3,382,762	35,996,167	386,624 (29.0)
1873	1,142,065	2,957,813	37,731,239	397,077 (34.8)
1874	776,116	2,487,522	31,190,256	275,721 (35.5)
1875	947,827	2,457,306	25,747,271	367,907 (38.8)
1876	910,005	2,224,470	20,737,410	357,333 (39.3)
1877	882,059	2,346,370	20,094,562	364,899 (41.4)
1878	923,080	2,296,860		
1879	1,223,436	2,883,484		
1880	1,632,343	3,792,993		
1881	1,482,354	3,818,338		
1882	1,758,152	4,350,297		

Notes: Measured in tons. ᵃPercentage proportions of total pig iron production of the United Kingdom.

Source: Modern Records Centre, Univ. of Warwick, MSS 365/CIA, Minute Book, Vol. 2; Secretary's Report, 1880; Iron, Steel, and Allied Trades, Annual Report to Members (1878), pp. 19, 39.

Table 2.9. Coastal Sales of Cleveland Pig Iron from Middlesbrough, 1877–82

Destination	1877	1878	1879	1880	1881	1882
Scotland	317,249	300,554	205,846	283,463	323,748	253,258
Wales	60,339	58,740	70,267	89,204	97,696	87,527
Newcastle	48,478	30,716	35,492	52,332	45,541	55,972
Other ports	34,324	32,470	28,300	39,944	34,165	27,880
Total	460,390	422,480	339,905	464,943	501,150	424,637

Note: Measured in tons.
Source: Iron, Steel, and Allied Trades, Annual Report to Members (1883), p. 19.

Leeds, Bradford and other towns, where pig iron was smelted in foundries or cupolas into cast iron, or worked at forges into wrought iron.[20]

In 1877, of pig iron manufactured in Cleveland, 2,124,831 tons in total, 364,899 tons (18%) were exported. Of this, 321,946 tons (88% of exports) were shipped from the port of Middlesbrough. To the coastwise domestic market, 460,390 tons (21% of the total) left by sea and about 500,000 tons (23%) were carried by railway to the inland market. The rest, about 800,000 tons, or 38% of total production, was consumed within the Cleveland region.[21] In the late-nineteenth century, Middlesbrough became not only a

---

[20] *Iron, Steel, and Allied Trades, Annual Report*, 1881, pp. 12–13, 19.
[21] Modern Records Centre, Univ. of Warwick, MSS 365/CIA, Secretary's Report for 1880, Minute

Table 2.10. Export of Pig Iron from North-east Ports, 1881–2

Ports	1881		1882	
	Tons	(%)[a]	Tons	(%)[a]
Middlesbrough	430,261	(77.9)	506,636	(71.7)
Newcastle	65,423	(11.8)	102,396	(14.5)
Sunderland	240	(–)	494	(0.1)
Hartlepool	32,210	(5.8)	57,974	(8.2)
Stockton	13,060	(2.4)	19,693	(2.8)
South Shields	8,659	(1.6)	8,610	(1.2)
North Shields	2,650	(0.5)	10,710	(1.5)
Total	552,503	(100.0)	706,513	(100.0)

Note: [a]Percentage proportion of total export from north-east ports.

Source: Modern Records Centre, Univ. of Warwick, MSS 365/CIA, Minute Book, vol. 2; Secretary's Report, 1880.

Table 2.11. Export and Coastal Sales of Cleveland Pig Iron from Middlesbrough, 1873–80

	1873	1874	1875	1876	1877	1878	1879	1880
Export	339,916	232,422	316,830	320,698	321,946	337,559	395,658	495,638
Coastwise	182,565	244,394	296,284	384,735	460,390	422,480	419,905	464,943
Total	522,481	476,816	613,114	705,428	782,336	760,039	815,563	960,581

Note: Measured in tons.

Source: Modern Records Centre, Univ. of Warwick, MSS 365/CIA, Minute Book, Vol. 2; Secretary's Report, 1880.

nodal centre for production, but also an export base in the Cleveland iron and steel industry. This process is clearly evident in Table 2.10, which indicates that of all exports of pig iron from north-east ports, Middlesbrough accounted for over 70% in 1881 and 1882.

Although the effects of recession after 1873 were not so severe in Cleveland as elsewhere, one feature that can be observed in the aftermath is a gradual shift towards the domestic market, demonstrated in Table 2.11. These figures are only for pig iron exported and transported coastwise from Middlesbrough, but it is discernible from 1874 that sales for the domestic market tended to rise, accounting for 50% to 60% of sales from Middlesbrough after 1876. This may have been because import-substituting industrialization was then proceeding in some of the main Cleveland marketplaces, of Germany, France and America.

In the 1870s, British finished wrought-iron products – which ranged from rails, plates, bars and angles, to bolts and rods, hoops, sheets or tinplates – found their main export markets in the United States of America, British

North America, Russia, Germany, the Netherlands, Belgium, France, India and Australia. The most important item until the mid-1870s was rails, followed by bars, angles, bolts and rods, hoops and sheets. The largest market for British wrought-iron products was America, where extensive railway investment in the 1870s boosted demand for rails, bars and angles. After this, railway construction in Russia, Australia and India sustained the British export market. In particular, rails sold to India, over 100,000 tons in 1877, compensated for a falling European market. Germany, Belgium, France and the Netherlands lost their position as main markets for British wrought-iron products in the late 1870s, but remained important purchasers of pig iron. The Netherlands imported on average 221,843 tons of pig iron per annum between 1870 and 1877, close behind Germany with 226,568 tons.[22]

Institutional Framework and Industrial Agglomeration

Mid-Victorian Cleveland has long been a focus of interest to economists interested in industrial agglomeration. Towards the end of the nineteenth century, Alfred Marshall referred to the Cleveland example in his *Principles of Economics*. Later, for the American classical location theorists North, Isard and Hoover, Cleveland was a favourite target for the study of industrial clustering. Recent investigations upon this theme, by North, Porter, Wilson and Popp, Casson, Staber and Hudson, have helped our understanding of mechanisms working to accelerate industrial clustering in Cleveland from the late 1860s.[23] Informed by this literature, the following section examines the location of industry, technological diffusion, and product specialization among manufacturers. It also explores diversification of the economic structure and how far this can be attributed to an existing institutional framework.

When the formation of an industrial agglomeration is considered in historical perspective, two interrelated but different dimensional questions should be distinguished. One is about the genesis, that is, how a certain industry was initially established in a particular region. The other is about the process whereby it developed: how the localized industry matured and clustered; how, as clustering advanced, the industrial structure became more diverse; how further subsidiary, complementary industries were generated within and beyond the region.[24] This latter point poses a question about the constituents needed for the region to achieve sustainability and to seek economic rationalism.

---

[22] *Iron, Steel, and Allied Trades, Annual Report*, 1878, pp. 40–6.

[23] Marshall, *Principles of Economics*, p. 330; North, 'Location Theory and Regional Economic Growth', pp. 243–58; Isard, 'General Theory of Location and Space-Economy', p. 483; 'Some Locational Factors in the Iron and Steel Industry', pp. 203–15; Hoover, *The Location of Economic Activity*, pp. 7–9, 15–115; cf. North, *Institutions, Institutional Change and Economic Performance*, pp. 3–140; Porter, *On Competition*, pp. 237–45; Piore and Sabel, *Second Industrial Divide*, pp. 28–35, 213–16; Wilson and Popp, 'Conclusion', *Industrial Clusters and Regional Business Networks in England*, pp. 3, 280; Casson, 'Economic Approach to Regional Business Networks', pp. 31–4; Staber, 'The Social Embeddedness of Industrial District Networks', pp. 148–74; Hudson, 'Industrial Organization and Structure', pp. 28–56.

[24] See especially Porter, *On Competition*, pp. 237–45.

In their recent econometric analysis of industrial location in Britain between 1871 and 1931, Crafts and Mulatu consider on the matter of comparative advantage that 'the importance of the traditional factor endowment variables in the pattern of industry location in pre-1931 Britain is confirmed by [our] results', and that 'factor endowments played the central role in industry location decisions before World War II. In particular, the continuing roles of natural resources in terms of coal abundance and of human capital are apparent.' They reaffirm that their results 'give much greater support to explanations for industrial location based on the traditional HO (Heckscher–Ohlin) model rather than those derived from the NEG (New Economic Geography)'.

However, Crafts and Mulatu qualify this conclusion, adding that 'the correct interpretation of the factor endowments variables may not always be straightforward', giving as example that interaction between coal abundance and steam power use is significant, whereas the one between coal abundance and coal use is not. Thus 'in the context of the historical literature a possible explanation for this is that proximity to coal *per se* mattered for the initial location of steam-powered industry but, as time passed, it was external economies of scale that sustained the attractiveness of the region', for 'steam power was installed in factories, foundries, mills, etc., which acted as repositories of technical knowledge and greatly reduced access costs to that knowledge'.[25]

In contrast, based on the Spanish experience in the nineteenth century, Rosés argues that factor endowments with economic geography specifications explain about 90% of variation in these aggregates, so that 'the fortunes of a region are assumed to depend not only upon its own endowments but also on market-size effects'. He also suggests that a common pattern emerges, where 'regions industrialized or failed to do so according to a combination of comparative advantage (HO model) and IRS (Increasing Returns) forces'.[26]

Viewed in the context of this region's industrial achievement in the late-nineteenth century, the line of discussion advanced by Crafts and Mulatu seems a more appropriate fit with the case of industrial agglomeration in Cleveland. The initial advantages which enabled Cleveland to industrialize, based on factor endowments – abundant and low-cost coal and ironstone – were accentuated by the benefits of a larger and integrated market, alongside substantial transport improvements, besides a developing institutional framework, all of which features promoted further agglomeration.

As already noted, the worldwide reduction in freight rates, together with liberal trade reforms in Europe from the 1870s, generated an upsurge in international trade. The peak in Cleveland's iron trade coincided with this.[27]

---

25 Crafts and Mulatu, 'What Explains the Location of Industry?', pp. 509, 512.
26 Rosés, 'Why Isn't the Whole of Spain Industrialized?', pp. 1015–16.
27 Tirado *et al.*, 'Economic Integration and Industrial Location', p. 348.

Locally, lower transportation costs were due largely to improvements in the Tees Navigation, the extension of the Stockton and Darlington Railway, and new export harbour facilities in the port of Middlesbrough. These advances enabled easier access to domestic and foreign markets at much lower cost. Of especial significance in improving navigation and reducing costs were the opening of the Tees Navigation Company's second cut in 1832, and the establishment of the Tees Conservancy Commission in 1852.[28]

It is revealing to set the case of Cleveland against North's model of stages in the process of industrial location in his classic article 'Location Theory and Regional Economic Growth'. In this analysis, first, settlers in new regions usually experimented with many different products before discovering one that was economically feasible. For Cleveland and Middlesbrough, this stage fell during the 1840s and 1850s, when pioneering enterprises such as Bolckow, Vaughan and Co. and Gilkes Wilson were casting around for viable products.[29]

Second, developing an exportable commodity reflected a comparative advantage in relative costs of production, which included transport costs.

Third, from a regional viewpoint, demand for exportable commodities was an exogenous factor, whereas both processing and transfer costs were not. Newly industrialized regions did apply themselves to reducing such costs in a concerted drive to promote their own economic well-being. To reduce transport costs to better the competitiveness of their exports, they would improve railways, river navigation and harbour facilities.

Fourth, as regions grew around the export base, external economies developed, improving the competitive cost position of exportable commodities. Specialized marketing organizations, improved credit and transport facilities, a trained labour force and complementary industries developed, all of them oriented to the export base. This stage would apply to the peak period of the Cleveland iron and steel industry, the late 1860s, when institutional arrangements such as the chamber of commerce, the exchange, the Warrant Stores and various industrial associations such as the Cleveland Ironmasters' Association, the North of England Iron Manufacturers' Association, and the Board of Arbitration and Conciliation, were established.

Fifth and finally, concerted collaborative steps were taken to improve the technology of production. Experiment stations, technical colleges and local research institutions grew up to provide the exporting industries with services, and to conduct research in technological improvements for the industries which made up the region's export base. This stage would fit the phase during which institutions were founded in Middlesbrough that shared techno-

---

[28]   Lillie, *History of Middlesbrough*, pp. 53–4, 121–2.

[29]   North, 'Location Theory and Regional Economic Growth', p. 248; National Archives, RAIL 667/1428; Teesside Archives, U/OME/8/9; Jeans, *Notes on Northern Industries*, pp. 143–9, 162; Armstrong *et al.*, *Industrial Resources of the District of the Three Northern Rivers*, pp. 252, 258, 267; Lillie, *History of Middlesbrough*, pp. 70–1.

logical information among entrepreneurs, engineers and even artisans. Such bodies included the Mechanics' Institute, the Cleveland Institution of Engineers and the Iron and Steel Institute. A distinctive method of technological improvement based on 'collective invention', which Allen has pointed out as prevailing in Cleveland in the second half of the nineteenth century, is an equally significant element in this stage of agglomeration.[30]

An especially notable movement which came into being in Cleveland in the latter part of the 1860s was conceived as a joint endeavour to deal with industrial disputes collectively and across the region as a whole, instead of having individual firms or their employees confront the issues alone. This initiative was embodied in the form of two industrial associations, the Board of Arbitration and Conciliation in which both employers and employees joined, and the ironworkers' trade union. These two bodies were created at a time of crisis in Cleveland region, with the Great Strike and other serious industrial conflicts between 1865 and 1866. The various new institutions were a result as well as a cause of industrial agglomeration. The steady progression of industrial clustering in Cleveland had brought the actors together, and the range of associations created by joint collaborative efforts improved technology, and provided information on outputs, domestic and export markets, prices, stocks, customs, about strikes, lockouts and other labour disputes in the region, wages, and so on, for the mutual benefit of firms, and ultimately bringing more success to the region overall.[31]

As will be further discussed in Chapter 4, the North of England Iron Manufacturers' Association and the Cleveland Ironmasters' Association were founded, respectively, in 1865 and 1866. The latter was organized by perhaps 22 pig-iron manufacturers, and the former by about 20 wrought-iron makers in north-east England, in Northumberland, Durham and the North Riding of Yorkshire. The objectives of the association included the exchange of information 'on all matters connecting with the iron trade, especially in regard to rate of wages and current selling prices', besides that on all other subjects affecting the interests of the trade, securing united action and mutual support for general welfare, attending to parliamentary bills and proposed alterations in employment law and other similar matters.[32]

These objectives suggest that the associations resembled the early forms of cartel seen in the German iron industry of this period. Between 1879 and 1882, about 18 cartels in Germany represented firms producing pig iron, semi-manufactured items, sheets and pipes. In Düsseldorf in 1896, there was formed the Pig Iron Syndicate, and in 1904, 27 large-scale steel manufacturers joined to form the German Steel Works Association. The Cleveland

30 Allen, 'Collective Invention', pp. 1–24.
31 Howard, 'Strikes and Lockouts in the Iron Industry', p. 419; Cockcroft, 'Great Strike in the Cleveland Iron Industry', pp. 4–5; Hudson, 'Industrial Organization and Structure', p. 46.
32 Modern Records Centre, Univ. of Warwick, MSS 365/NEI, vol. 1; MSS 365/BAC, Board of Arbitration Rules, 1869, p. 5; Mr. Waterhouse's Returns (Sale of Manufactured Iron), vol. 1, 1869; MSS.365/CIA, Minute Book, vol. 1, ff. 1–6, 30–1.

Ironmasters' Association seems to have been particularly cohesive, establishing strong control over its members' decision-making processes, as can be seen in the association rules, which prescribe united action in matters relating to the pricing of products, wage rates of their members' employees and strikes.[33]

The sharing of information among Cleveland employers about the technology of production and the state of the iron market was institutionalized when the Cleveland Institution of Engineers and the Iron and Steel Institute were established. The progress of industrial agglomeration brought a further three noteworthy new institutions in the early 1860s: the Middlesbrough Chamber of Commerce, the Middlesbrough Royal Exchange and the Cleveland Warrant Stores. These bodies were intended as means to lower transaction costs, including that of information; to promote collective activities by employers; and to set up a specialized marketing organization especially for the benefit of Cleveland ironmasters.

The Middlesbrough Chamber of Commerce, founded in 1861 by 40 influential trade and manufacturing concerns, dealt especially with affairs relating to the rapid expansion of the local iron trade, in particular the marked increase in export activity. The founders had in mind a central agency to promote commercial interests, collect trade statistics and represent their views to legislators. The chamber of commerce, originally a voluntary association financed through subscriptions from individual and company members, was incorporated under the Companies Act 1873. Its main concerns were to furnish statistics on merchant shipping and customs, to translate forms and information necessary to exporters and importers, and to liaise with equivalent overseas institutions in collecting information about the state of foreign markets, and furthermore on the latest technology employed in foreign countries.[34]

The chamber also issued annual publications, Middlesbrough Chamber of Commerce Reports, which included a range of useful commercial information. The 1877 edition, for instance, gave the number of furnaces in blast at Middlesbrough's 17 ironworks, quarterly figures of pig-iron manufacture, figures of stocks held in the ironworks and in the Cleveland Warrant Stores, tonnages of sales of pig-iron and wrought-iron products to domestic and foreign markets, import and export statistics for coal, coke, pottery, timber and chemical goods, and the number of ships newly built. These reports also provided prices of rails, bars, plates, angles, potash for industrial and agricultural use, Epsom salts, sulphuric acid, wires, nails and loading of other products. After it was incorporated in 1873, besides its annual reports the chamber issued a *Monthly Journal of the Middlesbrough Incorporated Chamber of Commerce*, which changed in 1928 to the *Teesside Chamber of Commerce Monthly Journal* upon the merger between the Middlesbrough and Stockton

[33] Crew, *Town in the Ruhr*, p. 34; Modern Records Centre, Univ. of Warwick, MSS.365/CIA, Minute Book, vol. 1, ff. 30–2.
[34] Lillie, *History of Middlesbrough*, pp. 106–7.

chambers of commerce. The journals published academic papers on iron-making technology, and on the state of trade and markets.[35]

To Middlesbrough as a nodal centre, an export base for the Cleveland industrial region, the chamber of commerce offered essential support, channelling as it did a range of specialist expertise, particularly in connection with the export trade.[36] Along with collecting and sharing customized intelligence about the export of pig- and wrought-iron products, commercial practice, and transaction techniques, the chamber of commerce acted as intermediary between the government and Cleveland ironmasters in petitioning for changes in policy to promote the ironmasters' interests. For example in 1864, immediately after the opening of the chamber, Henry Bolckow, its first president, and William Fallows tried to affiliate themselves to the national body of associated chambers to coordinate their lobbying activities in parliament. They intended to persuade the government to approach foreign countries to lower duties on British iron imports, thus helping boost Cleveland's staple export. Overall, the Middlesbrough Chamber of Commerce, like those of other municipalities, along with various industrial associations and research institutes, had a pivotal role in consolidating existing trade circles in the region. These groups also created a new economic sphere, by organizing a local and national business network that established a wider linkage function.[37]

Following the chamber of commerce's foundation, the Middlesbrough Royal Exchange was launched in 1862 by members of the chamber and of the Literary and Philosophical Society. There had been an earlier attempt, in 1835, when the Middlesbrough Exchange Association was set up with offices for dealing commodities, a hotel lounge and accommodation. This was funded by subscriptions of £100 from 17 influential members, £200 from two others and £600 from Joseph Pease. This facility was intended mainly for Stockton traders, and the commodity dealt was coal. As the local industrial structure changed from the mid-nineteenth century, and the iron industry came into the ascendant, the Exchange Association's results fell short of expectations, and the building was sold to the town.[38]

Middlesbrough in the late-nineteenth century needed an exchange to support activity within its extensive industrial agglomeration, and the foundation of the Royal Exchange had a significant impact in improving systems for distribution and dealing. The project originated in the proposition that

---

35 Middlesbrough Central Lib., C669.14, Chamber of Commerce Report, 1877; Lillie, *History of Middlesbrough*, p. 107.
36 Casson, 'Economic Approach to Regional Business Networks', p. 41.
37 Cf. Porter, *On Competition*, p. 241; *Middlesbrough Weekly News and Cleveland Advertiser*, 5 Feb. 1864. Respecting the coordination of local economic interests with national organizations and a network of firms sharing a common purpose in appealing to government, see Casson, 'Economic Approach to Regional Business Networks', pp. 22, 28–9; Staber, 'The Social Embeddedness of Industrial District Networks', p. 164.
38 Lillie, *History of Middlesbrough*, pp. 67–8.

Table 2.12. Applications for Shares in the Middlesbrough Exchange, 1864–8

Occupations	Applicants	Total Shares Applied for	Total Shareholding (%)
Ironmasters	23	377	48.1
OME[a]	3	300	38.3
Iron ship builders	1	10	1.3
Manager	1	10	1.3
Gentlemen	2	40	5.1
Iron merchant	1	25	3.1
Royal Navy Captain	1	10	1.3
Accountant	1	2	0.2
Other	1	10	1.3
Total	34	784	100.0

Note: [a]The Owners of the Middlesbrough Estate.

Source: Green, 'Royal Exchange', p. 37, Table II.

in order to perform prompt and smooth transactions, a market space was urgently needed, where sellers and buyers of iron products could meet to exchange information on the state of the iron trade. It was modelled on systems already operating in Glasgow and Birmingham. Previously, there had been a weekly iron market at Middlesbrough Town Hall.[39]

The exchange was launched as the Middlesbrough Exchange Company Ltd under the terms of the Companies Act 1862, with a share capital of £20,000 divided into 1,000 shares of £20 each. Its income came from rentals paid for offices and shops incorporated into the building, from members' subscriptions and from fees charged for the hall.[40] The exchange's main purpose was to deal in pig-iron warrants, backed by the security of pig-iron stocks carried by ironmasters into the Cleveland Warrant Stores, and to provide information to Cleveland ironmasters, merchants and speculators about Scottish pig-iron prices settled daily at the Glasgow Exchange.

Table 2.12 shows the applicants' occupations, and the number and proportion of shares applied for between 1864 and 1868. It is apparent that ironmasters predominated both in terms of total shares applied for and proportion of total shareholding. This is to be expected, since the initial object was to lower transaction costs by increasing efficiency in Cleveland pig-iron dealings, and to strengthen the ironmasters' relative position in the pig-iron market. At the same time, it is interesting to note that Joseph Pease and other members of his family who were partners in the Owners of the Middlesbrough Estate, were sufficiently enthusiastic about the project to apply for 300 shares, about 40% of the £15,180 taken up in the first six months.[41]

To be eligible, subscribers had to be situated within a boundary drawn three miles around the town. As many as 31 of the members in 1868, and 45

[39] Green, 'Royal Exchange', p. 72.
[40] Green, 'Royal Exchange', pp. 19–20, 73; Lillie, *History of Middlesbrough*, p. 108.
[41] Green, 'Royal Exchange', pp. 40–1.

of those in 1873, were tenants in the Exchange house. They consisted of nine ironmasters, five metal brokers, three iron merchants, two wine merchants, a club proprietor, solicitor, tea dealer, broker, company secretary, iron ship-builder, architect, heating and ventilator dealer, bookseller and newspaper proprietor, tea, tobacco and wine dealer, and two others in 1868, paying total rents of £1,580. In 1873, 11 ironmasters, nine iron and coal mine-owners, three iron merchants, two booksellers and newspaper proprietors, a colliery proprietor, banker, merchant, club proprietor, insurance broker, solicitor, brandy importer, iron puddler, engineering company, metal broker, ore merchant, timber merchant, company secretary, land and commercial agent, architect, hair dresser, and one other, occupied the offices and paid rents amounting to £2,047 10s.[42]

In the Exchange building, large quantities of pig iron and other commodities were bought and sold, and the prices settled weekly. Mercantile news-papers, lists of stocks and shares, and mining records were supplied there. From 1869 to 1873, both the Exchange's membership and income increased, from 168 to 429, and from £249 2s 3d to £634 19s 6d, respectively. As with the Manchester Royal Exchange, that in Middlesbrough acted as 'a coffee house, a news room and trading floor, centralizing the supply of information both private and public, and providing a congenial place for the conduct of business'.[43]

Apart from these formal associations which aimed to give opportunities to gather and share relevant information among people with interests in common, there were similar, but more loosely organized, associations or clubs. The largest among them, the Cleveland Club, had 400 members who were mainly manufacturers, merchants and professionals. Its subscriptions grew from £1,051 to £1,720 between 1869 and 1873. In 1873, the Erimus Club for gentlemen was opened. To use Casson's terminology, two kinds of non-profit associations served to consolidate networks in the region, 'representative associations, such as trades unions and employers' associations', and 'accrediting associations, such as professional associations', as well as groups for religious and political purposes, sports, leisure, social contact and various other clubs.[44]

The Cleveland Warrant Stores followed shortly upon the exchange's foundation, in 1864. Its aim was to make the iron trade more efficient and to regulate output and prices by mutual agreement on behalf of the Cleveland ironmasters.[45] In tandem with the movement to create the exchange, the iron-

---

[42]   Green, 'Royal Exchange', pp. 95–6.

[43]   Lillie, *History of Middlesbrough*, p. 108; Hudson, 'Industrial Organization and Structure', p. 5.

[44]   Green, 'Royal Exchange', pp. 70, 86; Casson, 'Economic Approach to Regional Business Networks', p. 39, original emphasis.

[45]   'Current Topics' by a correspondent describes an attempt at the beginning of the twentieth century by the Cleveland ironmasters to replace the Warrant Store system with a new central selling agency to 'cooperate and control amongst themselves the selling price of their iron': *Econ. Jnl*, XXIII (1913), pp. 463–4.

masters cooperated in establishing this second institution, intended to more closely reflect their interests in settling iron prices. In fact the exchange and Warrant Stores were inseparably interconnected. At first the Stockton and Darlington Railway Co. managed the Cleveland Warrant Stores, and afterwards the exchange seems to have served as storekeeper alongside its usual business.

The warrants issued by the stores, against the security of pig iron deposited into the warehouses by ironmasters, originated from the system of Scottish scrips promising to deliver a certain tonnage of pig iron at some future date. This practice, which spread across other regions in the 1840s, was a means of providing ready cash for ironmasters and a marketable security for scrip owners. However, the system of future trading carried risk, as 'some of the ironmasters sold more scrip than they could expect to honour, and the purchasers often acquired it not because they wanted iron, but purely as a speculative counter'. As a result, in 1845, the Scottish Pig Iron Association was formed to put the trade on a solid foundation, under which iron was kept at a neutral store, so that the warrants gained some guarantee of security and contracts were properly executed. With the introduction of warrants issued on condition that iron was actually brought into warehouses, from about 1850 the scrip system lost its element of future trading.[46]

The Cleveland Warrant Stores were established in 1864 by William Connal, a substantial warehouseman in Glasgow. Map 2.1 locates the Cleveland Iron Store Yards No.1 and No. 2, in 1895. Warrants issued, at first by the Stockton and Darlington Railway Co. and later by Connal and Co. as a recognized storekeeper, against iron brought into the store yards by ironmasters, could be cashed by iron merchants and were marketable. Occasionally, ironmasters could expect to be granted bank loans against iron warrants, or to receive discounts for cash by paying commissions.[47]

The warrants served as a kind of document of title, acting as warehouse receipts, and were sometimes called dock warrants, which demanded the delivery of pig iron to parties recorded in a warrant or endorsed upon it. The system enabled ironmasters to increase output and stocks, keeping furnaces in blast even when the market was slack. It also had the benefit to producers of smoothing their cash flow and moderating fluctuations in iron prices. The Cleveland Warrant Stores in the 1860s worked well, evident from reports on the output and stocks of the 16 member ironworks recorded in the minutes of the Cleveland Ironmasters' Association.[48] During this period, 70–80% of output was kept in exchange for warrants in the stores, and then sold in due course to iron merchants.

---

[46] Carr and Taplin, *History of the British Steel Industry*, p. 9.
[47] Carr and Taplin, *History of the British Steel Industry*, p. 9.
[48] Modern Records Centre, Univ. of Warwick, MSS 365/CIA, Minute Book, vol. 1, ff. 56–8.

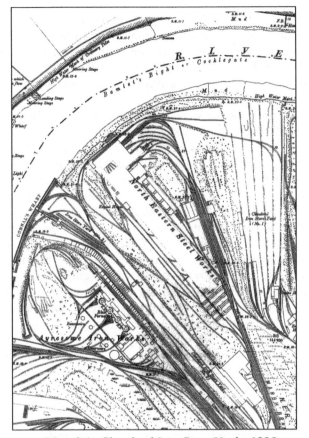

Map 2.1. Cleveland Iron Store Yards, 1895

The local newspaper carried reports of the earliest quotations following the establishment of the Cleveland Warrant Stores:

> Middlesbrough, Wednesday – The tone has been firm today – buyers offering 51s cash, and 52s three months; sellers asking 51s 6d cash, 52s 6d three months, for Stockton and Darlington Company warrants. Closing prices: F.o.b. warrants, cash buyers 51s, seller 51s 3d; three months' open buyers 52s, sellers 52s 3d. About 6,000 tons done.

> Middlesbrough, Wednesday – Market very quiet. Mixed numbers warrants 53s buyers, sellers 53s 6d, No. 1 GMB. 54s No. 3 GMB 51s.

> Glasgow, Wednesday – Market steady at 58s buyers, 58s 1½d sellers. No. 1 GMB 57s 6d, No. 3 GMB 56s 9d.[49]

49 *Middlesbrough Weekly News and Cleveland Advertiser*, 15 Jul. 1864; 19 Aug. 1864.

North pointed out that various means of reducing the cost of information, such as measuring the valued attributes of goods and services, enforcement and policing of agreements, such as 'warranties, guarantees, trademarks, the resources devoted to sorting and grading' and so on, were useful in promoting market operation by lowering transaction costs. By establishing the exchange and Warrant Stores, and concentrating together reliable information on the iron trade, an important step forward was made in improving the efficiency of the Cleveland iron market. Hudson has a slightly different perspective on the contribution of these institutions: 'Specialized, regionally concentrated mercantile institutions could significantly reduce transaction costs in the purchase of raw materials and the sale of finished or semi-finished goods, facilitating the finance and operation of a range of types and sizes of business.'[50]

The overriding objective of these three institutions established early in the 1860s, the chamber of commerce, exchange and Warrant Stores, was to make transactions more efficient, and to organize the market by improving transparency. Under the old iron market system, iron merchants and speculators had monopolized information on export prices, thus exerting a strong influence on pricing. The producers sought to restrict the control of information by merchants and speculators, and so to limit their influence over prices. The Warrant Stores in particular were intended to enable producers to participate in the iron market on equal terms with merchants and speculators, and to share profits arising from high prices of iron. To that extent, it can be argued that iron producers succeeded in making dealing in iron more efficient, and in lowering transaction costs. The establishment of these institutions which controlled exports and inland iron trade tended further to reinforce Middlesbrough's location as an export base, a centre of production as well as of collection and distribution for the Cleveland iron and steel industry.

Diffusion of Technology

Middlesbrough Mechanics' Institute was founded as early as 1844, its main purpose evidently to train young workers in rudimentary knowledge, rather than in specific technology or in scientific understanding. Its rules reported the institute's objects as to 'promote the diffusion of useful knowledge among the working class', by 'instruction, in classes of the members, in the practical branches of science'.[51] Although the society exercised little direct effect on the diffusion of technology or upon practical technological training, it seem likely that influential local industrialists, William Fallows and John Vaughan as vice-presidents, Henry Bolckow as treasurer, intended this as a centre through which the public might be enlightened about the iron industry generally, as it became a staple industry in the region.

---

[50] North, *Institutions, Institutional Change and Economic Performance*, pp. 30–1; Hudson, 'Industrial Organization and Structure', p. 52.
[51] Middlesbrough Central Lib., MMI 374/ MI 606, 80702, pp. 1–4.

Far more significant in terms of building practical technological expertise in the Cleveland industrial agglomeration were the Cleveland Institution of Engineers and the Iron and Steel Institute, established in 1864 and 1868, respectively. Both were regional research organizations with regular issues of journals which aimed to disseminate details of iron-making technology, and to inform about prices and outputs in the various iron-producing areas in Britain. They also covered trends in export and domestic markets for iron-stone, pig and wrought iron, and finished products. Within these media, the *Proceedings of the Cleveland Institution of Engineers*, and the *Transactions* (from 1871, the *Journal*) *of the Iron and Steel Institute*, they disclosed new iron-making techniques, published precise accounts of various experiments in fuel, furnace and manufacturing processes, as well as detailed plant designs and descriptions of improvements in efficiency of mechanical equipment, which brought with them higher productivity and better quality. They often organized lectures and tours of ironworks, 'to which free access was given, all the processes of manufacture being duly explained'.[52]

These journals also contained a range of information associated with the iron and steel industry, including outputs in ironstone, pig and wrought iron in Britain, numbers of blast and puddling furnaces in operation, details of cutting-edge iron-making technology prevailing in foreign countries, the names of overseas journals dealing with metallurgical engineering, and levels of exports of British pig iron and wrought iron products. They were effective media sharing information on technology and markets among engineers and entrepreneurs in the region.

While some engineers did in fact obtain patents, these journals were full of pages illustrating design specifications and drawn plans of machinery alongside results of experiments. As the contents of the *Transactions of the Iron and Steel Institute* illustrate, these media were an open market, a pool full of technological knowledge, of which members took advantage when they saw a possible benefit:

Vol. I, 1869
'On the Development of Heat, and its Appropriation in Blast Furnaces of Different Dimensions', by Mr. I.L. Bell
'On a New Process for Removing Silicon from Pig Iron', by Mr. J. Palmer Budd
'On Siemens' Regenerative Furnace, and its Application to Re-heating Furnaces', by Mr. J.T. Smith
'On the Manufacture of Rails', by Mr. E. Williams
'On the Siemens-Martin Process of Manufacturing Cast Steel', by Mr. Howson
'On Improved Machinery for Rolling Rails', by Mr. W. Menelaus
'On the Production and Application of Combustible Gases under Pressure', by Mr. G.H. Benson

---

[52] Carr and Taplin, *History of the British Steel Industry*, p. 45; *The Times*, 25 Sep. 1869.

Vol. II, 1870
'A Method of Designing Rails', by Thomas Gillott
'Fire-Brick Hot Blast Stoves', by T. Whitwell (Discussion on)
'Generation of Combustible Gases under Pressure', by G.H. Benson
(Discussion on)
'Improved Machinery for Rolling Rails', by William Menelaus
(Discussion on)
'Iron as a Material for Shipbuilding, and its Influence on the Commercial and Armament of Nations', by C.M. Palmer, and Discussion[53]

The pattern of technical innovation, its diffusion and accumulation in the Cleveland industrial agglomeration, appears to fit the idea of 'collective invention' studied by Allen. Based on formal or informal disclosure of technological information, collective invention was not the work of individual inventors or firms, but the outcome of firms as a group in collaboration. Specifically the Cleveland practice of iron-making, briefly described above, can be categorized as a collective invention. The increase in height of furnace stacks from an average 40 feet to 80 feet, with a resulting capacity of 25,000 to 30,000 cubic feet which more efficiently utilized heat generated at the base of the furnace upon materials being charged in at the top, was a remarkable achievement of vast importance for productivity growth in Cleveland iron and steel.[54]

Allen's hypothesis rests upon a specific set of historical circumstances in the mid-nineteenth century British iron and steel industry. The first is that nineteenth-century British iron industries were competitively organized, and that invention important for productivity growth was not novel in the legal sense and not patentable. In such a case, individual inventors or a firm allocating resources to invention could expect an economic return which was far lower than the social value of any invention. Collective invention was a partial solution to this, because firms did not allocate resources to invention but generated technical material as a by-product of their normal activity. Hence, 'as long as the rate of investment was high, the rate of experimentation and the discovery of new technical knowledge was also high'.[55] Between 1850 and 1875, the Cleveland iron and steel industries had a high rate of gross capital formation, and thus a high rate of invention.

A second assumption is that technical expertise was disseminated freely and openly in the region, evident in the media produced by local research institutions publicizing technological knowledge and market conditions. We have seen that the Cleveland Institution of Engineers and the Iron and Steel Institute served as forums for exchanging technological information,

[53] *Trans. Iron and Steel Institute*, vol. I (1869) and vol. II (1870), and indices.
[54] Allen, 'Collective Invention', pp. 1–24; Porter, *On Competition*, pp. 197–8, 222–3; Casson, 'Economic Approach to Regional Business Networks', p. 42; Sabel and Zeitlin, 'Historical Alternatives to Mass Production', p. 144.
[55] Allen, 'Collective Invention', p. 3.

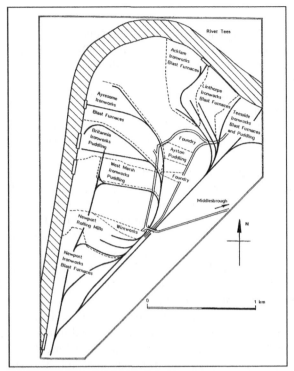

Map 2.2. Agglomeration and Product Specialization
in Ironmasters' District

via publication of their proceedings and members' discussions of specialist technical topics.

Allen's last premise is about entrepreneurs' possible attitudes towards collective invention. Why did firms publish important design and cost information to their competitors? One explanation could be that company owners released information to competitors or potential entrants because they took pride in exhibiting their achievements. It is possible also that too many people were in possession of the relevant information to keep it secret without incurring high costs. And last, circulating such information may have delivered great benefits to the industrialists, for instance in the way larger Cleveland blast furnaces increased the value of local iron ore deposits, so brought in higher rents to the owners of ironstone royalties, who were also the ironmasters. At the same time, such technological innovation provided considerable advantage to iron manufacturers across the region, so that 'by spreading cost and risks among firms, collective invention meant that competitive industries could have high rates of invention even if the inventions were not patentable', and collective invention was not inconsistent with private profit maximization.[56]

---

[56] Allen, 'Collective Invention', pp. 13, 20.

Table 2.13. Product Specialization in Cleveland Iron and Steel, 1870

Ironmakers	Puddling Furnaces[a]	Rails	Plates	Bars	Angles
A[b]	74		1,986		388
B	75	12,587			
C	31	3,854		421	506
D	28	3,491		210	331
E	26		5,257		
F	150	7,161	13,029		
G	38				
H	99	25,304			2,175
J	24		2,944		
K	57	300	6,173		3,983
L	32			2,106	2,459
M	200	7,425			
N	44		8,006		
O	57			300	1,000
P	20			2,252	
Q	103	2,500	2,688		
R	62	27,082			
S	183	13,250	1,008		
Total	1,303	102,964	38,147	8,233	10,842

Notes: Measured in tons. [a]Number of puddling furnaces owned by each ironmaker.
[b]No company names are given in the documents.
Source: Modern Records Centre, Univ. of Warwick, MSS 365/BAC, Vol. 1, pp. 22–3,
Mr. Waterhouse's Returns (Sales of Manufactured Iron).

The case of Cleveland iron and steel, as the industry developed over the second half of the nineteenth century, has provided interesting insights into the process of industrial agglomeration. Regarding the origin of industrial clustering in the region, the findings of Tirado *et al.* concerning the Spanish experience are pertinent. When factor mobility is high and elements that favour industrial agglomeration such as scale economies and external economies are present, the integration process will accentuate the genesis of forces favouring concentration of production in a limited number of productive centres, and hence will produce an increase in the geographical concentration of production.[57]

From the mid-nineteenth century, in particular from the latter half of the 1860s, the cumulative effects of industrial agglomeration around Middlesbrough, including external economies resulting from the mix of ironstone mining, pig and wrought iron, and finished products such as rails, plates, bars and angles, brought to the region a more diverse economic structure. This development delivered benefits of economic rationalization, including an increasing tendency of firms to specialize and concentrate on specific areas of production.

[57] Tirado *et al.*, 'Economic Integration and Industrial Location', p. 361.

Table 2.14. Wrought Iron Production in Middlesbrough, 1873

Ironmakers	Rails	Plates	Bars	Angles	Puddling Furnaces	Mills and Forges
Britannia Iron Works Co. Ltd	10,248		120		3	
Hopkins, Gilkes & Co.			535	2,622	100	5
Clay Lane Iron Works		1,450				
Jones Brothers & Co.		1,093			23	2
Jackson, Gill & Co. Ltd			446		32	2
Bolckow, Vaughan & Co. Ltd	16,212	2,587			67	11

Note: Measured in tons.

Source: Modern Records Centre, Univ. of Warwick, MSS 365/BAC, Vol. 1, pp. 54–6,
Mr. Waterhouse's Returns (Sales of Manufactured Iron); Griffiths, *Griffiths' Guide*, pp. 272–3.

Table 2.15. Number of Blast Furnaces, Pig and Wrought Iron Production per Week in Middlesbrough, 1856–61

Name of Works	Name of Firm	Furnaces In Blast	Furnaces Out of Blast	Pig Iron	Malleable Iron
Middlesbrough	Bolckow & Vaughan	3	0	450	300
Eston	Bolckow & Vaughan	6	0	900	–
Eston	Elwyn & Co.	3	0	430	–
Clarence	Bell Brothers	3	0	400	–
Middlesbrough	Gilkes, Wilson & Co.	4	0	500	–
Ormesby	Cochrane & Co.	2	2	250	–
Eston	B. Samuelson & Co.	3	0	400	–
Middlesbrough	Snowden & Hopkins	0	0	0	200

Note: Measured in tons.

Source: Griffiths, *Griffiths' Guide*, p. 315.

This trend can be seen within the iron and steel companies clustering in the Ironmasters' District of Middlesbrough, the agglomeration and product specialization in about 1875 illustrated on Map 2.2. There was a loose inter-firm division of production, for example, between Bell Brothers specializing in manufacturing pig iron, Fox, Head and Co. in the rolling process, Bolckow, Vaughan and Co. with various processes vertically integrated from coal- and iron-mining, blast furnaces, puddling and rolling to finished wrought-iron production, and engineering companies such as Gilkes and Wilson, which concentrated on making engines and machinery.[58] As demonstrated in Table 2.13, product specialization can be identified among those firms making finished wrought iron products. Of these 18 companies, all of them members

[58] With respect to agglomeration in the Ironmasters' District in about 1875, see Harrison, *John Gjers, Ironmaster*, p. 7, fig. 3; Gott, *Henry Bolckow*, pp. 35, 43.

Table 2.16. Number of Blast Furnaces in Middlesbrough, 1873

Name of Works	Name of Firm	Furnaces	In Blast	Furnaces being built
Lackenby	Lackenby Iron Co.	3	2	1
Eston	Bolckow, Vaughan & Co.	7	7	1
South Bank	T. Vaughan & Co.	9	7.5	
Clay Lane	T. Vaughan & Co.	6	6	
Cargo Fleet	Swan, Coates & Co.	4	4	
Normanby	Jones, Dunning & Co.	3	3	
Ormesby	Cochrane & Co.	4	3	2
Tees	Gilkes, Wilson, Pease & Co.	5	4.75	
Middlesbrough[a]	Bolckow, Vaughan & Co.	3	3	
Tees Side[a]	Hopkins, Gilkes & Co.	4	4	3
Linthorpe	Lloyd & Co.		6	6
Acklam	Stevenson, Jaques & Co.	4	4	
Ayresome	Gjers, Mills & Co.	4	4	1
Newport[a]	B. Samuelson & Co.	8	7.5	1
Clarence	Bell Brothers		8	8
Felling Gateshead[b]	H.L. Pattison & Co.	2	0	

Notes: [a]Firms owning puddling furnaces and also making wrought iron products.
[b]Middlesbrough branch of Tyneside Company.
Source: Griffiths, *Griffiths' Guide*, pp. 259–60.

Table 2.17. Number of Puddling Furnaces, Rolling Mills and Forges in Middlesbrough, 1873

Name of Works	Name of Firm	Puddling Furnaces	Mills and Forges
Middlesbrough	Bolckow, Vaughan & Co. Ltd	67	11
Tees Side	Hopkins, Gilkes & Co. Ltd	100	5
Newport	Fox, Head & Co.	42	4
Imperial	Jackson, Gill & Co. Ltd	32	2
West Marsh	West Marsh Iron Co.	20	2
Britannia	Britannia Iron Co. Ltd	120	3
Ayrton	Jones Brothers & Co.	23	2

Source: Griffiths, *Griffiths' Guide*, pp. 272–3.

of the Board of Arbitration and Conciliation for the North of England Manu-factured Iron Trade, not one made all kinds of wrought iron products in 1870.

Most firms concentrated on producing one or two specific items. While rail-producing firms predominated, 30% of firms made only one product. Table 2.14 shows contracts in hand for wrought-iron products in six Middles-brough firms in 1873. Excepting Bolckow, Vaughan and Co. and Hopkins, Gilkes and Co., there was an overwhelming focus on one product. Tables 2.15 to 2.17 give numbers of furnaces in blast, puddling furnaces, rolling mills, forges, and outputs of pig and wrought iron in 1856 and 1873 in

Cleveland (excluding Stockton and Whitby). Among the ironworks of the Middlesbrough area, 13 firms concentrated exclusively on the manufacture of pig iron, while three others also had rolling mills and forges. Seven firms specialized in finished wrought iron products, using pig iron either produced themselves, or bought from other ironmakers in the region.

Other iron-related industries expanded at this time. A steam hammer and engine maker, Joy and Co.; bolt and nut manufacturer, Cleveland Bolt and Nut Works; specialist pipe makers, Acklam Pipe Foundry; Cochrane, Grove and Co., who made components for railways: Anderston Foundry and Jones Brothers, both cut-nail makers; the wire-drawers Hill and Ward; iron tube makers, Crewdson, Hardy, and Co.; and a shipbuilder, which consumed large quantities of plates, Raylton, Dixon and Co., were all enterprises recognizably part of the increasing agglomeration. A division of work between firms producing materials, intermediate goods and finished items, is very evident. As displayed in Table 2.18, in addition to the core industries of iron and steel, with its complementary trades producing bridges, railway and marine engines, wagons, tenders, metal tubes, pipes, nails, bolts and nuts, other subsidiary industries grew up, notably a chemical industry which made slag wool, alizarine, aniline, sulphuric acid, oxalic acid, potash, benzoles, creosote, naphthas, and salt.[59]

Marshall's remarks on industrial agglomeration in his *Principles of Economics* are a neat summary of these developments in the Cleveland iron and steel trade:

> When then an industry has once chosen a locality for itself, it is likely to stay there long: so great are the advantages which people following the same skilled trade get from near neighbourhood to one another. The mysteries of the trade become no mysteries; but are as it were in the air, and children learn many of them unconsciously. Good work is rightly appreciated, inventions and improvements in machinery, in processes and the general organization of the business have their merits promptly discussed; if one man starts a new idea it is taken up by others and combined with suggestions of their own; and thus becomes the source of yet more new ideas.[60]

---

59 Armstrong *et al.*, *Industrial Resources of the District of the Three Northern Rivers*, p. 267; Jeans, *Notes on Northern Industries*, plan of Middlesbrough and South Stockton; Lillie, *History of Middlesbrough*, pp. 100, 102–3, 289, 290; regarding industrial clustering in the North East, see Milne, *North-East England*, pp. 59–63.
60 Marshall, *Principles of Economics*, p. 33.

Table 2.18. Industrial Agglomeration in Cleveland, Late-nineteenth and Early-twentieth Centuries

Iron, Steel, Wires and Mining
Bolckow & Vaughan
Bell Brothers (Clarence Works)
Middlesbrough Iron Works
Witton Park Iron Works
Teesside Iron Works (established in 1853)
Hopkins & Co.
Hopkins, Gilkes & Co.
Newport Iron Works
Eston Iron Works (founded in 1852, Bolckow & Vaughan)
Cochrane & Co. (established in 1854)
Cochrane, Grove & Co.
Gilkes, Wilson & Leatham
Gilkes, Wilson, Pease & Co.
Gjers, Mills (Ayresome Ironworks)
Acklam Pipe Foundry (established in 1878)
Anderston Foundry (established in 1876)
Brown Brass Foundry (established in 1860)
W. Richard Britannia Foundry (North Ormesby) (established in 1880)
Cargo Fleet Iron Co. (established in 1864)
Swan, Coates & Co.
Acklam Iron Works
Dorman Long (steel)
Ormesby Iron Works
Hopkins' Teesside Ironworks
North Eastern Steel Co. (established in 1881)
West Marsh Iron Co.
Pease & Partners Foundries Ltd (Teesside Iron & Engine Works)
Normanby Ironstone Mines
Wilson, Pease & Co.
Westgarth English Tees Furnace Co. Ltd
Furnace Westgarth Co.
Eston Mines
Erimus Iron Co.
Jones Brothers
Lackenby Iron Works
Richard Hill Wire Works
Hill & Ward, Wire Works
Joseph Pease & Partners (coal mining)
J.W. Pease & Co. (ironstone and limestone)

Continued

Table 2.18. Continued

Engineering, Cut-nails, Pipe, Tubes, and Bolt and Nuts

Gilkes, Wilson & Co. Tees Engine Works (Gilkes, Wilson & Leatham)
Warlick Patent Fuel Works
Tees Bridge & Engineering Co.
Crewdson, Hardy & Co. (Yorkshire Tube Works)
Messrs. Jones (the Nail Works)
Cleveland Nuts & Bolt Works
Wrought Iron Co.
Jones, Dunning & Co.(Normanby)
Richardson, Westgarth & Co.
Joy & Co.

Shipbuilding and Related Industries

Irwin & Co.
Rake, Kimber & Co.
Richardson & Duck
R. Craggs & Sons (originally at Stockton)
William Harkess & Sons
J.G. Holmes (Laing)
North Yorkshire & South Durham Shipping Co.
West Hartlepool Harbour & Dock Co.
Major Dickson (company name unknown)
Taylor's Middlesbrough & London Shipping Co.
Tees Tug Co.
Tees Union Shipping Co.
Scarborough Steam Shipping Co. Ltd
Cleveland Dockyard
Sir Raylton Dixon & Co. Ltd

Pottery

Middlesbrough Pottery Co. (founded by Richard Otley)
Middlesbrough Earthenware Co.
Company name unknown (founded by Isaac Wilson)
Linthorpe Art Pottery

Railway Company

Stockton & Darlington Railway
Port Clarence Railway Co.
North Eastern Railway Co.

Salt and Chemical

Cleveland Salt Co.
Pease & Partners
United Alkali Co.
The Salt Union
Brunner Mond

Note: Companies that changed their names during the period are included.

Source: Teesside Archives, catalogue; Armstrong, *Industrial Resources of the District of the Three Northern Rivers*, pp. 162, 179–81; Griffiths, *Griffiths' Guide*, pp. 259–60, 272–4; Jeans, Notes on Northern Industries, pp. 65–7, plan of Middlesbrough and South Stockton facing p. 162; Bullock, 'Spatial Adjustments', pp. 379, 383, 395, 405, 409, 411–12.

3

Demography and Urban Growth

> Various circumstances contribute to promote this immigration from the more distant parts of the country, such as the vicinity of competing towns, or the demand for a particular class of labour which surrounding country is not able to furnish... Middlesbrough affords a suitable illustration of this type of towns. Its rapid growth, the heterogeneous composition of its population, and the preponderance of the male sex, recall features generally credited only to the towns of the American west.[1]

In a survey of historical studies of nineteenth-century European geographical mobility, Jackson and Moch divided migration analysis into five basic emphases: (1) migrants defined by age, gender, landholding, education, income and so on; (2) motivation for mobility; (3) flows of movers, especially return migration and multiple moves; (4) the impact of mobility on the places people left and on their destinations; and (5) consequences of migration for those who migrated, for instance in experiencing urban crime or mental disorders. These five interrelated questions will be addressed here to establish a migration profile for Victorian Middlesbrough.[2]

This chapter seeks to challenge limitations in the sources available for the study of geographical mobility in nineteenth-century Britain, and address these five points as specifically as possible. In contrast with the kind of migration studies possible in other countries, most notably Germany, where detailed and accurate migration registration data were kept in the larger cities from the nineteenth century, for England no such comprehensive source material is available. In Germany, a combination of census manuscripts and population residency registers enables specific patterns of mobility to be studied in a way that is not possible elsewhere in western or central Europe.[3]

In the absence of such direct and complete figures, any study of nineteenth-century Britain must seek the evidence for a longitudinal migration profile, for individuals or for households, from a diverse range of sources. Census enumerators' books, directories, electoral rolls or rate books, can be linked together to yield information on individual or household movements over time, provided that these records are more or less complete. However,

---

[1] Ravenstein, 'Laws of Migration', p. 215.
[2] Jackson and Moch, 'Migration and the Social History of Modern Europe', pp. 29–31.
[3] For migration sources for nineteenth-century Germany, see Jackson, *Migration and Urbanization in the Ruhr Valley*, pp. 17–18, 347–54; Hochstadt, *Mobility and Modernity*, pp. 51–2.

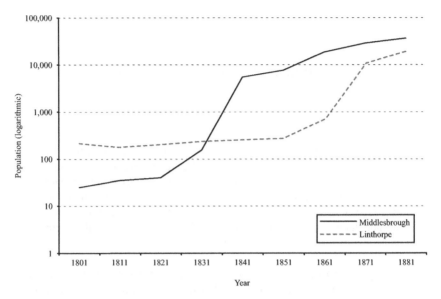

Figure 3.1. Population of Middlesbrough and Linthorpe, 1801–81

in the case of mid-Victorian Middlesbrough, the only useful data that are available, through which a migration profile can be analysed, come from the returns of census enumerators.[4]

In this chapter, demographic aspects of Middlesbrough's growth are illuminated through computer-aided record linkage drawing on the census enumerators' books to trace demographic behaviour. A longitudinal migration profile, of individuals as well as households, has been drawn by matching consecutive censuses, 1851 with 1861, and 1861 with 1871. The resulting dataset, containing individuals and households who appear in, and perhaps disappear from, census records, enables a migration profile of the town during these years to be fairly well established.

There have not as yet been enough quantitative migration studies based on record linkage of census enumerators' returns in other Victorian industrial towns to make systematic comparison possible. However, the detailed migration pattern described here, for the newly built and rapidly expanding industrial town of Middlesbrough, can be contrasted with several American and European industrial towns during the same period.[5] Above all the pioneering work of Thernstrom as early as 1973, *The Other Bostonians*, has stood the test of time. Thernstrom made extensive use of census enumerators' data to describe in-migration and the making of an American metropolis from 1880

4   Regarding available data and problems in their use for British nineteenth-century migration studies, see Lawton, 'Mobility in Nineteenth-century British Cities', pp. 207–8, 210.
5   For recent trends in historical studies on German migration, and a summary of research into migration in nineteenth- and early twentieth-century central Europe, see Jackson, *Migration and Urbanization in the Ruhr Valley*, pp. 22–4.

to 1970, and his work remains a starting point for migration studies based on census enumerators' books.

Profile of the Middlesbrough Population

Before embarking on a detailed exercise in record linkage, we should examine more generally the profile of Middlesbrough's population in the second half of the nineteenth century, and consider how far it was representative of Victorian industrial towns.

A first and most striking demographic feature is Middlesbrough's extraordinarily rapid population growth. Figure 3.1 shows the dramatic rise in population from the mid-nineteenth century in both Middlesbrough and Linthorpe, the adjacent suburban parish. This remarkable increase is typical of a boom town. The population growth in Middlesbrough between 1831 (154 residents) and 1841 (5,463), and Linthorpe between 1861 (702) and 1871 (10,551), was astonishing.[6]

Middlesbrough's growth was one of the most spectacular experienced by any British town in the nineteenth century.[7] Fortunately for our purposes, six local censuses were taken in the borough of Middlesbrough between 1854 and 1866, so that additional data – albeit merely head counts – are available on population trends between the censuses of 1851 and 1871. The local censuses were carried out for the purposes of acquiring Acts of Parliament, to incorporate the borough and establish an improvement commission and a local board of health. These surveys show that the most rapid population increase occurred in the middle of the 1850s. While the borough boundary was extended in 1858, the land taken into it was not then built upon, remaining undeveloped apart from the graveyard, industrial estates and wharf. The increase in population recorded between 1854 and 1859 was therefore a real growth within the area of the old borough. The first half of the 1850s had seen increases averaging 8% to 9% per annum; between 1855 and 1856 the rate of growth was 24%.[8]

Of the four panels in Figure 3.2 illustrating changes over time in the age structure of the Middlesbrough population between 1851 and 1881, those for 1861 and 1871 bear close similarity in shape, peaking at a plateau in the male age groups of 20 to 24 and 25 to 29. This is noticeably different from the panels for 1851 and 1881, which show for both males and females a rather

---

[6] PP, XXXVII,1831 Census, enumeration abstract; 1851 [1691-I] LXXXVIII, Part I; PP, 1851–53 [1631] LXXXV, 1851 Census of Great Britain, Population Table I, map facing xlvi; PP, 1873 [872] LXXII, Census of England and Wales 1871, Pt. I, Vol. III; PP, 1883 [3722] LXXX, Census of England and Wales 1881, Vol. III.

[7] For the rapid growth of population in late-nineteenth century British industrial towns, see for example Daunton, *Coal Metropolis*, pp. 9–12; Welton, 'On the Distribution of Population', pp. 531, 547; for population change and economic development in late-nineteenth century Middlesbrough, see Leonard, 'Urban Development and Population Growth', pp. 266–450, 500–15.

[8] Teesside Archives, CB/M/C 1/6, p. 40; CB/M/C 1/8, p. 75; CB/M/C (2) 9/57; Lillie, *History of Middlesbrough*, pp. 473–4.

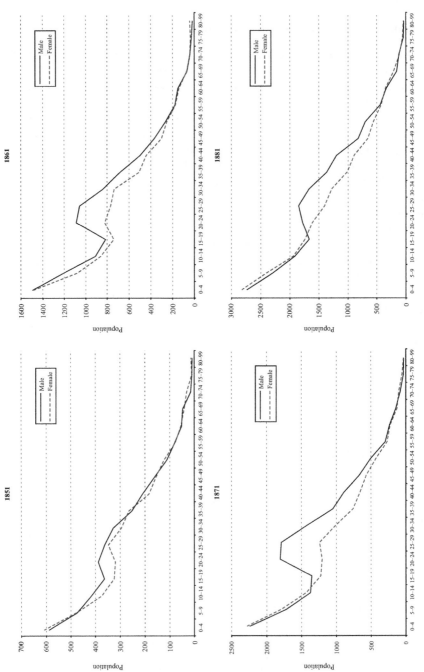

Figure 3.2. Age Structure of the Middlesbrough Population, 1851–81

Table 3.3. Migrants in Selected Industrial Towns in England, 1871,
with Sex Ratio

Provenance	Middlesbrough (%)	Liverpool (%)	Manchester (%)	Birmingham (%)	Leeds (%)	Sheffield (%)
Wales	3.9	4.3	1.5	0.8	0.2	0.2
Ireland	9.2	15.6	9.0	2.6	3.9	2.5
Scotland	2.9	4.1	1.9	0.4	0.8	0.6
Total	16.0	24.0	12.4	3.8	4.9	3.3
Foreign Countries	1.0	1.2	0.9	0.3	0.4	0.2
England	83.0	74.8	86.7	95.8	94.7	96.5
Grand Total	100.0	100.0	100.0	100.0	100.0	100.0

Sex Ratio of Migrants in Selected Industrial Towns in England, 1871

Provenance	Middlesbrough	Liverpool	Manchester	Birmingham	Leeds	Sheffield
Wales	127	83	66	90	81	105
Ireland	194	89	76	95	93	120
Scotland	151	106	116	129	121	133
Total	161	91	80	98	97	121

Source: Parliamentary Papers, Census of England and Wales, 1871, 1873 [c.872] LXII, Pt.1, Vol. III.

smooth decline from the left-hand side, with by and large fewer females throughout all the age groups.[9]

Economic fluctuations are clearly mirrored in the shapes of the age- and sex-specific population from 1851 to 1881. The shapes reflect the burgeoning in-migration of young males aged 20–24 and 25–29 during the boom in iron-making between 1851 and 1871, and lessening in-migration or increasing out-migration after the downturn in the iron and steel industries from the 1880s onwards. Throughout the period, notably in 1861 and 1871, the sex ratio, that is, the proportion of males to females, was heavily weighted towards males because of a continuing higher net migration rate for males than for females.

Undoubtedly the extraordinary age and sex structures evident in this middle period, 1851 to 1871, came about because of the radical developments in local industry. After some 20 years, between 1871 and 1881 the population returned to its original configuration. Figure 3.2, taken in conjunction with detailed analysis of the migration profile to be described below, suggests that the pattern of change was fundamentally related to major re-arrangements in the economic and social structure of the town.

Nineteenth-century Middlesbrough had a further distinctive demographic feature in the geographical origins of its inhabitants. Table 3.3 compares the percentage of migrants from Ireland, Wales, Scotland and foreign countries

[9]   National Archives, HO 107 2383 (1851); RG 9 3685-3689 (1861); RG 10 4889-4895 (1871); RG 11/4852 [4851] (1881).

Table 3.4. Sex Ratio of Middlesbrough, 1851–81

		Population	*Ratio*
1851 Census Enumerators' Books	Male	3,788	105
	Female	3,621	
	Total	7,409	
1851–1861 In-migrant Population	Male	8,055	115
	Female	7,013	
	Total	15,068	
1861 Census Enumerators' Books	Male	9,502	115
	Female	8,297	
	Total	17,799	
1861–1871 In-migrant Population	Male	11,872	114
	Female	10,372	
	Total	22,244	
1871 Census Enumerators' Books	Male	15,242	117
	Female	13,041	
	Unknown	118	
	Total	28,401	
1881 Census Enumerators' Books	Male	19,036	109
	Female	17,418	
	Unknown	10	
	Total	36,464	

Source: National Archives, HO 107 2383 (1851); RG 9 3685–3689 (1861); RG 10 4889–4895 (1871); RG 11/4852 (1881); record linkage from Middlesbrough Census Enumerators' Books, 1851–61 and 1861–71.

into selected industrial towns in England in 1871.[10] Middlesbrough shows the second highest proportion after Liverpool of in-migrants from Ireland, Wales, Scotland and foreign countries, respectively. Although Middlesbrough was not located closest to their home countries, Irish, Welsh and Scottish people, as well as foreigners, made up as many as 16% of its inhabitants in 1871. Manchester, Birmingham, Leeds and Sheffield attracted relatively few in-migrants from these places. Although there was substantial movement into Middlesbrough from other parts of England, longer-distance migration into the town appears to have been a distinctive feature at this time.

There was also a remarkable bias towards male migration from these places. The town attracted many more men than women from all places, in particular from Ireland where male in-migration was virtually twice that of females. It seems likely that the Middlesbrough labour market during its heyday owed much to skilled and semi-skilled male ironworkers from Wales, and to unskilled, casual male labourers from Ireland. The exceptional features of Middlesbrough's nineteenth-century population patterns noted here can be explained only by the extraordinary level of in-migration. Such demographic features could not have been brought about by any natural increases in the urban population.

[10]   PP, 1873 [872] LXXII, Census of England and Wales 1871, Pt. I, Vol. III.

From 1851 onwards, men outnumbered women in the population as a whole, the figures shown in Table 3.4 taking account also of the results of record linkages, 1851–61 and 1861–71. Sex ratios as high as 115 and 117, recorded in 1861 and 1871, can undoubtedly be attributed to the heavy influx of males at this time, to be discussed in more detail below. In contrast with all the main industrial towns of England, Middlesbrough was unique in having more men than women. From the mid-nineteenth century, Middlesbrough might be characterized as a young masculine urban community. A parallel can be drawn with the German industrial town of Duisburg, where in the late 1860s new smelting technology was introduced and new factories founded, and where the sex ratio was 110, while the sex ratio of in-migrants in 1867 and 1868 rose as high as 300.[11]

Table 3.5 draws upon vital statistics presented in the Registrar General's annual report for 1881. Although the best single measure of mortality prevailing at any time and place is the figure for life expectation at birth based on a life table, we compare crude death rates irrespective of age-specific mortality. The reason is the difficulty in producing life tables for smaller towns such as Middlesbrough, with a population of less than 100,000, as the age-specific mortality figures for individual smaller urban communities are not generally available in the records.[12]

The distinctive demographic features of late nineteenth-century Middlesbrough are illustrated in Table 3.5. The height of the crude birth rate of Middlesbrough, 40.5 per 1,000, in a population of 56,677 in 1881, was impressive, while mortality, 17.7 per 1,000, was extraordinarily low. In both fertility and mortality, the town showed extreme levels, with the difference between them as much as 22.8 points. Its fertility was much higher than large towns with populations over 100,000, and was far above the national average of England and Wales. In terms of birth and death rates affecting overall population growth rates, Middlesbrough was remarkable.[13]

Mortality was below the national average, and below the average for the 15 largest towns. Even compared with crude death rates observed in comparable smaller rapidly growing industrial towns in 1881, Middlesbrough's low mortality was striking. For instance, Merthyr Tydfyll, a centre of the Welsh iron and steel industry, had a crude death rate of 27.6 and crude birth rate of 35.0, the difference being merely 7.4 points. The mortality in other

---

[11] National Archives, HO 107 2383 (1851); RG 9 3685-3689 (1861); RG 10 4889-4895 (1871); RG 11/4852 [4851] (1881), and record linkage from Middlesbrough census enumerators' books, 1851–61 and 1861–71. Migration and other population figures for Middlesbrough which follow derive from this record linkage exercise; Yasumoto, 'Migrants in Middlesbrough', pp. 4–8; Jackson, 'Migration in Duisburgp', p. 165.

[12] *Forty-Fourth Annual Report of the Registrar General of Births, Deaths, and Marriages in England (Abstracts of 1881)*, 1883; *Supplement to the Forty-Fifth Annual Report of the Registrar General of Births, Deaths, and Marriages in England*, 1885; Szreter, *Health and Wealth*, pp. 188–90.

[13] For relationships between migration, fertility, mortality and population growth in early-modern towns, see Sharlin, 'Natural Decrease in Early-modern Cities', pp. 127–8, 134–8.

Table 3.5. Population of 15 Large Towns and Middlesbrough, 1881

Towns	Population	CBR	Illegitimacy	CDR	Infant Mortality	Suicide Rate	Marriage Rate	Female Minority Marriage Rate	Literacy M	F	T
Middlesbrough	56,677	40.5	3.1	17.7	143	1.5	8.4	33.8	82	77	79
London	3,814,571	34.8	3.9	21.3	148	3.8	9.1	18.3	93	90	92
Portsmouth	127,986	34.4	3.4	19.7	120	4.1	10.0	17.9	93	90	92
Norwich	87,843	33.6	6.2	19.4	149	4.1	8.7	25.0	89	86	87
Wolverhampton	145,440	36.3	4.8	19.3	136	2.0	7.0	24.5	72	69	70
Birmingham	246,352	36.9	4.5	22.0	157	4.1	8.6	25.3	82	76	86
Leicester	122,351	38.5	4.6	21.9	202	3.4	9.4	24.0	90	80	85
Nottingham	159,346	35.9	7.1	22.8	169	3.6	11.6	25.5	90	82	86
Liverpool	210,161	33.0	5.1	34.1	217	1.9	14.4	26.2	80	71	75
Salford	181,525	39.1	4.5	23.2	165	2.1	8.2	25.9	85	69	77
Manchester	148,805	36.5	4.1	25.1	171	3.0	10.0	25.8	84	63	74
Oldham	168,459	34.6	3.8	22.2	156	4.6	7.8	22.7	88	68	78
Leeds	190,863	35.8	6.3	22.0	168	2.6	10.1	26.3	87	76	81
Sheffield	183,138	39.5	5.9	22.4	159	2.5	11.8	34.5	81	72	76
Sunderland	139,376	39.8	3.6	20.4	147	2.4	9.8	28.1	83	76	79
Newcastle	150,121	36.9	5.2	21.7	153	3.0	12.1	23.4	89	81	85
Total 15 Urban	6,076,337	35.5	4.3	22.0	154	3.5	9.4	21.7	90	84	87
England & Wales	25,968,286	34.0	4.9	18.9	130	3.3	7.6	21.4	87	82	84

Notes: For suicide rates, figures are means between 1871 and 1881 with Middlesbrough for 1875–80 and Manchester for 1874–80. Figures for infant mortality of Middlesbrough, Ormesby and Thornaby. CBR: crude birth rate per 1,000 population, CDR: crude death rate per 1,000 population, Illegitimacy: percentage of Illegitimate births to all births, Infant Mortality: Deaths under 1 year of age per 1,000 births, Suicide Rate: Suicide deaths per 1,000 deaths, Marriage Rate: Marriages per 1,000 population, Female Minority Marriage Rate: Females not of full age married per 1,000 female married, Literacy: % of those who signed the marriage registers to all married, M = male, F= female, T = total.

Source: Forty-Forth Annual Report of the Registrar General of Births, Deaths and Marriages in England (Abstracts of 1881), London, 1883; Supplement to the Forty-Fifth Annual Report of the Registrar General of Births, Deaths, and Marriages in England, London, 1885.

smaller industrial towns, Gateshead (21.0), West Bromwich (20.0), Barrow-in-Furness (19.8) or Newport (18.9) was above that of Middlesbrough. The neighbouring north-east industrial towns of Stockton and Darlington also had lower crude birth rates, of 39.6 and 35.7, while their crude death rates were higher or almost equal, 19.1 and 16.9, respectively.[14]

In the mid-nineteenth century these smaller towns had mortality levels higher than the national average, but a significant improvement was seen in the 1870s or 1880s. Yet even compared with the diminishing mortality in the 1880s of these smaller industrial towns, Middlesbrough's position was extreme.[15] Along with the influx of young in-migrants, a resident population with similarly young age structure contributed to the high crude birth rates and low death rates which increased Middlesbrough's population so rapidly.

Because more than 80% from each group aged between 20 and 39 in 1861 had migrated into the town, fertility rates were raised and mortality rates reduced. Comparative crude death rates for large cities with populations of over 100,000 in 1851 are: Liverpool (34.1, expectation of life at birth: 36); Manchester (25.1, expectation of life at birth: 37); Salford (23.2); Nottingham (22.8); Sheffield (22.4); Oldham (22.2); Birmingham (22.0); Leeds (22.0). Middlesbrough's lower mortality was due to its exceptionally low age structure caused by the influx of younger population. Like Duisburg in western Germany in the late-nineteenth century, Middlesbrough was not an urban graveyard but a centre of demographic vitality, full of young families.[16]

One of the sensitive indices of urban amenity is infant mortality, which in 1881 averaged 154 per 1,000 births across the 15 large cities, while the national average stood at 130 per 1,000. The Middlesbrough figure of 143 fell between the two. The mean suicide rate in Middlesbrough, 1.5 per 1,000 deaths between 1871 and 1881, was much lower than that for the 15 large towns and less than half the national average. While the Middlesbrough marriage rate was slightly higher than national average, it was evidently lower than average for the 15 large towns. Conversely, illegitimacy expressed as the percentage of illegitimate births among all births was well below the national and the 15 large towns' averages.

The female minority marriage rate shows the number per 1,000 females who married younger than full age, and in this too Middlesbrough was exceptional among urban centres. Its rate of 33.8 was very high, and can be explained by the young age structure of the population as a whole, and by the high

[14] *Forty-Fourth Annual Report of the Registrar General of Births, Deaths, and Marriages in England (Abstracts of 1881)*, 1883; *Supplement to the Forty-Fifth Annual Report of the Registrar General of Births, Deaths, and Marriages in England*, 1885.

[15] For mortality in smaller industrial towns in the late-nineteenth century, see Szreter, *Health and Wealth*, pp. 189–90.

[16] With respect to mortality in British cities in the late-nineteenth century, especially the low life expectancies in Liverpool and Manchester, see Szreter, *Health and Wealth*, pp. 169–73, 185–6; regarding age structure and demographic features in Duisburg, see Jackson, 'Migration in Duisburg', p. 169.

Table 3.6. Causes of Death in 15 Large Towns and Middlesbrough, 1881

Towns	Infectious Diseases	Phthisis	Nervous System	Circulatory System	Respiratory System	Digestive System	Violent Death	Others	Total Deaths	(Inquest)
Middlesbrough	249 (13.4)	157 (8.5)	283 (15.3)	112 (6.1)	366 (19.7)	97 (5.2)	111 (6.0)	436 (25.8)	1,856 (100.0)	160 (8.6)
London	364 (17.1)	225 (10.5)	247 (11.6)	131 (6.1)	418 (19.6)	119 (5.6)	80 (3.7)	602 (25.8)	2,133 (100.0)	145 (6.8)
Portsmouth	348 (17.7)	225 (11.4)	262 (13.3)	133 (6.7)	324 (16.5)	100 (5.1)	49 (2.5)	638 (26.8)	1,970 (100.0)	104 (5.3)
Norwich	195 (10.0)	167 (8.6)	223 (11.5)	120 (6.2)	261 (13.5)	105 (5.4)	57 (2.9)	768 (41.9)	1,936 (100.0)	121 (6.2)
Wolverhampton	244 (12.6)	124 (6.4)	250 (13.0)	131 (6.8)	395 (20.5)	122 (6.3)	68 (3.5)	538 (30.9)	1,931 (100.0)	102 (5.3)
Birmingham	304 (13.8)	207 (9.4)	269 (12.2)	130 (5.9)	513 (23.3)	102 (4.6)	123 (5.6)	527 (25.2)	2,203 (100.0)	230 (10.4)
Leicester	432 (19.7)	154 (7.1)	304 (13.9)	134 (6.1)	354 (16.2)	78 (3.6)	74 (3.4)	606 (30.0)	2,190 (100.0)	168 (7.6)
Nottingham	437 (19.1)	205 (9.0)	297 (13.0)	135 (5.9)	382 (16.7)	113 (4.9)	65 (2.8)	601 (28.6)	2,285 (100.0)	129 (5.7)
Liverpool	559 (16.4)	309 (9.1)	315 (9.2)	206 (6.0)	960 (28.1)	147 (4.3)	188 (5.5)	897 (21.4)	3,411 (100.0)	246 (7.2)
Manchester	293 (11.7)	232 (9.2)	319 (12.7)	120 (4.8)	630 (25.1)	130 (5.2)	171 (6.8)	595 (24.5)	2,510 (100.0)	347 (13.8)
Salford	477 (13.4)	398 (11.2)	463 (13.0)	179 (5.0)	871 (24.5)	161 (4.5)	93 (2.6)	851 (25.8)	3,559 (100.0)	157 (4.4)
Oldham	234 (10.6)	234 (10.6)	337 (15.2)	145 (6.5)	567 (25.6)	128 (5.8)	62 (2.8)	470 (22.9)	2,215 (100.0)	66 (3.0)
Leeds	302 (13.7)	204 (9.3)	315 (14.3)	138 (6.3)	448 (20.4)	115 (5.2)	91 (4.1)	557 (26.7)	2,204 (100.0)	144 (6.5)
Sheffield	282 (12.6)	203 (9.0)	329 (14.6)	139 (6.2)	574 (25.6)	103 (4.6)	85 (3.8)	532 (24.3)	2,244 (100.0)	118 (5.3)
Sunderland	277 (13.6)	175 (8.6)	336 (16.5)	119 (5.8)	380 (18.6)	115 (5.6)	74 (3.6)	517 (27.7)	2,043 (100.0)	103 (5.1)
Newcastle	278 (12.8)	210 (9.7)	316 (14.6)	160 (7.4)	326 (15.0)	125 (5.7)	92 (4.2)	625 (30.6)	2,170 (100.0)	151 (7.0)
Total 15 Urban	351 (16.0)	220 (10.0)	267 (12.2)	134 (6.1)	449 (20.5)	117 (5.3)	85 (3.9)	572 (26.0)	2,195 (100.0)	150 (6.8)
England & Wales	230 (12.1)	183 (9.7)	261 (13.8)	137 (7.3)	358 (18.9)	111 (5.8)	70 (3.7)	520 (28.8)	1,894 (100.0)	105 (5.5)

Notes: Infectious diseases are smallpox, measles, scarlet fever, diphtheria, whooping cough, typhus fever, enteric fever, simple continued fever, diarrhoea and dysentery, cholera. Figures for Middlesbrough comprise Middlesbrough, Ormesby and Thornaby. Figures are rate for each group of diseases per 100,000 population. Those in the parentheses are the proportion (%) of each group of diseases of the total deaths.

Source: Forty-Fourth Annual Report of the Registrar General of Births, Deaths and Marriages in England (Abstracts of 1881), London, 1883.

ratio of men to women, resulting in a sellers' marriage market for women. The younger age at marriage also contributed to the town's high fertility rate. The high proportion of males in Middlesbrough did not in fact have a negative impact on fertility levels.[17] The literacy level, especially among males, expressed as those who signed the marriage registers as a percentage of all marriages, was understandably lower in Middlesbrough than the averages nationally and for the 15 large towns. This can be explained partly by the large number of unskilled labourers pouring into the town at this period.

A final element to be considered of Middlesbrough's late nineteenth-century demographic history is causes of death. Table 3.6 shows these in 1881, as observed in Middlesbrough and the same 15 large towns as in Table 3.5. The violent death rate – both in terms of proportion of all causes of death (shown in parentheses) and of the ratio for each group of diseases per 100,000 population – was substantially higher than the averages, nationally and for 15 large towns. The proportion of violent deaths in Middlesbrough related to all causes of death was the second highest after Manchester. This could be accounted for by the frequency of industrial accidents in both towns.

Deaths into which inquests were held, and those from illnesses of the nervous system, were much more frequent than the national average and slightly above the average for the 15 large towns, and indeed higher than in most smaller industrial towns. The high number of inquests is likely to have been related to the numbers of vagrants moving into town, in some cases lying dead by the roadside unidentified, and also because so many workers were killed by industrial accidents. The frequency of death from nervous system ailments was presumably a result of excessive drinking, habitual among many manual labourers engaged in the iron, steel and other heavy industries.[18] Otherwise, Middlesbrough in the late nineteenth century did not show any unusual patterns in the causes of death recorded. In fact it could be argued that in 1881 the town was relatively healthy, for despite the intensity of population increase and urban growth, various measures of mortality were comparatively good for such a rapidly expanding urban centre.

Migration Study Methodology

To investigate exactly how these demographic patterns emerged in Middlesbrough, a process of record linkage has been employed to create a longitudinal migration profile. The principle of record linkage is reasonably straightforward. Using all information available from census enumerators' books for 1851 onwards, gender, first name and surname, age and birthplace of individuals are linked and matched to identify the same person. That is

[17] For the relationship between a high sex ratio and high fertility as observed in Duisburg in the late nineteenth and early twentieth centuries, see Jackson, 'Migration in Duisburg', p. 169.

[18] *Forty-Fourth Annual Report of the Registrar General of Births, Deaths, and Marriages in England (Abstracts of 1881)*, 1883; *Supplement to the Forty-Fifth Annual Report of the Registrar General of Births, Deaths, and Marriages in England*, 1885.

why this method is usually called 'nominal record linkage'. Although it is designed to identify individuals who remain in a community between two consecutive censuses, this record linkage method throws an incidental light on the longitudinal migration profile of individuals and families.

From a number of methods now available, the system adopted here is that developed by Kingston University's Centre for Local History Studies, selected for the reliability of resultant record linkages. In the Kingston procedure, no linkage is automatic. All potential links are reviewed visually by the researcher.

To achieve this, and to enable further analysis to be developed from the results of the linkage exercise, information about surname, relationship to head of household, marital status and occupation needs to be encoded. Also, since place names were recorded inconsistently depending on individual enumerators, or even spelt in a variety of ways by the same enumerator, it is most reliable to use a county or country of birth rather than the name of a parish. For the most important variable for nominal record linkage, the surname, a Soundex code is used.

To identify potential links, the Kingston method uses five algorithms: initial letter of forename, Soundex surname, gender, county of birth, year of birth plus or minus four-year margins from a difference of 10 years between the censuses. Beyond the algorithms, during the review process by the researcher, potential matches can also be identified for other members of the same household that have not been revealed by the algorithms. Thus by the Kingston method, two kinds of matching results are available, '*true*' (T) *matches* revealed by the algorithms and '*possible*' (P) *matches* obtained through from the researcher's review of other members of the same household. This method is comparable with similar research undertaken in Germany by James H. Jackson, a migration study of Duisburg which used census data for 1810, 1843, 1867 and 1890 to produce algorithms of names, ages, occupations, household statuses, family characteristics, denominational affiliations, addresses and other information, for nearly 23,400 residents.[19]

Although our nominal record linkage based on two, three or more consecutive enumerators' books, by collating successive snap-shots overcomes the flaws in cross-sectional analysis of a single-year census, 10-year periods are too long to analyse continuing residency in a very mobile society such as mid-Victorian Middlesbrough.[20] Neither does this record linkage procedure reveal specifically the dates and stages of migration, let alone motivation or reason, nor the relation to life cycle or circulatory movement. Furthermore this method of intercensal nominative migration analysis is much more reliable in tracking the male population than the female one, as some females

[19] Tilley and French, 'Record Linkage for Nineteenth Century Census', pp. 122–32; Jackson, *Migration and Urbanization in the Ruhr Valley*, p. 17.
[20] For the shortcomings of cross-sectional census-based migration study, see Pooley and Turnbull, 'Migration and Urbanization in North-West England', p. 187.

would change their name upon marrying and become unidentifiable in subsequent census enumerators' books.

Owing to the difficulties involved in tracing females, the following demographic analysis will focus mainly on the experiences of males. A further problem in using this method is that, in contrast with isonymy analysis, it carries an intrinsic defect, an inability to trace the second generation, for example of Irish migrants, because the census enumerators' books recorded the birth places of the first generation only.[21] Despite these caveats, in the absence of other direct migration evidence, this technique when reinforced by other relevant analysis, for example, of tracing stepwise migration based on evidence of the birthplaces of surviving co-resident offspring in the household, can potentially shed light on features of in- and out-migration.

With this system of record linkage, the population breaks down into three categories of individual. The first group consists of those who can be linked, identifiable in consecutive census enumerators' books. These, presumably, would have stayed in the Middlesbrough area between censuses, although it is likely that some of them moved away and returned in the decade between the two censuses. This pattern has been investigated by analysing the birthplaces of surviving co-resident children in these supposedly persistent households in Middlesbrough between 1851 and 1861.

There were 866 households in 1861 whose male household heads can be found in both the 1851 and 1861 census enumerators' books. Of these, 650 households had surviving co-resident offspring. For any household containing children recorded as having been born in a place other than Middlesbrough, we would regard that family as having temporarily moved away some time after 1851, afterwards returning to the town before 1861. We have identified 62 such households, accounting for almost 10% of all those with surviving co-resident offspring.[22]

It seems, then, that at least one-tenth of families assumed to have remained in the town between censuses, in fact temporarily out-migrated during the period. It is likely that some of these cases of temporary out-migration left the town when they were young, to establish a family and bear children away from Middlesbrough, returning to their former home town in their 30s or 40s. The birthplaces of children in these families indicate that the movements tended to be over a relatively short distance, with most of the places situated in adjacent Co. Durham and Yorkshire.

A similar pattern is suggested in the census records of Breslau and Karlsruhe in Germany during this same period. Six per cent of Breslau natives in 1885 had migrated out and then come back in. In 1905, 28% of those aged over 27 and born in Karlsruhe had been migrants. Overall, German censuses

---

[21] Smith, *Human Biology and History*, pp. 1–124.
[22] The figure is based on record linkage from the Middlesbrough census enumerators' books, 1851–61.

Table 3.7. Migration in Middlesbrough, 1851–61

	1851			*1861*	
Out-migrants	Male	2,341	Persistent	Male	1,447
	Female	2,337		Female	1,284
	Total	4,678 (63.1%)		Total	2,731 (15.3%)
Persistent	Male	1,447	In-migrants	Male	7,412
	Female	1,284		Female	6,390
	Total	2,731 (36.9%)		Total	13,802 (77.6%)
			Children born	Male	643
			after 1851	Female	623
				Total	1,266 (7.1 %)
Total	Male	3,788	Total	Male	9,502
	Female	3,621		Female	8,297
	Total	7,409 (100.0 %)		Total	17,799 (100.0 %)

Source: Record linkage from Middlesbrough Census Enumerators' Books, 1851–61.

show that 15–30% of urban native-born adults had migrated at least twice before returning to their place of birth.[23]

The second category in this analysis is those individuals who cannot be traced in subsequent census enumerators' books. These people, it might be supposed, had out-migrated, died or, in the case of females, changed their names after marriage, so becoming unidentifiable in the later census returns. A rough estimate of actual out-migration rates can be reached by taking into account the prevailing level of age-specific mortality, a point to be considered in more detail below in Tables 3.14, 3.15 and 3.16.

It follows that the larger the number of matched pairs between censuses identified in the procedure of record linkage, the smaller the number of people coming into and moving out of a specific locality – and vice versa. Therefore a technique for yielding a longitudinal migration profile can be said to be a spin-off of conventional nominal record linkage. As for the females who changed their names after marriage, they could be traced by referring to marriage records. Unfortunately, though, the Middlesbrough marriage registers during this period are not complete, and in any case the task of identifying marriages in the parish registers of such a large and dramatically growing town as Middlesbrough would be daunting. Presumably in the case of many brides whose home villages lay in the neighbouring countryside, weddings would have taken place there.

The third and final category is those individuals who cannot be traced backwards to a previous census enumeration, and who presumably arrived in the locality at some time between the two censuses. Thus out- and in-migrants are remainders, groups to be investigated as a spin-off from the record linkage study. The core of the analysis below derives from those matched individuals

---

[23] Hochstadt, *Mobility and Modernity*, p. 156.

Table 3.8. Migration in Middlesbrough, 1861–71

		1861			*1871*
Out-migrants	Male	6,195	Persistent	Male	3,315
	Female	5,670		Female	2,619
	Total	11,865 (66.7%)		Total	5,934 (20.9%)
Persistent	Male	3,315	In-migrants	Male	10,584
	Female	2,619		Female	9,032
	Total	5,934 (33.3%)		Total	19,616 (69.1%)
			Children	Male	1,343
			born after	Female	1,390
			1861		
				Unknown	118
				Total	2,851 (10.0%)
Total	Male	9,510	Total	Male	15,242
	Female	8,289		Female	13,041
				Unknown	118
	Total	17,799 (100.0%)		Total	28,401 (100.0%)

Source: Record linkage from Middlesbrough Census Enumerators' Books, 1861–71.

identified and interpreted using computer-aided procedures developed by Kingston University's Centre for Local History Studies.

The Migration Profile of Middlesbrough

Middlesbrough's population in 1861 measured 17,799, with in-migrants predominant, as shown in Table 3.7. As many as 78% had arrived in the town during the previous decade, while only 15% had been in Middlesbrough 10 years earlier. The balance, 7%, was made up of babies born since the previous census. Similarly, though not quite so dramatically, as Table 3.8 illustrates, those who had migrated into the town since 1861 made up 69% of the 1871 population of 28,401. This was still an overwhelming proportion of the town's inhabitants, while the persistent population, those recorded by the census in both 1861 and 1871, accounted for 21%.

Rough estimates of male in-migration as well as out-migration rates, calculated as an average number per year of in-migrants and out-migrants per total population, are as follows: between 1851 and 1861, the in-migration rate was 7.8% (yearly average number of male in-migrants of 741, excluding those who left or died after having in-migrated between 1851 and 1861, per total male population of 9,502 in 1861); while the out-migration rate was 2.5% (yearly average number of male out-migrants of 234 including those who died between the censuses). Corresponding rates between 1861 and 1871 were 6.9% and 4.1% respectively.

Compared with in-migration rates observed in some German regions or cities during the same period, those for Middlesbrough were roughly equivalent to the Düsseldorf district, somewhere between 7% and 9%. Berlin was 5.5%, Quedlinburg 5.5%, Aachen 6.6%, Münster 8.0%, Köln 9.5% and

Magdeburg an exceptional 18.5%. In many German cities, especially older and established urban centres, in-migration rates peaked before 1880, most often during the 1870s, immediately before the onset of the Great Depression.[24]

However, Middlesbrough's annual levels of out-migration, 2.5% between 1851 and 1861 and 4.1% between 1861 and 1871, were substantially lower than those seen in German districts and cities. Düsseldorf district experienced out-migration rates of 5–9% between 1850 and 1865, in contrast with Berlin's 4.9%, Quedlinburg 5.7%, Aachen 5.4%, Münster 8.0% and Köln 7.1% between 1859 and 1865.[25] For as long as the rapid industrial expansion continued, it appears that Middlesbrough attracted many more new residents than it lost. Though in- and out-migration data have not been calculated after 1871, it seems likely that the trends were reversed, the rates of in-migration falling below those of out-migration once the town lost its economic vigour in the late 1880s.

This is in striking contrast with the experience of some American urban communities during the same period. Here there were recorded much higher rates of persistence, calculated as a percentage of residents still settled in the community at the end of a decade. The male populations of Boston (39%), Philadelphia (32%), Waltham (44%) and Northampton, Massachusetts (53%) between 1850 and 1860, as well as Waltham (45%) and Poughkeepsie (49%) between 1860 and 1870 were more stable than their counterparts in Middlesbrough.[26]

More precise figures are not available for female in-migrants. Yet we can be confident that among the male population, approximately 70–80% of those living in the town in 1861 and 1871 had migrated into Middlesbrough during the preceding decade, while only 15–21% of the male inhabitants of 1851 and 1861 remained there at the end of the following decade. Mid-Victorian Middlesbrough was more fluid than most of the American urban communities where 'city dwellers in general and poor people in particular were highly transient, leaving a single faint imprint on the census schedule or city directory files, and then vanishing completely'.[27]

Between 1861 and 1871, the Middlesbrough population became slightly less volatile, though it was by no means stagnant. Compared with in-migration rates in some German towns of similar industrial structure, for example, Bochum in Ruhr, where quite recent in-migrants accounted for 67% of the population in 1871, Middlesbrough's rate stood higher.[28] While it is now

---

24 Hochstadt, *Mobility and Modernity*, pp. 68–71, 74–5, 81, 83, 87, 114–16, 118, 135; for in- and out-migration rates in Duisburg from the 1850s, see Jackson, *Migration and Urbanization in the Ruhr Valley*, pp. 191–3; and regarding Duisburg's total migration rates in the nineteenth century, p. 15.

25 Hochstadt, *Mobility and Modernity*, pp. 68, 81, 87.

26 Thernstrom, *The Other Bostonians*, pp. 25, 221–2.

27 Thernstrom, *The Other Bostonians*, p. 41.

28 See Crew, *Town in the Ruhr*, p. 60.

Table 3.9. Age-specific In-migration Rates in Middlesbrough, 1851–61

	1861 Population		In-migrants (1851–61)		In-migrants (%)	
Age	Female	Male	Female	Male	Female	Male
0–4	1,466	1,475	1,162	1,179	79.3	79.9
5–9	1,065	1,191	775	869	72.8	73.0
10–14	845	896	559	616	66.2	68.8
15–19	724	801	515	579	71.1	72.3
20–24	809	1073	725	899	89.6	83.8
25–29	754	1043	708	928	93.9	89.0
30–34	721	825	628	708	87.1	85.8
35–39	496	668	400	560	80.6	83.8
40–44	431	488	297	370	68.9	75.8
45–49	291	358	182	251	62.5	70.1
50–54	242	254	156	178	64.5	70.1
55–59	164	169	103	108	62.8	63.9
60–64	132	142	75	86	56.8	60.6
65–69	62	59	38	40	61.3	67.8
70–74	33	32	20	21	60.6	65.6
75–79	27	18	19	10	70.4	55.6
80–99	34	9	28	9	82.4	100.0
Total	8,296	9,501	6,390	7,411	77.0	78.0

Source: Record linkage from Middlesbrough Census Enumerators' Books, 1851–61.

Table 3.10. Age-specific In-migration Rates in Middlesbrough, 1861–71

	1871 Population		In-migrants (1861–71)		In-migrants (%)	
Age	Female	Male	Female	Male	Female	Male
0–4	2,237	2,199	1,573	1,549	70.3	70.4
5–9	1,755	1,686	1,094	1,042	62.3	61.8
10–14	1,400	1,341	775	733	55.4	54.7
15–19	1,196	1,323	808	794	67.6	60.0
20–24	1,178	1,771	979	1,401	83.1	79.1
25–29	1,213	1,755	1,115	1,467	91.9	83.6
30–34	986	1,397	792	1,121	80.3	80.2
35–39	740	1,025	531	752	71.8	73.4
40–44	639	867	372	572	58.2	66.0
45–49	551	651	321	397	58.3	61.0
50–54	410	488	217	303	52.9	62.1
55–59	253	277	144	155	56.9	56.0
60–64	209	218	113	115	54.1	52.8
65–69	113	129	53	65	46.9	50.4
70–74	88	66	50	37	56.8	56.1
75–79	43	23	24	8	55.8	34.8
80–99	23	17	15	10	65.2	58.8
Total	13,034	15,233	8,976	10,521	68.9	69.1

Source: Record linkage from Middlesbrough Census Enumerators' Books, 1861–71.

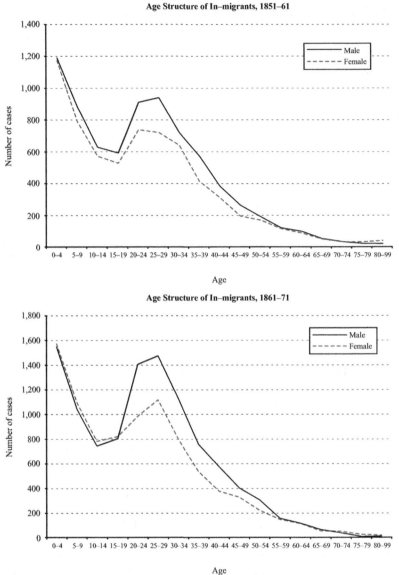

Figure 3.11. Age Structure of In-migrants to Middlesbrough, 1851–61 and 1861–71

generally accepted that natural increase was a more important component of urban growth than migration in most towns after the mid-nineteenth century, Middlesbrough seems to have been exceptional. The town was utterly dependent on in-migration for its rapid population growth from 1850. The explanation for this lies in the fact that Middlesbrough was a new town, planned as late as the early 1830s.

The age structure of in-migrants coming into Middlesbrough between 1851 and 1861 and between 1861 and 1871 is shown in Tables 3.9 and 3.10, and Figure 3.11. For both males and females, as illustrated in Table 3.9, more than 80% of those recorded in 1861 as aged 20 to 39 had migrated into the town during the previous decade. The peak appears in the 25 to 29 age group, of whom 89% of males and 94% of females were recent in-migrants.

Almost the same pattern can be seen between 1861 and 1871, with the highest in-migration rates observed in the group aged 25 to 29 in 1871, both for males (84%) and females (92%). The age structure profile of the incoming population almost matches that of the overall population in 1871, shown above in Figure 3.2. So most in-migration was undertaken by those in their late 20s, producing the extraordinary age structures seen in the 1861 and 1871 populations.[29] Another remarkable feature of migrants moving to the town during this period is their sex ratio. The in-migrants were chiefly males, so that Middlesbrough's sex ratio pressed upwards, far beyond 100 throughout the period, as already noted. This male bias is especially conspicuous among the young and middle groups aged from 20 to 39.

Yet more than 63% of Middlesbrough inhabitants recorded in the 1851 census have not been matched for record linkage purposes, as they moved out, died or changed their names after marriage. Of the 1861 population of 17,799, 11,865 people, that is, 67%, have not been traced in the 10-year interval between 1861 and 1871. As discussed above, this method of record linkage profiles the male population much more reliably than the female one. Among the male population, in the decade between 1851 and 1861 as little as 37% of the population remained, while perhaps 63% of the initial population migrated outwards or died. Similarly in the next decade, from 1861 to 1871, only 33% of male residents recorded in 1861 stayed in the town, with the remaining 67% of the 1861 population migrating outwards or dying.

Out-migration rates were remarkable, especially among young adults aged 20–24 and 25–29. Tables 3.12 and 3.13 illustrate out-migration rates between consecutive censuses, including people who died or are unidentifiable after changing surname after marriage. They also present the proportion of residual population in the town in 1861 and 1871, related to total population for that year. More than 70% of the 20–24 age group recorded in 1851 has not been traced in the 1861 census enumerators' books.

Similarly, for both males and females, as discussed above, more than 80% of those recorded as aged 20–39 in 1861 have not been traced in 1851. The figure is particularly high for the 25–29 age group, peaking there at 89% for males and 94% for females. Likewise, in the decade to 1871 more than 70% of the male population recorded as aged 20–29 in 1861 moved out or died, whereas almost 80% of the 1871 population aged 20–34 were newly arrived

---

[29] For age-specific in-migration rates in German cities in the latter half of the nineteenth century, see Hochstadt, *Mobility and Modernity*, pp. 145–50; for those observed in Duisburg in the late nineteenth century, see Jackson, *Migration and Urbanization in the Ruhr Valley*, pp. 203, 205–9, 226–7.

Table 3.12. Age-specific Out-migration Rates from Middlesbrough, 1851–61

Age	1851 Population Female	Male	Out-migrants[a] (1851–61) Female	Male	Persistent (1851–61) Female	Male	Out-migrants (%)[a] Female	Male
0–4	602	582	337	333	265	249	56.0	57.2
5–9	473	470	273	241	200	229	57.7	51.3
10–14	368	411	287	241	81	170	78.0	58.6
15–19	318	357	274	246	44	111	86.2	68.9
20–24	313	382	231	273	82	109	73.8	71.5
25–29	341	356	224	225	117	131	65.7	63.2
30–34	289	321	168	209	121	112	58.1	65.1
35–49	260	248	139	140	121	108	53.5	56.5
40–44	179	205	95	126	84	79	53.1	61.5
45–49	150	156	81	92	69	64	54.0	59.0
50–54	118	107	68	64	50	43	57.6	59.8
55–59	74	76	51	51	23	25	68.9	67.1
60–64	51	48	36	37	15	11	70.6	77.1
65–69	38	44	31	38	7	6	81.6	86.4
70–74	28	12	24	12	4	0	85.7	100.0
75–79	8	7	7	7	1	0	87.5	100.0
80–99	11	6	11	6	0	0	100.0	100.0
Total	3,621	3,788	2,337	2,341	1,284	1,447	64.5	61.8

Note: [a]Including those who died between the censuses.

Source: Record linkage from Middlesbrough Census Enumerators' Books, 1851–61.

in the town.[30] The numbers for females roughly correspond. This comparison, of the age structure of out-migrants between 1851 and 1861, and between 1861 and 1871, with the total population of 1851 and 1861, is a means of understanding the patterns of in- and out-migration through this period.

David Crew and William Hubbard found similarly high rates of transiency, and low persistency rates, in the German town of Bochum in the Ruhr region, and also in Graz in Austria, in the late nineteenth and early twentieth centuries. Their researches were also based on record linkage from census enumerators' books. Crew and Hubbard demonstrated that percentages of urban populations still found in the same towns after 10 years are less than 50%, which they interpret as confirming a high degree of overall geographic mobility.[31]

The male out-migration rates thus calculated for Middlesbrough have been obtained by taking account of the number of deaths between censuses. They can be further refined by counting the death rates in each age group. Table 3.14 presents the rates of age-specific mortality in Middlesbrough for both sexes in 1875–80 and 1881, drawn from the Registrar General's annual reports.[32]

---

30 Regarding age-specific migration rates in England and Wales at the beginning of the twentieth century, see Friedlander and Roshier, 'Study of Internal Migration', p. 247.
31 Langewiesche and Lenger, 'Internal Migration: Persistence and Mobility', p. 96.
32 *Forty-Fourth Annual Report of the Registrar General of Births, Deaths, and Marriages in*

Table 3.13. Age-specific Out-migration Rates from Middlesbrough, 1861–71

Age	1861 Population Female	Male	Out-migrants[a] (1861–71) Female	Male	Persistent (1861–71) Female	Male	Out-migrants (%)[a] Female	Male
0–4	1,466	1,475	925	936	541	539	63.1	63.5
5–9	1,065	1,191	674	674	391	517	63.3	56.6
10–14	845	896	663	526	182	370	78.5	58.7
15–19	724	801	622	534	102	267	85.9	66.7
20–24	809	1,073	617	779	192	294	76.3	72.6
25–29	754	1,043	545	761	209	282	72.3	73.0
30–34	721	825	447	542	274	283	62.0	65.7
35–39	496	668	291	429	205	239	58.7	64.2
40–44	431	488	236	302	195	186	54.8	61.9
45–49	291	358	165	227	126	131	56.7	63.4
50–54	242	254	149	163	93	91	61.6	64.2
55–59	164	169	104	108	60	61	63.4	63.9
60–64	132	142	94	112	38	30	71.2	78.9
65–9	62	59	50	47	12	12	80.6	79.7
70–64	33	32	29	29	4	3	87.8	90.6
75–79	27	18	26	17	1	1	96.3	94.4
80–99	34	9	32	9	2	0	94.1	100.0
Total	8,296	9,501	5,669	6,195	2,627	3,306	68.3	65.2

Note: [a]Including those who died between the censuses.

Source: Record linkage from Middlesbrough Census Enumerators' Books, 1861–71.

Applying these age-specific levels to the results of our record linkage, we can revise the out-migration rates to take account of expected death rates among the male population, 1851–61 and 1861–71. The exercise rests on an assumption that the Registrar's age-specific mortality data for 1875–81 is in line with levels applicable in 1851–71 (see Tables 3.15 and 3.16).

The outcome of this exercise suggests that while levels diminished somewhat over time, in both decades, 65% of the male population aged 20–24 moved out of the town, and 56% to 62% of the 25–34 age group also left. In a study of the mid-nineteenth century German town of Düsseldorf, Lenger took account of death rates in reckoning actual out-migration levels of about 25% of the population over 10 or 12 years. Middlesbrough's estimated out-migration rates during the same period were much higher. The estimated overall male out-migration rates for Middlesbrough adjusted for mortality are 43.2% between 1851 and 1861, and 46.6% between 1861 and 1871. Contrast this with male out-migration rates for Graz in Austria between 1857 and 1869 of 50.9%, and 22.1% between 1869 and 1880.[33]

England (Abstracts of 1881), 1883; Supplement to the Forty-Fifth Annual Report of the Registrar General of Births, Deaths, and Marriages in England, 1885.

[33] For age-specific out-migration rates in Graz, see Hubbard, 'Aspects of Social Mobility in Graz', pp. 6; 17, Table 1; 19, Table 4; Langewiesche and Lenger, 'Internal Migration: Persistence and Mobility', p. 96.

Table 3.14. Age-specific Mortality in Middlesbrough, 1875–81

	Age-specific Mortality in 1881 (per 1,000)												
Age	0	1–4	5–9	10–14	15–19	20–24	25–34	35–44	45–54	55–64	65–74	75–	Total
No. of Deaths	533	298	74	35	41	56	116	130	121	120	79	65	1,668
Population	3,723	10,467	12,307	9,874	8,309	8,033	14,597	10,938	6,476	3,362	1,264	398	89,853
Mortality	143.2	28.5	6.0	3.5	4.9	7.0	7.9	11.9	18.7	35.7	62.5	163.3	18.6

	Age-specific Mortality, 1875–80 (per 1,000)											
Age	0	1–4	5–9	10–14	15–19	20–24	25–34	35–44	45–54	55–64	65–74	75–
Mortality	152.0	36.2	6.6	3.0	4.6	5.7	8.3	11.5	14.8	29.0	61.6	174.4

Source: Parliamentary Papers, Census of England & Wales, 1881, Vol. III, Ages, Condition as to Marriage, Occupations, and Birth Places of the People, 1883 [C. 3722] LXXX, p. 383; Forty-Fourth Annual Report of the Registrar General of Births, Deaths, and Marriages in England (Abstracts of 1881), 1883, pp. 78, 83; Supplement to the Forty-Fifth Annual Report of the Registrar General of Births, Deaths, and Marriage in England, 1885, p. 320.

Table 3.15. Middlesbrough Out-migration Rates (Male) Adjusted
to Reflect Deaths, 1851–61

Age	Population (1851)	Max. Mortality (1851–61)	No. of Max. Deaths (1851–61)	Out-migrants (1851–61)	Out-migration Rates (%)
0–4	582	586[a]	(341)	(333)	–
5–9	470	60	28	213	45.3
10–14	411	35	14	227	55.2
15–19	357	49	17	229	64.1
20–24	382	70	27	246	64.4
25–34	677	79	53	381	56.3
35–44	453	119	54	212	46.8
45–54	263	187	49	107	40.7
55–64	124	357	44	44	35.5
65–74	56	625	35	15	26.8
75–	13	(1,000)	13	0	0.0
Mean	3,788	186	705	1,636	43.2

Note: [a]Measured per 1,000.

Source: Record Linkage from Middlesbrough Census Enumerators' Books, 1851–61;
Parliamentary Papers, Census of England & Wales, 1881, Vol. III, Ages, Condition as to
Marriage, Occupations, and Birth Places of the People, 1883 [C. 3722] LXXX, p. 383; Forty-
Fourth Annual Report of the Registrar General of Births, Deaths, and Marriages in England
(Abstracts of 1881), 1883, pp. 78, 83; Supplement to the Forty-Fifth Annual Report of the
Registrar General of Births, Deaths, and Marriage in England, 1885, p. 320.

Table 3.16. Middlesbrough Out-migration Rates (Male) Adjusted
to Reflect Deaths, 1861–71

Age	Population (1861)	Max. Mortality (1861–71)	No. of Max. Deaths (1861–71)	Out-migrants (1861–71)	Out-migration Rates (%)
0–4	1,457	586[a]	864	72	4.9
5–9	1,191	60	71	603	50.6
10–14	896	35	31	495	55.2
15–19	801	49	39	495	61.8
20–24	1,073	70	75	704	65.6
25–34	1,868	79	148	1,155	61.8
35–44	1,156	119	138	593	51.3
45–54	612	187	114	276	45.1
55–64	311	357	111	109	35.0
65–74	91	625	57	19	20.9
75–	27	(1,000)	27	0	0.0
Mean	9,501	186	1,767	4,428	46.6

Note: [a]Measured per 1,000.

Source: Record Linkage from Middlesbrough Census Enumerators' Books, 1861–71;
Parliamentary Papers, Census of England & Wales, 1881, Vol. III, Ages, Condition as to
Marriage, Occupations, and Birth Places of the People, 1883 [C. 3722] LXXX, p. 383; Forty-
Fourth Annual Report of the Registrar General of Births, Deaths, and Marriages in England
(Abstracts of 1881), 1883, pp. 78, 83; Supplement to the Forty-Fifth Annual Report of the
Registrar General of Births, Deaths, and Marriage in England, 1885, p. 320.

Table 3.17. Relationship to Heads of Households of In-migrant, Persistent and Out-migrant Population of Middlesbrough, 1851–61 and 1861–71

| | | 1851–61 | | | | 1861–71 | | | |
| | | Lodgers and Boarders | | Head (Wife) | | Lodgers and Boarders | | Head (Wife) | |
		No.	%	No.	%	No.	%	No.	%
Out-migrants[a]	Male	277	11.8	726	31.0	1,253	20.2	2,049	33.1
	Female	51	2.2	836	35.8	189	3.3	1,871	33.0
Persistent	Male	61	4.2	736	50.9	221	6.7	1,582	47.7
	Female	11	0.8	634	49.4	12	0.5	1,323	50.5
In-migrants	Male	1,460	18.1	2,414	30.0	2,696	25.5	3,196	30.2
	Female	209	3.0	2,714	38.7	209	2.3	3,777	41.8

Note: [a]Including those who died between the censuses.

Source: Record linkage from Middlesbrough Census Enumerators' Books, 1851–61 and 1861–71.

A further question is whether there were any differences in household status between migrants and the more settled population. Apart from members of conjugal family units, lodgers and boarders represented considerable numbers among the population of in-migrants. Moving into lodgings or boarding was clearly related to migration, and the status of lodger or boarder often followed the first move from the parental home. As shown in Table 3.17, they made up 18.1% of male and 3.0% of female in-migrants, in contrast to only 4.2% and 0.8% respectively among the persistent population for 1861. Corresponding figures are higher, 25.5%, among the male in-migrant population between 1861 and 1871, with 2.3% for females.

The proportion of lodgers as a proportion of all male in-migrants was 18.8%, and 1.8% for females, while among the male persistent population of 3,315, 4.9% were lodgers, with 0.2% for females of the total 2,619 persistent population in 1871. The proportions of lodgers as seen among the population which moved out or died between the two censuses roughly correspond with those for the previous decade with 12.9% for males and 2.2% for females.

There remains a question of the family circumstances of those people migrating into Middlesbrough. It is likely that between any two censuses, young single males and females would move into the town and marry there, subsequently appearing as married in the next census return. This clearly does not amount to family migration in its entirety. However, in such cases it is impossible to ascertain the exact time at which they arrived in the town, and there are great difficulties in identifying such marriages in parish registers. Without source material to fill this gap, it is not easy to distinguish a 'genuine' family migration from those people who moved into Middlesbrough unattached and formed families there between censuses.

In any case, as the life-cycle migration behaviour of individuals over time cannot be reconstructed by this method of census linkage, it is difficult to establish the percentage accounted for by this category, of couples moving in together after marriage. Yet we know that more mature adults were most likely to move in a family grouping. From this, a technique suggests itself which may help answer this question: examining the migrants' nuptiality and comparing this with the nuptiality of other groups in this study, while controlling the difference in age structure between them.

Analysing the marital status of all in-migrants, shown in Table 3.18, suggests that migration by entire families was substantial between 1851 and 1861. Among the male peak age group for in-migrants, that is, 25–29, 62% were married or widowed, while an overall proportion of males ever-married throughout all age groups from 15 upwards, accounts for 57.9%. The proportions of women ever-married are also supplied for information, although the figures in Table 3.18 include women who arrived in the town after marriage, those who came unattached and subsequently married between censuses, and also women who were persistent residents but by changing their names upon marriage became unidentifiable by record linkage and are consequently regarded as in-migrants. The numbers presented here must therefore be treated with some caution. They suggest that more than 81% of females in 1861 aged 20–44 were married or widowed; the overall rate from age 15 upwards was 73.5%.

Similarly, in the peak age groups among females we suppose to have migrated into Middlesbrough between 1861 and 1871, that is those aged 20–29 in 1871, married or widowed women account for 67.1% of the age group 20–24, and 86.5% of those 25–29. These percentages are substantially higher than the corresponding figures in those age groups among the 1871 population of Middlesbrough as a whole. It is interesting to note that during these 20 years in the mid-nineteenth century, 'ever-married' proportions were high among the incoming younger age groups. This is true in particular of females, who predominate in the total in-migrating population, when compared to both persistent and total populations for the same year.

This 'ever-married' proportion among the in-migrating population corresponds roughly to a national trend from the eighteenth century, reconstructed by C. G. Pooley and J. Turnbull from different sources, which seems to support the consistency of our own findings. Pooley and Turnbull suggest that movement as a family group was a common experience, and that numerically the largest categories of movers were married people and nuclear families, making up 60–70% of migrants compared with the 20% who moved alone.[34]

---

[34] Pooley and Turnbull, *Migration and Mobility in Britain*, pp. 17, 49, 63, 68–9, 73–6 *et passim*.

Table 3.18. Age-specific Proportion Ever Married of In-migrants and Persistent Population of Middlesbrough, 1851–61 and 1861–71

Age Group	1851–61 (Male)				Age Group	1861–71 (Male)			
	Persistent		In-migrants			Persistent		In-migrants	
	No.	%	No.	%		No	%	No	%
15–19	–	–	5	0.9	15–19	4	0.7	9	1.1
20–24	50	28.7	219	24.4	20–24	72	19.7	312	22.4
25–29	78	68.7	577	62.2	25–29	143	51.3	756	51.6
30–34	105	89.7	547	77.3	30–34	217	80.4	746	66.6
35–39	102	94.4	475	84.8	35–39	237	88.1	574	76.3
40–44	114	96.6	328	88.6	40–44	272	93.2	417	72.9
45–49	99	92.5	219	77.7	45–49	232	93.2	337	84.9
50–54	75	98.7	160	89.9	50–54	173	95.1	247	81.5
55–59	57	93.4	91	84.3	55–59	116	95.9	134	86.5
60–64	55	98.2	78	90.7	60–64	101	99.9	94	81.7
65–69	18	94.7	37	92.5	65–69	63	82.8	56	86.2
70–	18	94.7	31	77.5	70–	51	98.0	47	85.5
Total	771	64.7	2,767	57.9	Total	1,680	60.8	3,729	51.8

Age Group	1851–61 (Female)				Age Group	1861–71 (Female)			
	Persistent		In-migrants			Persistent		In-migrants	
	No.	%	No.	%		No.	%	No.	%
15–19	2	0.1	57	11.1	15–19	2	0.5	86	10.7
20–24	10	11.9	467	64.4	20–24	22	11.3	657	67.1
25–29	17	37.0	600	84.7	25–29	47	49.0	965	86.5
30–34	85	91.4	544	86.6	30–34	172	91.0	725	91.5
35–39	87	90.6	366	91.5	35–39	201	97.1	486	91.5
40–44	116	86.6	269	90.6	40–44	255	96.6	351	94.4
45–49	96	88.1	166	91.2	45–49	221	98.7	301	3.8
50–54	79	91.9	140	89.7	50–54	185	97.4	209	96.3
55–59	51	83.6	91	88.3	55–59	102	95.3	141	97.9
60–64	52	91.2	72	96.0	60–64	94	98.9	108	95.6
65–69	22	91.7	35	92.1	65–69	56	94.9	49	92.5
70–	26	96.3	55	82.1	70–	60	95.2	82	93.2
Total	643	62.7	2,862	73.5	Total	1,417	68.7	4,160	75.2

Source: Record linkage from Middlesbrough Census Enumerators' Books, 1851–61 and 1861–71.

Further detail of family migration into Middlesbrough can be found in local newspapers. The *Middlesbrough News and Cleveland Advertiser* reported in 1873 under the heading 'Increase of Middlesbrough' that 'upwards of 70 labourers, with their families, have left Wisbech in Cambridgeshire for Middlesbrough, intending to obtain employment in the ironworks'. The

English experience is in contrast with that of Germany, where single adult in-migrants predominated in the nineteenth century.[35]

Finally we have investigated how frequently residents changed their local addresses within the town. Some Middlesbrough evidence suggests that intra-urban mobility during the period was very high. The turnover during 16 years between 1846 and 1862 of those who rented houses built and owned by Joseph Pease was unexpectedly large. For instance, in less than three years from April 1846 to January 1849, seven out of 13 occupiers moved, a turnover rate of 54%. From January 1858 to June 1861, six occupiers were replaced, with the turnover rate 46%. The high intra-urban mobility apparent among town dwellers in the period most probably arose because of shifts in attitudes about changing residence, the ease and low cost of moving, and a buoyant housing market with cheap rented housing readily available. Working-class residents in particular seem to have moved most frequently as they had limited household goods and possessions.[36]

Patterns of Persistence

Among Middlesbrough's population in this period, there was a strikingly low rate of persistence. Of men moving into the town between 1851 and 1861, 7,412 in all, record linkage shows that almost 70% (5,183) had left the town or died between 1861 and 1871. In other words, 30.1%, as few as 2,229 of males entering the town between 1851 and 1861, remained there for the following decade. If a rigid norm for record linkage, *true match*, is adopted, only 25.2% of male in-migrants have been traced who remained in 1871. In fact in late-nineteenth century Middlesbrough, the high volumes of in-migration were matched by similar streams of outward movement.

Comparatively little attention has been paid, at least in Britain, to the transiency and persistency of migrant population in urban areas. Although information is available on persistence by age and by socio-economic group in mid-Victorian Liverpool, it is not clear whether transiency rates observed for in-migrants to Middlesbrough during the period were exceptionally high, or not, given the paucity of comparable studies on other Victorian industrial towns.[37]

The interesting point, however, as mentioned above, is that very similar

---

35 *Middlesbrough Weekly News and Cleveland Advertiser*, 24 Jan. 1873; see Hochstadt, *Mobility and Modernity*, pp. 93–106, 150–2, 166–7. In- and out-migration rates in Duisburg by marital status indicate overwhelmingly high rates for single males: Jackson, *Migration and Urbanization in the Ruhr Valley*, pp. 205–7.

36 Teesside Archives, CB/M/T, Poor Rate books, 25 Apr. 1846, pp. 3–5; 17 Sep.1849, p. 5; 13 Dec. 1856, p. 53; 8 Jan. 1858, p. 59; 15 Jun. 1861, p. 55. For intra-urban mobility in North-West England, see Pooley and Turnbull, 'Migration and Urbanization in North-West England', p. 196; and for that in the German city of Duisburg in the late-nineteenth century, see Jackson, *Migration and Urbanization in the Ruhr Valley*, p. 190.

37 Lawton, 'Mobility in Nineteenth-century British Cities', pp. 220–1. See also for net-migration rates in nineteenth-century Prussian urban centres, Ehmer, *Bevölkerungsgeschichte und historische Demographie*, pp. 20–1, 84.

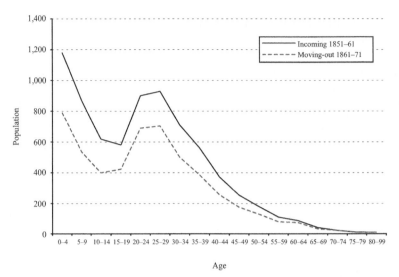

Figure 3.19. Age-specific Net Migration in Middlebrough, 1851–61
and 1861–71

or even lower levels of persistence, for male populations including not only in-migrants of the previous decade, but also longer-term residents, were recorded in many American towns of the period. Between 1800 and 1968, 31 urban communities in America experienced overall low persistence ranging from 32 to 64%. Thernstrom points out that in America, irrespective of differences in the types of communities, 'their populations were leaving them for other destinations at a rapid and surprisingly uniform rate. Approximately half of their residents at any date were destined to disappear before 10 years had elapsed, to be replaced by other restless newcomers who had lived elsewhere a decade before. This was not a frontier phenomenon, or a big city phenomenon, but a national phenomenon.'[38]

Studies of modern western European urban centres also confirm high, and virtually equal, rates of in- and out-migration. Likewise in Britain, evidence supports the notion that migration was circulatory and repeat, rather than migrants being sucked into large cities never to return. The corroboration comes from surveys which use different methods of analysing spatial patterns of mobility during the same period. Much movement was not a simple one-way process.[39]

Age-specific persistence rates confirm the mobility of Middlesbrough's population. So the town attracted a large population, mainly from the younger age groups, 20–24 and 25–29, and then pushed out as many as 70% of that young immigrant group (the figure also includes those who died) within the following decade. Age-distributions of males who had migrated into the town

---

38   Thernstrom, *The Other Bostonians*, p. 222, Table 9.1; p. 227.
39   Pooley and Turnbull, 'Migration and Urbanization in North-West England', pp. 201, 211.

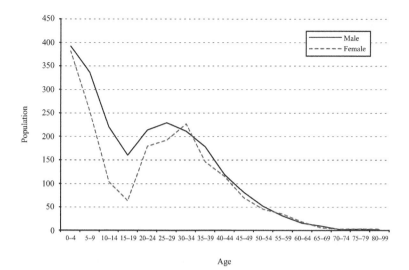

Figure 3.20. Age Structure of In-migrants, 1851–61, living in Middlesbrough in 1871

between 1851 and 1861, and those of the males who left or died between 1861 and 1871, are very similar, as illustrated in Figure 3.19. The analysis is based on ages recorded in 1861. The exact age at which they migrated (or died) cannot be ascertained.

Figure 3.20 breaks down by age those who migrated into the town between 1851 and 1861, and who stayed there until at least 1871. Ages are those recorded in 1861. It appears that younger male migrants into Middlesbrough, aged between 20 and 29 in 1861, were much more likely to migrate out again, or die, during the following decade, than were other age groups. The persistent population of males in 1871 peaks in the age group of 25–29, who were much more likely to be married than were the younger population aged 15–24. In line with observations in other European industrial towns, young bachelors were the most mobile group, while married couples tended to be more stable.[40]

Similarly high rates of transience were found in American towns, as well as in many European urban communities, during this time. Northampton (56%), Rochester (47%), Poughkeepsie (80%), Atlanta (70%) and Boston white residents (57%) are among them. Eighteen large German towns experienced high turnover rates, with that of Krefeld as high as 60%. Bochum in the Ruhr experienced a rapid rate of turnover, the majority of immigrants staying in the town for less than a year.[41]

In Middlesbrough, 50.9% of the male household heads remained between

---

[40] Regarding differential persistence rates between single men and those with wives and children, see Crew, *Town in the Ruhr*, p. 62.
[41] Hubbard, 'Aspects of Social Mobility in Graz', p. 5; Crew, *Town in the Ruhr*, pp. 60–2.

Table 3.21. Male In-migrants to Middlesbrough, 1851–61, from Elsewhere in the United Kingdom, and Re-migration Rate, 1861–71

Countries	Incoming 1851–61	Moving-out[a] 1861–71	Re-migration Rate (%)
Wales[b]	627	504	80.4
Ireland	1,057	848	80.2
Scotland	202	157	77.7
Foreign Countries	65	49	75.4
England	5,158	3,066	59.4
Total	7,109	4,624	65.0

Notes: [a]Including those who died between the censuses. [b]Including Monmouthshire.
Source: Record linkage from Middlesbrough Census Enumerators' Books, 1851–61 and 1861–71.

1851 and 1861, and 47.7% between 1861 and 1871. In Graz in Austria, persistence rates for male household heads and lodgers were much higher, 60% for the household heads and just over 30% for lodgers. In contrast, persistence rates for male lodgers in Middlesbrough were as low as 4.2% between 1851 and 1861, and 6.7% between 1861 and 1871.[42]

Of 1,057 Irish males recorded in the 1861 Middlesbrough census who had moved in during the previous decade, 848 (80.2%) left the town or died within the next 10 years (see Table 3.21). In the same period, 202 Scottish males had migrated inwards, 77.7% of whom could not be identified in the 1871 census enumerators' books. There were 627 Welsh immigrants noted in 1861, 80.4% of them migrating from the town or dying between 1861 and 1871. However, from among the 5,158 males born in English parishes in-migrating between 1851 and 1861, 3,066 (59.4%) moved out of the town or died during the next decade. The long-distance migrants seem to have been more transient, short-term settlers, perhaps less comfortable in this new English community. The German experience in the late-nineteenth and early-twentieth centuries, explored by Köllman and Becker, also indicates that the number of migrants who came to live permanently in a town represented only a very small proportion of all the migratory population.[43]

Taking the analysis to a level more birthplace-specific, Table 3.22 considers the re-migration rates of those born in English counties. Middlesbrough received 103 male migrants from Lancashire between 1851 and 1861, of whom 86 (83.5%) left the town or died in the subsequent decade. Monmouthshire also shows a high re-migration rate, of 82.0%, as do Staffordshire (78.4%), Northumberland (74.1%), Worcestershire (72.2%), and Warwickshire, with 15 males incoming between 1851 and 1861 of whom 14 moved out or died between 1861 and 1871. Lancashire's high re-migration rate is attributable to the fact that the county's migrants to Middlesbrough

---

42 Hubbard, 'Aspects of Social Mobility in Graz', pp. 7, 10.
43 Langewiesche and Lenger, 'Internal Migration: Persistence and Mobility', p. 88.

Table 3.22. Male In-migrants from English Counties, 1851–61, and
Re-migration Rate, 1861–71

Counties	Incoming 1851–61	Moving-out[a] 1861–71	Re-migration Rate (%)
Warwickshire	15	14	93.3
Lancashire	103	86	83.5
Monmouthshire	183	150	82.0
Staffordshire	250	196	78.4
Northumberland	162	120	74.1
Worcestershire	97	70	72.2
Norfolk	61	41	67.2
Durham	989	632	63.9
Yorkshire	2,964	1,900	64.1
Cumberland	98	56	57.1
Other Counties	419	312	74.5
Total	5,341	3,577	67.0

Note: [a]Including those who died between the censuses.

Source: Record linkage from Middlesbrough Census Enumerators' Books, 1851–61 and 1861–71.

were mainly unskilled labourers who were generally very mobile. On the other hand, Monmouthshire, Staffordshire, Northumberland and Worcestershire supplied many more skilled ironworkers, especially puddlers, who also showed a high incidence of re-migration.

The social and economic composition of migratory streams bear a more detailed examination. Table 3.23 illustrates what percentage of the Middlesbrough inhabitants of 1861 remained in the town in 1871, analysed by occupational groups to produce persistence rates by occupation. Grocers show the highest persistence rate, of 43.4%. There is a marked tendency for shopkeepers such as grocers, tailors, drapers and butchers, with more secure roots in the town, to be more immobile than other groups of inhabitants. At the other end of the spectrum, as few as 20.8% of unskilled industrial labourers recorded in the 1861 census have been identified in 1871.[44]

In comparison, examples from Central Europe show that in Bochum, day labourers' persistence rates were 42% between 1880 and 1890, with as few as 17.8% of them remaining in 1901. Migration rates for clerks, accountants and other white-collar employees in trade and commerce in Duisburg were higher than those for other middle-class groups. Contrasted with occupational differentials in an American city, Boston, between 1880 and 1890, where persistence for unskilled manual labourers stood at 56%, Middlesbrough's labourers were highly transient.[45]

---

[44] For persistence rates of day labourers in Bochum towards the end of the nineteenth century, see Crew, *Town in the Ruhr*, 81.

[45] See Jackson, *Migration and Urbanization in the Ruhr Valley*, pp. 214–15; Thernstrom, *The Other Bostonians*, pp. 39–41, 229, 230, Table 9.3.

Table 3.23. Persistence by Occupation (Male), 1861–71

Occupations in 1861	No. of Cases	Remaining in 1871	Persistence Rates (%)
Grocers	99	43	43.4
Accountants	14	6	42.9
Shipwrights	68	28	41.2
Blacksmiths	162	65	40.1
Iron founders	25	10	40.0
Tailors	89	35	39.3
Forgemen	16	6	37.5
Carpenters	36	13	36.1
Drapers	25	9	36.0
Boiler makers	69	24	34.8
Agricultural labourers	24	8	33.3
Moulders	273	90	33.0
Butchers	65	21	32.3
Surgeon	10	3	30.0
Rollers	95	28	29.5
Shinglers	17	5	29.4
Clerks (specified & un-specified)	90	25	27.8
Chemists (druggists)	18	5	27.8
Joiners	157	40	25.5
Innkeepers	30	7	23.3
Engineers	258	59	22.9
Labourers (industry defined and undefined)	1,660	346	20.8
Puddlers	402	46	11.4

Source: Record linkage from Middlesbrough Census Enumerators' Books, 1861–71.

Levels of persistence in Middlesbrough were higher not only among craftsmen and artisans such as shipwrights, blacksmiths, carpenters, and boiler-makers, but also for skilled iron workers, for instance, iron founders, forgemen, moulders, rollers and shinglers. Among the skilled workers, however, puddlers have been identified by record linkage as exceptionally mobile, even more so than unskilled labourers. Only 11.4% of puddlers recorded in the 1861 census have been traced as resident in the town in 1871. Among skilled workers employed in the iron and steel industries, they had without doubt the highest propensity to move, numbering among a body of highly mobile and skilled workers ready to migrate from one industrial centre to another, wherever their skills were in demand.

It is interesting that one-third of agricultural labourers stayed in the town. They would have been employed occasionally in the iron and steel industries, especially in slack times in agriculture. An analogous situation arose in Germany, with a new community like Middlesbrough, isolated in the midst of an agrarian region, emerging from the Georgs-Marien Mining and Foundry Co.'s foundation in 1856. In Georgsmarienhütte in western Lower Saxony the agricultural workers employed on the landlord's property, Heuerleute, supplemented their income through 'occupational emigration', for it was possible to work in the new industry that was developing on their doorstep without leaving home.[46]

Compared with the persistence by occupation observed in Graz in Austria during the same period, Middlesbrough's experience differed in that unskilled workers were more mobile, their persistence rate as low as 20.8% while their counterparts in Graz showed a rate of 42%. Excepting puddlers, though, skilled workers in Middlesbrough were more persistent residents than those in Graz.[47]

In the town of Bochum in the Ruhr, which with its iron and steel, coal and metal manufacture had almost the same industrial structure as Middlesbrough, a high turnover rate of 53.2% was found among unskilled manual workers, while the rate for skilled workers was 28.5%.[48] In Boston in the United States, lower grade manual labourers were more likely to move than others. Thernstrom remarks that:

> The lower an individual ranked on the occupational ladder, the smaller the likelihood that he would still be found in Boston by the next census-taker a decade later; nearly half of the low-manual labourers living in the city in 1880 had left it by 1890; nearly two-thirds of the labourers of 1910 had departed by 1920.[49]

So where did the out-migrants go, and why? Out-migration is likely to have been a response to economic opportunities elsewhere. Yet the question is still *terra incognita*, since any search to establish destinations of those who moved away represents an enormous task of linkage. As tracing the fate of out-migrants has proved to be virtually impossible, we can only infer that the geographical sources of in-migrants nearly exactly match the destination of out-migrants, if the pattern observed by Jackson in Duisburg holds true in our case.[50] How far this relates to the Middlesbrough experience will be examined in the following chapter.

It seems, then, that there were two layers of population in Middlesbrough during this period. The upper layer consists of a rapidly replacing, restless population, moving into and leaving the town within a short period of time. Most unskilled labourers belong to this stratum. The population in this layer was in fact being speedily re-shuffled. The second layer contains a compara-

[46] Meyer, 'In-Migration and Out-Migration in an Area of Heavy Industry', pp. 177, 179, 198.
[47] Hubbard, 'Aspects of Social Mobility in Graz', pp. 22–3. For persistence by occupation in German cities, see Hochstadt, *Mobility and Modernity*, pp. 162–3.
[48] For high out-migration rates found among the Bochum unskilled and long-distance migrants during the same period, see Crew, *Town in the Ruhr*, pp. 65, 69–71.
[49] Thernstrom, *The Other Bostonians*, p. 39.
[50] Jackson, *Migration and Urbanization in the Ruhr Valley*, pp. 253–63.

tively stable, less fluid population made up of shopkeepers, craftsmen and skilled workers, underneath the upper, highly volatile, floating group.

As Crew remarks about the Ruhr town of Bochum at this time, 'those who had skilled jobs or non-manual employment, and therefore possessed a more secure livelihood, tended to remain in the city'. Langewiesche and Lenger have identified a similar phenomenon of persistence and mobility in late nineteenth- and early twentieth-century German cities. They find two cores of inhabitants, a stable core of residents and a far smaller segment of newly arrived migrants, often staying less than a year. The more stable element was composed of skilled workers and professionals, who could most easily take advantage of opportunities offered by the labour market. Although professionals were not present in large numbers at this time, 143 males and 50 females categorized as such moved into Middlesbrough between 1851 and 1861, and 251 males and 96 females during the following decade. Unskilled workers, who may have had more difficulty finding suitable employment, needed to be more mobile and seek their chances elsewhere.[51]

Unfortunately, record linkage from census enumerators' books cannot establish the exact length of time that either the volatile or the relatively persistent groups remained in the town. German migration studies of the same period do, however, offer an analogy. Langewiesche and Lenger, from their researches on Frankfurt and Düsseldorf, suggest that 'among the single migrants leaving a town, between two-thirds and three-quarters had been there for less than a year, quite a number staying only a few days'.[52]

As noted above, though, some of the in-migrating skilled workers, puddlers and engineers, were unusually mobile, with 80–90% of them moving out of the town or dying between censuses. Puddlers in the late nineteenth-century iron industry had a degree of independence from their ironmasters, enjoying a privileged position among the working classes. This position is attributed to the fact that mechanization of the puddling process had proved difficult despite repeated trials, so that the puddlers' bargaining power with employers was strengthened. They were therefore willing to tramp with their underhands in search of better working conditions and higher wages. Engineers' high mobility could be explained to some extent by trade unions' providing travelling expenses to members in search of employment, which eased the migration and mobility of unionized engineers around branches where there were greater opportunities for employment. This subject will be examined later in more detail.[53]

---

51 Crew, *Town in the Ruhr*, p. 72; for compositions of immigrant populations in German cities during the same period, see Langewiesche and Lenger, 'Internal Migration: Persistence and Mobility', pp. 96–7.

52 Langewiesche and Lenger, 'Internal Migration: Persistence and Mobility', p. 95.

53 About the difficulties involved in mechanizing puddling processes, and consequent strong bargaining position of puddlers, see Howard, 'Strikes and Lockouts in the Iron Industry', p. 427. For the high mobility of skilled workers in Duisburg, see Jackson, *Migration and Urbanization in the Ruhr Valley*, pp. 203, 206, 210–11, 214.

So the development of iron and steel, railway and chemical industries around Middlesbrough during this period rested not only on a large flow of labour into the town, but also out of it. High rates of in-migration were accompanied by high rates of out-migration. It is intriguing to note that in one of the west-central German towns, Duisburg, where the construction of major smelting plants in the mid-1850s marked the start of the industrial era, population flows and counter-flows were symmetrical, with in- and out-migration rates reaching virtually the same levels, 8% of all registered inhabitants.[54]

It seems, then, that Middlesbrough, like other industrializing towns, simultaneously attracted and ejected a large mass of human resources. As the town saw rapid population growth during this period, increasing 2.45 times from 7,631 to 18,714 between 1851 and 1861, and 1.5 times from 18,714 to 28,864 between 1861 and 1871, the lost population was clearly more than supplemented. Admittedly it would have been impossible for a community to sustain out-migration on the scale described above, while at the same time experiencing a rapid growth in total population, had not large-scale in-migration been taking place. The considerable net increase in younger men among the population generated those unusual age distributions seen in the 1861 and 1871 populations.

This seems to have been made possible partly because British labour markets, by and large, were loose and fluid before the 1870s. Additionally, Middlesbrough was a new, emergent community with fewer exclusive vested interests than older-established urban communities. This created a favourable climate for attracting new and heterogeneous population elements from other places.[55] But we must take full account, too, of the other element in Middlesbrough's rapid population growth: the crude birth rate observed among the resident population, as high as 40.5 per 1,000, while the crude death rate, 17.7 per 1,000, was by far the lowest among the 16 main English towns.

Jackson classified the major German cities of the Ruhr Valley and the lower Rhine into three categories in terms of demographic and economic characteristics. The first category includes towns which were regional administrative and commercial centres with moderate population growth, steady crude birth rates and moderate sex ratios. The second group comprised centres of textile manufacturing where higher birth rates and moderate population growth were accompanied by lower sex ratios. According to this classification, Middlesbrough belongs to a third major group of cities that includes Duisburg, Essen, Bochum and Dortmund. Compared with the first and second types of urban community, the third category towns had the highest crude birth rates, higher sex ratios and a rapid population growth in the late nineteenth century. The German towns belonging to the first and second categories experienced

[54]   Jackson, 'Migration in Duisburg', pp. 148–51.
[55]   Ravenstein, 'The Laws of Migration', p. 215.

Table 3.24. Persistence of Male In-migrants from the North East and Other
Counties of England, 1861–71

(In-migrants between 1851 and 1861)			
Origin	No. of Cases	Staying in 1871	Persistence Rates
North East	4,115	1,463	35.6%
			30.7% ('True Match' adopted)
Other Counties	1,226	316	25.8%
			22.3% ('True Match' adopted)

Source: Record linkage from Middlesbrough Census Enumerators' Books, 1851–61 and
1861–71.

average or lower migration rates, whereas the third category towns, of iron-
smelting, tool-making and rolling mills, showed the highest migration rates.[56]

In Graz in Austria during the same period, 'the frequency of persistence is
inversely related to the distance a migrant has come'. So immigrants from the
surrounding districts and from neighbouring provinces had the lowest rates of
persistence. Hubbard argues that his results suggest that these were probably
temporary migrants who came to the city for training and experience and
from the outset had no intention of staying in Graz.[57]

By contrast, as Table 3.24 shows, the persistence rate of those who came into
Middlesbrough from elsewhere in the North East of England was much higher
than those from other counties of England. Of 4,115 male in-migrants from
Yorkshire, Co. Durham and Northumberland between 1851 and 1861, 1,463
(35.6%) have been identified by record linkage as still resident in the town in
1871, whereas of 1,226 males from other counties of England, only 316 (25.8%)
remained there in 1871. The same tendency is apparent even when a rigid norm
in record linkage, *true match*, is adopted. More than 30% of in-migrants from
the North East continued to live in Middlesbrough, while 22.3% of those from
other counties of England remained in the town in 1871.[58]

Apart from skill-specific migration, which tended to be undertaken irrespective of distance, migration was also embarked upon to regions with
which migrants were familiar, in that they could easily find there relatives
or neighbours from their home villages or towns. Once migrants of this kind
found themselves in a new community, family and other ties, or a shared
territorial bond, seem to have held them there. Work-related reasons as well
as marriage, family, housing, caring responsibilities and a variety of other
motives played an important role in migration behaviour.[59]

To develop this point, it is possible to investigate whether natives of
Middlesbrough were a more stable group than in-migrants. Table 3.25 shows

---

56 Jackson, *Migration and Urbanization in the Ruhr Valley*, pp. 11, 14.
57 Hubbard, 'Aspects of Social Mobility in Graz', pp. 8, 21.
58 For a discussion about the inverse relationship between persistence and distance in German cities
   during the same period, see Hochstadt, *Mobility and Modernity*, pp. 164–5.
59 Pooley and Turnbull, *Migration and Mobility in Britain*, pp. 71–8.

Table 3.25. Persistence of Native-born and In-migrants (Male) in
Middlesbrough, 1851–71

Places of Birth	No. of Cases in 1851	Staying in 1861	Persistence (%)
Middlesbrough	904	419	46.3
Whitby	170	44	25.9
Stockton	164	83	50.6
Sunderland	83	40	48.2
Darlington	60	27	45.0
Hutton Rudby	52	26	50.0
Newcastle	50	13	26.0
Stokesley	47	17	36.2
Other parishes	2,258	778	34.5
Total	3,788	1,447	38.2

Places of Birth	No. of Cases in 1861	Staying in 1871	Persistence (%)
Middlesbrough	2,156	975	45.2
Stockton	267	115	43.1
Sunderland	145	55	37.9
Darlington	129	57	44.2
Newcastle	114	36	31.6
Whitby	100	37	37.0
Leeds	85	33	38.8
Hutton Rudby	76	41	53.9
Stokesley	69	30	43.5
Yarm	59	33	55.9
Other parishes	6,302	1,895	30.1
Total	9,502	3,307	34.8

(1851–1861–1871)

Places of Birth	No. of Cases in 1851	Staying in 1861 and 1871	Persistence (%)
Middlesbrough	904	210	23.2
Whitby	170	23	13.5
Stockton	164	52	31.7
Sunderland	83	18	21.7
Darlington	60	15	25.0
Hutton Rudby	52	14	26.9
Stokesley	47	14	29.8
Yarm	24	8	33.3
Other parishes	2,284	381	16.7
Total	3,788	735	19.4

Continued

Table 3.25. Continued

(1851–1861–1871)
('True Match' Linkage)

Places of Birth	No. of Cases in 1851	Staying in 1861 and 1871	Persistence (%)
Middlesbrough	904	168	18.6
Whitby	170	22	12.9
Stockton	164	47	28.7
Sunderland	83	17	20.5
Darlington	60	14	23.3
Hutton Rudby	52	13	25.0
Stokesley	47	12	25.5
Yarm	24	8	33.3
Other parishes	2,284	344	16.7
Total	3,788	645	17.0

Source: Record linkage from Middlesbrough Census Enumerators' Books, 1851–61 and 1861–71.

that persistence rates of males born in Middlesbrough between 1851 and 1861 and between 1861 and 1871, at 46.3 and 45.2%, respectively, were much higher than average persistence rates, whether based on *true match* or on *true* and *possible match* linkage. On average, 35.6% of male in-migrants were still present in 1861 and 31.7% in 1871. Also persistence rates for those remaining in the town for at least 20 years, throughout the period 1851 to 1871, indicate that those native-born were more stable than the average.

It cannot be said, however, that native-born males were the most persistent population in the town, for the rates for males born in some other North East places who had migrated into Middlesbrough, were higher than for native-born males. Those born in Stockton, Hutton Rudby and Yarm showed higher persistence over the 20 years than men born in Middlesbrough.

There is no significant observable difference between persistence rates for native-born and migrants among those males who remained in the town through the whole period from 1851 to 1871. Especially in rates based on *true match* record linkage, the native-born population tended to be only slightly more stable, and showed a lower persistence than in comparable figures for migrants born in many other towns in the North East. At least as far as the long-term is concerned, there seems to be no clear demonstrable pattern in persistence. No obvious distinction can be drawn between Middlesbrough-born residents and migrants, as has been shown in German cities during the same period.[60] The evidence available with which to study the persistence and transience of the mid-Victorian Middlesbrough population is limited, but it does suggest a general pattern of quite a mobile population.

---

[60] For high persistence ratios among the native-born observed in German cities during the same period, see Hochstadt, *Mobility and Modernity*, p. 139.

Table 3.26. Birth Countries of Wives of Irish-, Welsh- and
Scottish-born Men in Middlesbrough in 1861

Birth Countries of the Wives	No. of Cases	%
Irish Husbands		
Ireland	380	86.4
Wales	1	0.2
Scotland	13	3.0
England	46	10.4
Total	440	100.0
Welsh Husbands		
Wales	166	81.0
Ireland	1	0.5
Scotland	1	0.5
England	32	15.6
Foreign Country	1	0.5
Unknown	4	1.9
Total	205	100.0
Scottish Husbands		
Scotland	33	39.8
Ireland	3	3.6
England	48	57.1
Total	205	100.0

Source: National Archives, Census Enumerators' Books 1861, RG
9/3685–9.

Stepwise Migration

In all probability, some in-migrants moved into the town in stages. They would
have left home, formed households at home or on the way, had children and
made short or long stays in other locations before entering Middlesbrough.
Others would have arrived in Middlesbrough directly without staying elsewhere after leaving home. Generally the censuses note only migration from
birthplace to current residence at an unspecified past time, so that information
on stepwise, circular migration and frequent movement is not directly available from a conventional record linkage.[61]

To track the stepwise movement of Middlesbrough in-migrants at this
time, it is possible to use census enumerators' books to investigate how and
where they found their partners, and to identify the birthplaces of surviving
co-resident children of the household. For married household heads living
with children, this analysis displays, at least to an extent, a stepwise migration profile for those recorded in the 1861 census, ending with their last place
of residence, Middlesbrough.

Table 3.26 indicates countries of birth of the wives of migrants coming

---

[61] With respect to stepwise migration seen in late nineteenth-century Liverpool, see Lawton,
'Mobility in Nineteenth-century British Cities', p. 211.

Table 3.27. Birthplaces of the First to Seventh Surviving Co-resident
Offspring of Irish, Welsh and Scottish Parents in 1861

Birth Countries	No. of Cases	%
Irish Household Heads (485 households)		
Ireland	212	20.0
Scotland	33	3.1
Wales including Monmouthshire	22	2.1
England	788	74.5
Foreign Countries	1	0.1
Unknown	2	0.2
Total	1,058	100.0
Welsh Household Heads (244 households)		
Wales including Monmouthshire	305	53.8
Scotland	7	1.2
England	252	44.4
Ireland	1	0.2
Foreign Countries	2	0.4
Total	567	100.0
Scottish Household Heads (107 households)		
Scotland	51	24.7
Wales including Monmouthshire	1	0.5
England	154	74.8
Total	206	100.0

Source: National Archives, Census Enumerators' Books, 1861, RG 9/3685–9.

from Ireland, Wales and Scotland, and thus the degree to which ethnicity
might have influenced choice of spouse. Because the census enumerators
recorded the birthplace only of an individual himself or herself, in the case
of first generation residents, the figures do not reveal 'ethnicity'. Yet as
many as 86.4% of men born in Ireland who migrated into Middlesbrough
before 1861 had partners born in Ireland, while 81.0% of the wives of Welsh
husbands were from Wales. This suggests an 'ethnic' propensity to a certain
degree. Especially in the case of the Irish, most marriages were endogamous.
Religion may have accounted for this, as the Irish migrants, almost all of
them Catholic, were expected to marry within their own faith, whereas the
Welsh and Scots were overwhelmingly Protestant.[62] Only 40% of husbands
born in Scotland chose Scottish-born marriage partners, indicating that Scots
were likely to leave home when they were young and establish a family in
England, irrespective of their partners' ethnicity.

Table 3.27 shows birthplaces of the first to seventh surviving co-resident
offspring of household heads shown as having been born in Ireland, Wales,
including Monmouthshire, and Scotland. More than half (53.8%) of the surviving
offspring of Welsh household heads were born in Wales. In contrast, only 20%

---

[62] For social mixing in Liverpool observed in the 1871 census data, see Lawton, 'Mobility in Nineteenth-century British Cities', p. 218.

Table 3.28. Stepwise Migration to Middlesbrough: Birthplaces of In-migrating English Male Household Heads, 1861

Birth Places	No. of Cases	%
Stockton	81	4.2
Sunderland	47	2.5
Darlington	45	2.4
Stokesley	36	1.9
Whitby	35	1.8
Hutton Rudby	31	1.6
Newcastle	29	1.5
Leeds	25	1.3
Yarm	22	1.2
Guisborough	21	1.1
Other places	1,539	80.5
Total	1,911	100.0

Source: National Archives, Census Enumerators' Books, 1861, RG 9/3685–9.

of surviving children born to Irish household heads were born in Ireland. One-quarter of the Scottish households' surviving co-resident children were born in Scotland. As discussed further below, most of the households heads from Wales and Monmouthshire were skilled workers who learned their trade in iron-making, formed a family and had children born in Wales. They then migrated more or less directly to Middlesbrough as independent skilled workers such as master puddlers, rollers, shinglers or other craftsmen.

Their profile is typical of 'skill-specific migration'. Other iron and steel industrial towns all over the country must have experienced a substantial inter-urban movement based on this type of migration. Liverpool saw the same patterns of migration among different occupational groups. The Liverpool Irish tended towards direct migration, other types of migrants were likely to move stepwise, while workers with specialist skills were more inclined to re-locate direct to jobs over long distances.[63]

In contrast, numbers of the Middlesbrough Irish left home as single unskilled labourers and migrated directly to England, where they formed households in the town or in other localities. This is evident from the figure that 74.5% of their surviving co-resident children were born in England. Some of the migrants, however, would have travelled around the iron and steel areas of England and Wales, have been trained in the industry, moved into Middlesbrough, and then formed households. Scottish household heads show a similar pattern to that observed among their Irish counterparts.

As for those household heads born in England who migrated into Middlesbrough before 1861, a sizeable group originated in the neighbouring town of Stockton, as Table 3.28 shows. From Sunderland and Darlington came 47

---

[63] Lawton, 'Mobility in Nineteenth-century British Cities', pp. 211, 213.

Table 3.29. Stepwise Migration to Middlesbrough: Birthplaces of Wives of In-migrating English Male Household Heads, 1861

Birth Places	No. of Cases	%
Whitby	64	3.4
Stockton	61	3.3
Middlesbrough	49	2.6
Darlington	42	2.3
Sunderland	41	2.2
Stokesley	33	1.8
Hutton Rudby	27	1.4
Guisborough	25	1.3
Newcastle	24	1.3
Leeds	22	1.2
Other places	1,480	79.2
Total	1,911	100.0

Source: National Archives, Census Enumerators' Books, 1861, RG 9/3685–9.

and 45 household heads, while other commonly mentioned places of origin are small nearby towns such as Stokesley and Guisborough. But more than 80% of migrants' hometowns are spread widely across the whole of England.

The largest single group of marriage partners came from Whitby, as shown by Table 3.29. More than 30% of those men with Whitby-born wives were mariners, seamen or shipwrights. Stockton, Middlesbrough, Darlington and Sunderland also supplied many marriage partners. 'Marriage horizons' show a close geographical relationship to place of origin. Nine of the 10 places occurring most frequently in Tables 3.28 and 3.29 are the same. Relatively large proportions of couples who migrated into Middlesbrough before 1861 had found marriage partners from the North East of England.

Clearly, the motivation behind migration cannot be established through this method of record linkage. Yet from the evidence of the 'marriage horizon', perhaps short-distance moves, especially of women within the region, were for reasons of marriage or housing, rather than being prompted by work-related motives.[64]

Analysis of the places in which the first surviving co-resident child was born to English household heads suggests, as shown in Table 3.30, that about 43% came to Middlesbrough without staying in other places on the way. As for the second to seventh surviving co-resident offspring, more than half, from 52.4% up to 74.1% and increasing, were born in Middlesbrough. Overall, of a total 4,872 surviving children born to household heads from English parishes excluding Middlesbrough, 53.2% were born in Middlesbrough. This strongly indicates that of the household heads from England, more than half directly migrated into Middlesbrough.

64   Pooley and Turnbull, 'Migration and Urbanization in North-West England', pp. 201–2.

Table 3.30. Stepwise Migration to Middlesbrough: Birthplaces of Surviving
Co-resident Children of English-born Household Heads, 1861

Surviving Co-resident Children				Birth Places		
	Middlesbrough	Stockton	Darlington	Sunderland	Other Places	Total
1st	739 (42.9)	64 (3.7)	39 (2.3)	29 (1.7)	853 (49.5)	1,724 (100.0)
2nd	667 (52.4)	39 (3.1)	22 (1.7)	14 (1.1)	530 (41.7)	1,272 (100.0)
3rd	500 (58.3)	27 (3.2)	11 (1.3)	9 (1.0)	310 (36.2)	857 (100.0)
4th	354 (66.7)	10 (1.9)	4 (0.8)	3 (0.6)	160 (30.1)	531 (100.0)
5th	194 (65.8)	7 (2.4)	4 (1.4)	–	90 (30.5)	295 (100.0)
6th	100 (71.9)	5 (3.6)	–	–	34 (24.5)	139 (100.0)
7th	40 (74.1)	2 (3.7)	–	–	12 (22.2)	54 (100.0)
1st–7th	2,594 (53.2)	154 (3.2)	80 (1.7)	55 (1.1)	1,989 (40.8)	4,872 (100.0)

Source: National Archives, Census Enumerators' Books, 1861, RG 9/3685–9.

The remaining 47% most probably moved into the town stepwise, with Stockton, Darlington and Sunderland, all of them iron and steel, railway or engineering centres, frequent stopping-off points on the way. It is logical that these three places would form steps in the process of migration, given that they made up the three most frequent places of origins of household heads, already shown in Tables 3.28 and 3.29. Most family formation presumably occurred in the home town or village, and in neighbouring towns in the North East. Two of the towns linked most frequently to Middlesbrough in these movements had a similar population size in 1861 as that of Middlesbrough itself (18,714), Stockton with 13,487 and Darlington with 15,789. Sunderland was much larger at this time, having a population of 91,088. Taking account of Sunderland, a far bigger town, as a step in the process of migration, these findings appear to challenge the observation of Ravenstein that most movement was stepwise up the urban hierarchy. As observed in North West England during the same period, most moves were short-distance and between similar-sized towns, the predominant pattern being movement within an area that was well known to the people in transit.[65]

The brief analysis of migration patterns in late-nineteenth century Middlesbrough and the Cleveland region has revealed interesting trends and challenged some conventional assumptions about the internal geographical migration by people of mid-Victorian urban communities. Further research using the same methodology, and considered along with the numerous recent investigations of nineteenth-century North American, German and Austrian cities, is needed to confirm whether the migration patterns of mid-Victorian Middlesbrough have any general applicability to other urban centres in Europe and America.

[65] Ravenstein, 'The Laws of Migration', pp. 198–9; for the population of Sunderland in the late nineteenth century, see Cookson, *Sunderland: Building a City*, pp. 56, 118; Pooley and Turnbull, 'Migration and Urbanization in North-West England', pp. 198, 201.

Although, as Lind suggests, realistic explanations for migration can be found only by considering a number of economic variables besides employment and wage levels, as well as geographical, psychological and even political factors, it does seem here that employment opportunities and higher wages were the main motivations in the migration patterns observed.[66] Because the economic development and urbanization of Middlesbrough were proceeding at a rate which was unprecedented in its speed, so that demand for an industrial labour force was huge and immediate, work-related motives were more likely to be decisive. But the economic imperative did not necessarily arise from poverty. In most cases, movements in this region are explained by desires for economic and social betterment, rather than an escape from destitution. At least for skilled workers, as we will see in the next chapter, migration seems to have been well structured and organized, not just a haphazard outpouring.

Added to this is another factor outside economic explanation, which is recognized as attracting people from the countryside into large urban centres. A 'contagion of numbers', as Banks has pointed out, would be an important force pulling migrants towards 'the sense of something going on, the theatres and the music halls, the brightly lighted streets and busy crowds'.[67] A tight-knit sense of traditional rural community tended to exercise repressing effects on individuals, stifling initiative, so that many people in the countryside, especially young ones, would have viewed the prospect of town life as a kind of release.

Conversely, in urban centres, 'rural traditions and localism, lynchpin of identity, broke down in urban anonymity' and 'there was no focus, no sense of community except what the individual might create out of his organizational ties: the lodge, ethnic saloon, trade union, fire company, political club, literary society, church'. The individual became 'a great deal freer of collective bonds', much more so in a newly built town like Middlesbrough where there were few attachments to long-established conventions, and much less in the way of complicated human relationships, vested interests, territorial bonds or a strong sense of belonging to a certain social hierarchy and class, than would be found in older-established urban communities.[68]

A final point to consider is the environment into which migrants arrived, and the process of adaptation and assimilation which they underwent. For towns like mid-Victorian Middlesbrough, where extremely high migration was presumably a cause of friction in various aspects of daily life, the question of how new arrivals adapted and integrated into the

---

66 Lind, 'Internal Migration in Britain', p. 77; see also for a variety of motivations for moves, Bade, 'Introduction', p. 10.

67 Banks, 'The Contagion of Numbers', p. 112.

68 Lee and Reinders, 'The Loss of Innocence', pp. 182, 191; Durkheim, *De la Division du Travail Social*, pp. 297–8.

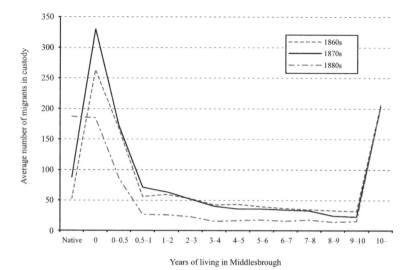

Figure 3.31. Crimes by Migrants According to Duration of Stay in
Middlesbrough, 1860s–1880s

host communities is particularly intriguing. This is Jackson and Moch's
fifth emphasis in migration studies, that dealing with the consequences
of migration for those who migrated, for instance as casualties of urban
crime or mental disorders.

Data showing crime rates of migrants according to how long they had
lived in the town, are available from the annual reports of chief superintendents, later chief constables, to the Middlesbrough Watch Committee.
These are illustrated in Figure 3.31.[69] They suggest, as might be expected,
that people temporarily dropping into the town and without a fixed
address, described as *strangers* in the records, as well as those resident
for a short period of time, less than six months, tended to commit crimes
most often. At least in the 1860s and 1870s, those born in Middlesbrough
were less likely to have offended against the law, though afterwards, in
the 1880s, those born in Middlesbrough showed the highest crime rate, a
trend which remains to be investigated. A tendency can be seen, that the
longer migrants lived in the town, the lower their crime rate. Given that
crime rates decreased radically among those who had lived in the town for
six months or more, this seems to have been a crucial period of adaptation
to a host community.

In this period, young adult males aged 20–29 were pouring into the
town in enormous numbers, pushing the sex ratio up far beyond 100.
Middlesbrough's male bias was firmly established from the mid-nineteenth century onwards, and the town could be characterised as a young

---

[69] Teesside Archives, CB/M/C2/100, 101 & 102; CB/M/P, 23 & 2; CB/M/C 39-60.

Table 3.32. Urban Crimes, 1861

| | No. of Crimes Committed and Persons Proceeded Against | | | |
| | | | | Proportions of Indictable |
Towns	I	II	Total (I+II)	Offences I / I + II (%)
Middlesbrough	72	865	937	7.7
London	1,029	5,749	6,778	15.2
Portsmouth	682	1,820	2,502	27.3
Norwich	279	853	1,132	24.6
Wolverhampton	451	2,677	3,128	14.4
Birmingham	836	6,905	7,741	10.8
Bristol	305	3,896	4,201	7.3
Leicester	204	1,145	1,349	15.1
Nottingham	239	424	663	36.0
Liverpool	3,954	41,153	45,107	8.8
Manchester	5,808	8,618	14,426	40.3
Salford	1,016	1,798	2,814	36.1
Oldham	212	1,438	1,650	12.8
Leeds	626	5,887	6,513	9.6
Sheffield	400	4,811	5,211	7.7
Sunderland	90	2,660	2,750	3.3
Newcastle	481	2,723	3,204	15.0
Bradford	337	1,741	2,078	16.2
Cardiff	155	2,150	2,305	6.7
Total	17,176	97,313	114,489	15.0

Notes: I Indictable offences: murder, attempts to murder, shooting at, wounding, stabbing, etc. to do bodily harm, manslaughter, etc. Figures are the number of crimes committed. II Offences determined summarily: assaults, bastardy orders, breaches of the peace, drunkenness, and drunk and disorderly, prostitutes, begging, etc. Figures are the number of persons proceeded against.

masculine community. In such a culture of masculinity, physical force tends to be exalted as a means of catharsis, while in many cases working men's pent-up frustrations arising from hard manual labour such as that in iron, steel and other heavy industries, are worked off by heavy drinking.

The coming together of a population with a young age structure, and a newly built town such as Middlesbrough, produces a form of urban life about which Durkheim might have been reflecting when he wrote that 'the prime of youth … is the time when men are most impatient with all restraint and most eager for change. The life circulating in them has not yet had time to congeal, or definitely to take determined forms, and it is too intense to be disciplined without resistance.'[70]

Infrastructure such as housing, the urban environment, public space, education, policing, entertainment and medical facilities, struggled to

[70] Durkheim, *De la Division du Travail Social*, p. 295.

keep up with the stream of younger generation migrants crowding in at unprecedented speed from the mid-nineteenth century. In particular, the extraordinary sex ratio and distorted age structure were a prescription for friction. These factors seem to have heightened tension in the town, making the crime rate rise rapidly. Yet in reality, Taylor suggests, 'the serious crime rate might have been below that of industrial regions in the north-west and Midlands'.[71]

Table 3.32 compares crime rates in the main towns in England and Wales in 1861 and shows that in fact for serious crime, expressed as a proportion of indictable offences to all crimes committed, Middlesbrough had the fourth lowest rate (7.7%). Only Sunderland, Bristol and Cardiff scored better. Its serious crime rate was substantially below those of Manchester (40.3%), Salford (36.1%), Nottingham (36.0%), Portsmouth (27.3%) and London (15.2%). However, if instead we examine cases of drunkenness per 1,000 population (13.4), as well as the proportion of offences determined summarily (28.4%), shown in Table 3.33, it is interesting to note that Middlesbrough shows the highest rate after Liverpool (22.2) for drunkenness, and comes second to Salford (30.6%) in percentage of total offences determined summarily.[72]

Felonies such as murder and manslaughter were few relative to the rate in other towns, whereas the incidence of misdemeanour like drunkenness, petty assault, violation of bastardy orders, breaches of the peace, prostitution and begging, was higher. This indicates what were the real frictions and tensions experienced by the mid-Victorian inhabitants of Middlesbrough. At least during the zenith of the Cleveland iron and steel industry, the town could be characterised not as a dismal haunt of the destitute, but as a centre of demographic vitality, full of youthful energy.

Moreover, migrants appear to have shared a strong feeling that they were *déraciné*, rootless above all, away from their native places. This in turn seems to have strengthened the solidarity among them, leading to the establishment of a wide variety of voluntary associations such as friendly societies, trade unions, benevolent societies, clubs and other institutions in the town. This newborn urban society was inadequately provided with fixed or disposable old endowments and legacies, whether spiritual, physical or institutional, from the past, so that the vacuum had to be filled by the migrants themselves forming fresh associations. It is clear that, in order to be effective, any such organizations demand some continuity of membership. Given the high transiency rates among lower manual labourers at this time, the voluntary associations which formed one after another in mid-Victorian Middlesbrough must have had at their core a more settled group of skilled workers and independent craftsmen. This

---

[71] Taylor, 'The Infant Hercules and the Augean Stables', p. 59; with respect to crime in Middlesbrough in the late-nineteenth century, see Taylor, *Policing the Victorian Town*, pp. 52–77.

[72] Calculated from National Archives, HO/63/8, Vols 1 & 2, annual police records, 1861.

Table 3.33. Urban Crimes: Arrest Rates for Drunkenness and Minor Offences, 1861

Towns	Population in 1861	Total Offences Determined Summarily	Drunkenness Apprehended	Proportions per 1,000 Population	Percentage of the Total Offences Determined Summarily
Middlesbrough	18,327	865	246	13.4	28.4
London		5,749	351	–	6.1
Portsmouth	94,546	1,820	287	1.9	15.8
Norwich	74,414	853	138	1.9	16.2
Wolverhampton	60,858	2,677	426	7.0	15.9
Birmingham	295,955	6,905	1,186	4.0	17.2
Bristol	154,093	3,896	560	3.6	14.4
Leicester	68,186	1,145	218	3.2	19.0
Nottingham	74,531	424	13	0.2	3.1
Liverpool	443,874	41,153	9,832	22.2	23.9
Manchester	338,346	8,618	2,284	6.8	26.5
Salford	105,334	1,798	550	5.2	30.6
Oldham	72,334	1,438	375	5.2	26.1
Leeds	207,153	5,887	1,287	6.2	21.9
Sheffield	185,157	4,811	989	5.3	20.6
Sunderland	78,699	2,660	502	6.3	18.9
Newcastle	109,291	2,723	706	6.5	25.9
Bradford	106,218	1,741	178	1.7	10.2
Cardiff	32,421	2,150	221	6.8	3.3
Total		97,313	20,349		20.9
Total excluding London	2,519,737	91,564	19,998	7.9	21.8

Source: National Archives, HO/63/8, Vols 1 & 2.

community, perhaps with a longer-term perspective on life in the town, sought a means of self-definition which was fulfilled through benevolent societies and similar social enterprises.[73]

[73] Briggs, *Victorian Cities*, pp. 242, 246; Turner, 'The Frontier Revisited', pp. 98–9; Praed, *Rise and Progress of Middlesbrough*, pp. 16, 21. For voluntary associations in America in the late-nineteenth and early-twentieth centuries, see de Tocqueville, *De la Démocratie en Amérique*, pp. 595, 605–6; Turner, *The Frontier in American History*, pp. 343–5, 347; Lee and Reinders, 'Loss of Innocence', pp. 177–80, 182, 191–2; Temperley and Bradbury, 'Introduction', *Introduction to American Studies*, p. 7.

4

The Labour Market in Cleveland Iron and Steel

> The iron-workers for the North being thus, owing to the character of
> the business in which they are engaged, dealt with not as individuals, or
> even as groups separated into as many bodies as there are employers,
> but as a *class,* it was natural that some organization should be formed to
> protect the interests of the body. This took the shape of an iron-workers'
> union. The employers shortly afterwards formed an iron manufacturers'
> association.[1]

The Industrial Context

This chapter will focus upon features of the labour market in the iron and steel
industry of mid-Victorian Middlesbrough and the Cleveland region. Like the
preceding demographic study, it draws for its main source on record linkage
results from census enumerators' books, between 1851 and 1861 and between
1861 and 1871. As Thernstrom suggests, 'migration is the prime mechanism
by which the labour force is redistributed in response to shifts in the location
of industry brought about by technological innovation, the discovery of new
resources and other circumstances'. Hence migration figures are a key to
understanding the formation of this region's labour market.[2]

The first point to consider is how the industrial structure of Middlesbrough changed over the period from 1851 to 1881. The town's industry at
this time was highly concentrated on manufacturing, with an insignificant
proportion of the working population engaged in the commercial or tertiary
sector.[3] Table 4.1 illustrates the dominance of staple industries, especially
marked in 1861 and 1871, in terms of the proportion of workers engaged in
the manufacturing sector overall, and Table 4.2 for those employed in the
iron and steel industry. In 1871, as many as 85% of the town's male labour
force of about 10,000 worked in manufacturing, with less than 10% in the
commercial sector. It appears that the staple industry reached its zenith in
the 1860s, for males employed in ironworks made up almost one-half the
manufacturing labour force in 1861. The figures reveal that the boom in this
industry had passed its peak by the beginning of the 1880s, when proportions

1 Modern Records Centre, Univ. of Warwick, MSS 365/BAC, Rules, p. 5; Mr. Waterhouse's
   Returns (Sale of Manufactured Iron), I (1869); Minute Book, Vol. 1.
2 Thernstrom, *The Other Bostonians*, p. 228.
3 Reeder and Rodger, 'Industrialization and the City Economy', pp. 564, 568–9.

of the manufacturing labour force and of those engaged in iron and steel fell back to match the levels found in 1851.

An obvious feature of the mid-nineteenth-century labour market in iron manufacture in England, Wales and Scotland was its overwhelmingly male bias. Women made up on average only 1% of the workforce, for they were not considered suited to the dangerous and physically challenging operations involved in iron making. Opportunities for female employment in the areas where iron and steel dominated were consequently much less than those on offer to men. A further striking feature of the sector was the youth of its male labour force. Among skilled and semi-skilled ironworkers such as puddlers, founders, moulders and forgers, as well as unskilled labourers, numbers peaked in the 20–24 age group, 19% of the whole, followed by those aged 15–19 (17%) and 25–29 (15%).[4]

In this, the iron and steel labour market of the late-nineteenth century was in sharp contrast to that of other industries, for instance textiles. More than half the woollen and worsted industry workforce was female, and it was predominantly aged 10–19. The peak for female employees there was in the age group of 15–19, making up 27%, while that for male textile workers was younger still, aged 10–15, accounting for 17.5%. The explanation for this is that many boys worked in unskilled textile occupations until they were 14, and old enough to start an apprenticeship. In flax-spinning, there was a similar trend, females predominant and the peak in the age group of 15–19, with next highest numbers in the 10–14 age group.[5]

The iron and steel labour market demanded a diversified labour force in terms of job types and skills. In 1866 William Menelaus of the Dowlais Iron Co., one of the largest iron manufacturers in South Wales where various iron-making processes were vertically integrated within the enterprise, produced a breakdown of occupations in his company. The workforce amounted to 8,500. Only 9% were engaged on the furnaces, with 26% in the forges and mills and 24% in the collieries. Those employed in ironstone mines and lime-stone quarries accounted for a further 20%. Fitters, pattern-makers, smiths, foundry workers, carpenters and boiler-makers made up a further 5%, while enginemen in the forge, furnaces, locomotion and pits were 4% of the total. If various simple and subsidiary jobs carried out by unskilled labourers are added, it can be seen that the Dowlais labour force ranged widely, from the most skilled and highly paid workers such as shinglers, rollers and puddlers, down to casual labourers.[6]

It was usual in South Wales for workers to be hired directly by ironmasters, whereas in other iron-making centres in England, sub-contracting, or the double-handed employment system, was widespread. It is likely that overall in iron and steel at this time, especially in the wrought and malleable iron-making

---

4   PP, 1851 [1691-I] LXXXVIII, Part I, pp. cxxxiv, cxxxix, cxliv, cxlviii.
5   Yasumoto, *Industrialisation, Urbanisation and Demographic Change*, pp. 126–7.
6   Glamorgan R.O., D/D G/C5/15–16.

Table 4.1. Industrial Structure of Middlesbrough, 1851–81

		Professional	Domestic	Commercial	Agricultural	Manufacturing	Total
1851	M	52 (2.2%)	6 (0.2%)	424 (17.7%)	84 (3.5%)	1,836 (76.4%)	2,402 (100.0%)
	F	29 (5.1%)	262 (46.4%)	11 (1.9%)	7 (1.2%)	256 (45.3%)	565 (100.0%)
	Total	81 (2.7%)	268 (9.0%)	435 (14.7%)	91 (3.1%)	2,092 (70.5%)	2,967 (100.0%)
1861	M	158 (2.6%)	21 (3.5%)	638 (10.6%)	119 (2.0%)	5,070 (84.4%)	6,006 (100.0%)
	F	70 (7.0%)	512 (51.1%)	8 (0.8%)	4 (0.4%)	407 (40.7%)	1,001 (100.0%)
	Total	228 (3.2%)	533 (7.6%)	646 (9.2%)	123 (1.8%)	5,477 (78.2%)	7,007 (100.0%)
1871	M	335 (3.4%)	78 (0.7%)	982 (9.8%)	68 (0.7%)	8,531 (85.4%)	9,994 (100.0%)
	F	131 (6.6%)	1,024 (51.7%)	25 (1.3%)	9 (0.5%)	791 (39.9%)	1,980 (100.0%)
	Total	466 (3.9%)	1,102 (9.2%)	1,007 (8.4%)	77 (0.6%)	9,322 (77.9%)	11,974 (100.0%)
1881	M	426 (3.5%)	150 (1.2%)	2,165 (18.0%)	143 (1.2%)	9,128 (76.0%)	12,012 (100.0%)
	F	232 (8.7%)	1,467 (54.9%)	26 (1.0%)	7 (0.3%)	938 (35.1%)	2,670 (100.0%)
	Total	657 (4.5%)	1,617 (11.0%)	2,191 (14.9%)	150 (1.0%)	10,066 (68.6%)	14,682 (100.0%)

Source: National Archives, HO 107 2383 (1851), RG 9 3685-3689 (1861), RG 10 4889-4895 (1871), RG 11/4852 (1881).

Table 4.2. Iron and Steel Workers as a Proportion of Middlesbrough's
Manufacturing Workforce, 1851–81

		Iron and Steel	Total Manufacturing
1851	M	619 (33.7%)	1,836 (100.0%)
	F	8 (3.1%)	256 (100.0%)
	Total	627 (30.0%)	2,092 (100.0%)
1861	M	2,431 (47.9%)	5,070 (100.0%)
	F	20 (4.9%)	407 (100.0%)
	Total	2,451 (44.8%)	5,477 (100.0%)
1871	M	2,797 (32.8%)	8,531 (100.0%)
	F	39 (4.9%)	791 (100.0%)
	Total	2,836 (30.4%)	9,322 (100.0%)
1881	M	2,728 (29.9%)	9,128 (100.0%)
	F	14 (1.5%)	938 (100.0%)
	Total	2,742 (27.2%)	10,066 (100.0%)

Source: National Archives, HO 107 2383 (1851), RG 9 3685-3689 (1861), RG 10
4889–4895 (1871), RG 11/4852 (1881).

processes, sub-contracting prevailed. In the blast furnace process, bridge-stockers and stock-takers employed under-hands to whom they paid wages. In forges, rolling and puddling mills, fore-hands or principal (that is, master) rollers, shinglers and puddlers employed under-puddlers, under-workers, under-hands or level-hands to whom they paid wages from their own income.

These under-hands were in most cases trained on the job by master workers. In the Middlesbrough census returns for 1861 can be found 'roller at ironworks employing three men and six boys', 'stock-taker in iron trade employing two men' and 'puddler under-hand'. For workmen employed in Cleveland wrought iron manufacture, information on the employment system and wage payment appears in work rules recorded in 1871 in the minutes of the North of England Iron Manufacturers' Association.[7]

Irrespective of job type, wages were paid weekly. There were two kinds of payment. Day workmen were paid by hours worked, which they entered on a time-board. Most of these were unskilled labourers. The other type of payment was for piece work, carried out mainly by skilled workers – puddlers, rollers, shinglers, mill furnacemen, forgemen or others. These employed under-hands and could delegate their work to assistants, with the permission of a foreman. In Cleveland most skilled workers were paid by piece, receiving tonnage prices out of which they paid their under-hands.[8]

In north-east firms producing wrought iron or finished iron in 1870, fore-hands and under-hands had a wage system so complicated and detailed that they could be paid by the day, shift, ton or charge, according to the type of work. Across the 28 puddling mills, 11 rail and heavy angle mills, 9 bar and

[7]   Birch, *The Economic History of the British Iron and Steel Industry*, pp. 256–7; National Archives, RG 9 3685-9, 1861; Modern Records Centre, Univ. of Warwick, MSS 365/NEI, 5 Jan. 1871.
[8]   Modern Records Centre, Univ. of Warwick, MSS 365/BAC, Rules, p. 5.

angle mills, 9 plate mills, and 10 guide mills, were occupations whose range of activities numbered between seven and 59 operations, for each of which a different rate was stipulated.[9]

Under the sub-contracting system, these fore-hands, principal or master workers employing under-hands, enjoyed a measure of independence from the ironmasters and were consequently difficult to control, a fact made clear in the workplace rules. These prescribed that every workman 'must attend at and during reasonable and usual times'; that 'puddlers, rollers, mill furnacemen, forgemen, or other workmen, shall not leave their work to assistants, or to any other persons, unless permitted at the time by their respective foremen'; that 'workmen are not to charge iron or use iron, different either in quantity or quality, from that ordered by their employers or their agents'; that 'puddlers, or their under-hands, or level-hands, shall not take iron or other material beyond the puddler's regular charge, for the purpose of making up the yield, or for any other purpose'; and that 'puddlers shall not shingle their own iron or pass iron that has been rejected'. These regulations reflect the difficulties of managing labour under a double-handed employment system.[10]

There were several exceptionally large-scale iron and steel enterprises in both South Wales and Cleveland. The Dowlais ironworks, with its collieries, iron-ore mines, forges and various mills producing rails, bars, plates and angles, employed as many as 7,000 workmen in 1845, and 8,500 in 1866. Bolckow and Vaughan's ironworks in Middlesbrough was said to have employed 1,600 workmen in the 1850s. However, while there were regional differences, iron-manufacturing firms in England and Wales in the late-nineteenth century on average employed quite small numbers of workmen. According to a survey of 754 iron-manufacturing firms in England and Wales in 1851, as many as 49% had fewer than 10 workmen. Those employing 10–20 men account for 21% of firms, 100–350 men for 7.5%, 350 and upwards for only 0.7%. In the mid-nineteenth century, firms with more than 1,000 workmen were very unusual. Yet by 1870, 761 iron and steel firms in England, Wales and Scotland employed in total 16,652 workers, a remarkable increase in the size of employers, with 219 men per firm on average.[11]

From the mid-nineteenth century, particularly after commercial quantities of Cleveland iron ore were discovered in nearby Eston, Middlesbrough and its neighbourhood prepared for a great transformation in industry and urban growth. Except for the period of the Great Strike and lockout from 1864 to 1866, at least up until the late 1880s, Middlesbrough was hungry for skilled workers in iron and steel, as the industry expanded at an unprecedented rate. The town benefited from Britain's plentiful reservoir of mobile and footloose

9 Modern Records Centre, Univ. of Warwick, MSS 365/NEI, Dec. 1870.
10 Modern Records Centre, Univ. of Warwick, MSS 365/NEI, 5 Jan. 1871. For the employment of under-hands by master puddlers, see Howard, 'The Strikes and Lockouts', p. 427.
11 Glamorgan R.O., D/D G/C5/15-16; Birch, *The Economic History of the British Iron and Steel Industry*, pp. 255, 254; Lillie, *History of Middlesbrough*, p. 100; PP, 1851 [1691-I] LXXXVIII, Part I, p. cclxxix.

population at this time. The attraction of this newly born boom town was its unprecedented opportunities for employment which offered higher wages to both skilled workers and unskilled manual labourers. While employment levels and wage rates are important determinants of geographical movement, there are generally multiple other factors, whether economic, geographical, psychological, ethnic or even political, to take account of. Yet in the case of Middlesbrough, economic factors seem to have been paramount. Workers were induced to move there above all because they saw prospects of improving their material standard of living and economic status.

At this time, it was most usual to recruit labour by word of mouth. Personal contacts still played an important role in how workers searched for employment. Another means of recruitment was through public notices, circulated in places such as chapel yards, announcing that workers were needed and supplying additional information about whether the company would cover the expense of removing goods and families. Otherwise employers often used agents to search for workers, especially unskilled labourers, in the surrounding agricultural district.[12] Iron companies sometimes used local newspapers to recruit specialist skilled workers or managers. Bolckow, Vaughan and Co. advertised for a manager of their ironstone works at Eston in 1868 in the *Cambrian*, one of the major Swansea newspapers:

> Wanted, by Messrs. Bolckow, Vaughan, and Co., Limited, a thoroughly competent MANAGER, for their Ironstone Mines. He will be required to give the whole of his time and attention to the duties of the position, and to reside at or near the Mines. Applications to be addressed, General Manager, Messrs. Bolckow, Vaughan, and Co., Limited, Middlesbrough-on-Tees...[13]

Conversely, work was sought by skilled workers or managers through the columns of Cleveland newspapers:

> Iron works assistant manager and engineer: A gentleman who has filled the above appointment is open to an engagement. Has for many years been engaged as Engineer to one of the largest Iron, Copper, and Tin-plate Works in South Wales, and for four years had the Management of Charcoal Blast Furnaces and Iron Works abroad, where the manufacture of Steel by the Bessemer, or Pneumatic process, was in operation. Unexceptionable reference given. Address ... Merthyr Tydfil.[14]

---

12 Birch, *The Economic History of the British Iron and Steel Industry*, p. 261.
13 *The Cambrian*, 28 Feb. 1868.
14 *Stockton Gazette and Middlesbrough Times*, 24 Oct. 1862.

Table 4.3. Occupational Structure of In- and Out-migrants, 1851–61

Manufacturing	Commercial	Agricultural	Domestic	Professional	Total
In-migrants					
Male					
4,085	464	99	15	143	4,806
(85.0%)	(9.7%)	(2.0%)	(0.3%)	(3.0%)	(100.0%)
Female					
299	7	4	400	50	760
(39.4%)	(0.9 %)	(0.5%)	(52.6%)	(6.6%)	(100.0%)
Out-migrants[a]					
Male					
1,169	289	58	5	40	1,561
(74.9%)	(18.5%)	(3.7%)	(0.3%)	(2.6%)	(100.0%)
Female					
192	6	6	232	22	458
(41.9%)	(1.3%)	(1.3%)	(50.7%)	(4.8%)	(100.0%)

Note: [a]Including those who died between the censuses. Occupational classification is based on the system developed by Woollard, *Classification of Occupations in the 1881 Census*.

Source: Record linkage from Middlesbrough Census Enumerators' Books, 1851–61.

Migration and the Labour Market

An analysis of in- and out-migrants by occupational sector is shown in Tables 4.3 and 4.4. Of gainfully employed males who came into the town, 4,806 between 1851 and 1861, and 7,164 between 1861 and 1871, those working in manufacturing made up as many as 86%, far outnumbering other sectors. The second highest proportion, those in the commercial sector, account for less than 10% in both periods. Of the female in-migrants, more than half were engaged in domestic service, with almost 40% in manufacturing.

The proportion of male out-migrants engaged in the manufacturing sector, including those who died, is lower than that for in-migrants by 10 points for the first period. In the second decade, the rate is almost the same as that of in-migrants. Of those 4,208 workers who left the town or died between 1861 and 1871, 86% had been engaged in manufacturing. The percentage of male out-migrants from the commercial sector during the first decade, 18.5%, is double that of in-migrants from that same group, though in real numbers, more migrated inwards, 464 compared with 289 out-migrants. Proportions of female out-migrants from manufacturing, 42% in the first decade and 37% in the second, as well as domestic services, 51% and 54%, respectively, are almost the same as for the corresponding groups of in-migrants.

The proportionate imbalance between males in the commercial sector entering and leaving the town had the effect of shifting the industrial structure further towards manufacturing. At least one-half (50.9%) of all male in-migrants engaged in manufacturing worked in the iron industry, whereas of male out-migrants, 1851–61, 36% of those in manufacturing came from that industry. Of female in-migrants and out-migrants in manufacturing,

Table 4.4. Occupational Structure of In- and Out-migrants, 1861–71

Manufacturing	Commercial	Agricultural	Domestic	Professional	Total
In-migrants					
Male					
6,173	634	47	59	251	7,164
(86.2%)	(8.8%)	(0.7%)	(0.8%)	(3.5%)	(100.0%)
Female					
527	18	8	776	96	1,425
(37.0%)	(1.3 %)	(0.6%)	(54.4%)	(6.7%)	(100.0%)
Out-migrants[a]					
Male					
3,598	390	74	18	128	4,208
(85.5%)	(9.3%)	(1.8%)	(0.4%)	(3.0%)	(100.0%)
Female					
325	6	4	475	77	887
(36.6%)	(0.7%)	(0.4%)	(53.6%)	(8.7%)	(100.0%)

Note: [a]Including those who died between the censuses. Occupational classification is based on the system developed by Woollard, *Classification of Occupations in the 1881 Census.*

Source: Record linkage from Middlesbrough Census Enumerators' Books, 1861–71.

proportions working in the iron industry were as low as 6.4% for in-migrants and 3.6% for out-migrants. Within a decade in the mid-nineteenth century, Middlesbrough lost 1,169 male workers to out-migration or death, corresponding to 64% of those engaged in manufacturing in 1851, while it attracted 3.5 times as many, 4,085 males, into local manufacturing. These account for 80% of those employed in the sector in 1861.

During the second period, from 1861 to 1871, of all gainfully employed in-migrant males, 32.3% were ironworkers, in contrast to 50% of their equivalents in the previous period. Numbers from the manufacturing workforce who left the town or died during this time, 3,598 in all, comprise a larger share, 71%, of that sector at the start of the decade, than during the first period. Meanwhile, the town drew in 1.7 times as many to the manufacturing workforce, as those leaving or dying. These in-migrants made up 72% of employees in manufacturing in 1871. In addition, our calculations from census data reveal that 48.9%, a much higher proportion of those engaged in the manufacturing sector than was the case in the previous decade, had been employed in the iron industry before they left the town. The occupational patterns observed in these two decades suggest that by the mid-1860s, Middlesbrough had emerged as the major iron-making centre of the region and had become an 'Export Base' as defined by Location Theory.[15]

[15] Cf. Andrews, 'Mechanics of the Urban Economic Base', p. 161; Hudson, 'Regional Perspective', p. 22; Hudson, *Industrial Revolution*, p. 102; Pollard, *Peaceful Conquest*, p. 39; North, 'Location Theory and Regional Economic Growth', p. 248; Piore and Sabel, *Second Industrial Divide*, pp. 28–35, 213–21; Porter, *On Competition*, pp. 237–45; Wilson and Popp, *Industrial Clusters and Regional Business Networks*, p. 3; Marshall, *Principles of Economics*, pp. 268–9; Isard, 'General

Table 4.5. Birthplaces of In-migrant Ironworkers, 1851–71

Country	Puddlers	Engineers	Moulders	Labourers
1851–61				
England	181 (48.1)	182 (81.6)	161 (84.7)	308 (40.5)
Wales	110 (29.3)	5 (2.3)	4 (2.1)	19 (2.5)
Ireland	62 (16.5)	6 (2.7)	4 (2.1)	397 (52.1)
Scotland	9 (2.4)	17 (7.6)	8 (4.2)	13 (1.7)
Foreign	2 (0.5)	2 (0.9)	2 (1.1)	9 (1.2)
Unknown	12 (3.2)	11 (4.9)	11 (5.8)	15 (2.0)
Total	376 (100.0)	223 (100.0)	190 (100.0)	761 (100.0)
1861–71				
England	139 (43.7)	375 (88.9)	192 (89.3)	305 (52.4)
Wales	33 (10.4)	5 (1.2)	6 (2.8)	9 (1.6)
Ireland	123 (38.7)	20 (4.7)	7 (3.3)	251 (43.1)
Scotland	20 (6.3)	14 (3.3)	7 (3.3)	9 (1.5)
Foreign	– (–)	6 (1.4)	1 (0.4)	7 (1.2)
Unknown	3 (0.9)	2 (0.5)	2 (0.9)	1 (0.2)
Total	318 (100.0)	422 (100.0)	215 (100.0)	582 (100.0)

Note: Percentages in parentheses.

Source: Record linkage from Middlesbrough Census Enumerators' Books, 1851–61 and 1861–71.

Skilled, semi-skilled and unskilled workers were recruited from all over the country, though a skill-specific migration pattern from other iron-making centres in England and Wales is especially marked. This pattern is different from the short-distance movements of unskilled labourers from nearby rural and urban areas, and from the large numbers of Irish migrants. The supply of, and demand for, unskilled non-Irish labourers could be met within a local labour market, whereas the requirements for highly skilled labour meant extending a search beyond the local, to regional and national levels.[16]

An unskilled labour force, lacking manual dexterity or training but fully able to carry and to perform other odd jobs, was quite abundant in the surrounding rural areas. There was a reservoir of agricultural labourers in the North Riding of Yorkshire and across the River Tees in Co. Durham, in the countryside and in the many large and small towns. Middlesbrough's staple iron and steel industry, and the railways, heavily depended on this unskilled workforce.

The overall driving force upon in-migrants was clearly the rapid growth in employment opportunities for skilled and unskilled workers, as well as the higher wages offered by the expanding iron and steel industry. It seems

---

Theory of Location and Space-Economy', p. 483; 'Some Locational Factors in the Iron and Steel Industry', pp. 203–15; Hoover, *Location of Economic Activity*, pp. 7–9, 15–115.

[16] For trends in internal migration in England and Wales, particularly in South Wales and the North East, based predominantly on coal and heavy industry, and changing patterns emerging in the twentieth century, see Friedlander and Roshier, 'Study of Internal Migration', pp. 265–6, 278; Richmond, 'Sociology of Migration', p. 247.

Table 4.6. Birthplaces of In-migrant Ironworkers from England, 1851–71

Counties	Puddlers	Engineers	Moulders	Blacksmith	Labourers
1851–61					
Durham	14 (7.3)	67 (36.8)	57 (35.4)	30 (35.7)	28 (9.4)
Yorkshire	15 (7.9)	50 (27.5)	49 (30.4)	42 (50.0)	148 (49.7)
Staffordshire	50 (26.2)	7 (3.8)	13 (8.1)	1 (1.2)	21 (7.0)
Worcestershire	5 (2.6)	2 (1.1)	18 (11.2)	1 (1.2)	8 (2.7)
Monmouthshire	53 (27.8)	2 (1.1)	1 (0.6)	– (–)	6 (2.0)
Northumberland	6 (3.1)	21 (11.6)	12 (7.5)	3 (3.6)	8 (2.7)
Others	48 (25.1)	33 (18.1)	11 (6.8)	7 (8.3)	79 (26.5)
Total	191 (100.0)	182 (100.0)	161 (100.0)	84 (100.0)	298 (100.0)
1861–71					
Durham	26 (20.2)	77 (21.3)	51 (27.7)	29 (22.0)	35 (11.8)
Yorkshire	37 (28.7)	115 (31.8)	46 (25.0)	58 (43.9)	112 (37.8)
Staffordshire	22 (17.0)	13 (3.6)	15 (8.1)	2 (1.5)	5 (1.7)
Worcestershire	2 (1.6)	6 (1.7)	19 (10.3)	– (–)	3 (1.0)
Monmouthshire	– (–)	1 (0.3)	4 (2.2)	– (–)	3 (1.0)
Northumberland	7 (5.4)	17 (4.7)	20 (10.9)	10 (7.6)	9 (3.1)
Others	35 (27.1)	132 (36.6)	29 (15.8)	33 (25.0)	129 (43.6)
Total	129 (100.0)	361 (100.0)	184 (100.0)	132 (100.0)	296 (100.0)

Note: Percentages in parentheses.

Source: Record linkage from Middlesbrough Census Enumerators' Books, 1851–61 and 1861–71.

unlikely, particularly in the case of skilled and semi-skilled ironworkers, that they would migrate into the town at random, without any particular prospect of employment and accommodation. Networks of communication must have operated between areas requiring and supplying labour and technology. It is often suggested that industrial South Wales had close links with Middlesbrough in the latter half of the nineteenth century, in terms of iron- and steel-making technology and personnel. John Vaughan of the Bolckow and Vaughan Iron Co. had once been employed at the Dowlais Ironworks in Glamorganshire, and he recruited Edward Williams and E. Windsor Richards, both from Merthyr Tydfil, as managers.[17]

The origins and migration patterns of those engaged in the town's staple trade, the iron and steel industry, can be analysed in more detail. The industrial cauldron of Middlesbrough drew in thousands of people in the latter half of the nineteenth century, from all over Britain and even from Europe. The geographical distribution of birthplaces of these ironworkers is shown in Table 4.5. Between 1851 and 1861, 30% of the iron puddlers were from Wales. Adding in those from Monmouthshire, 53 in number, increases to 43.4% this figure, which reflects a considerable distance movement to

---

[17] Briggs, *Victorian Cities*, p. 255; Pooley, 'Welsh Migration to England', pp. 298–303; 'Longitudinal Study of Migration', pp. 149–70; Gwynne and Sill, 'Welsh Immigration into Middlesbrough', pp. 19–22; Gwynne and Sill, 'Census Enumeration Books', pp. 74–9; Gott, *Henry Bolckow*, pp. 23–4; Lillie, *History of Middlesbrough*, p. 97.

Table 4.7. Marital Status of In-migrant and Persistent Skilled and Semi-skilled Workers, 1861–71

Proportion Ever Married of In-migrant Skilled & Semi-skilled Workers			*Proportion Ever Married of Persistent Skilled & Semi-skilled Workers*		
Age	*No.*	*%*	*Age*	*No.*	*%*
15–19	1	1.0	15–19	–	–
20–24	47	33.6	20–24	19	24.7
25–29	115	66.5	25–29	25	43.9
30–34	95	70.9	30–34	37	84.1
35–39	64	82.1	35–39	37	92.5
40–44	45	84.9	40–44	34	97.1
45–49	24	82.8	45–49	31	94.1
50–54	24	85.7	50–54	17	100.0
55–59	22	91.7	55–59	6	85.7
60–64	4	80.0	60–64	7	100.0
65–69	2	66.7	65–69	8	100.0
70–	1	50.0	70–	2	100.0
Total	444	57.6	Total	223	55.1

Source: Record linkage from Middlesbrough Census Enumerators' Books, 1861–71.

Middlesbrough. Glamorgan, from which came 34 puddlers, was of course an important centre of Welsh iron. It is also notable that many Irish puddlers, accounting for 16.5% of incomers in this occupational group, migrated into Middlesbrough. In the next decade, Irish puddlers had come to predominate over the Welsh, comprising nearly 40% of this set of incomers.[18]

It is worthy of note that, as illustrated in Table 4.6, of the incoming English puddlers during the first decade, those from nearby counties, Durham and Yorkshire itself, made up only 15.2%, while Staffordshire, a centre of British iron production at this time, provided 26.2%. By the second decade, Durham and Yorkshire supplied almost one-half of the English-born puddlers. Yet it seems to have remained the case that most longer-distance movement was undertaken by those with marketable skills, knowledge of employment opportunities and most probably access to transport.[19]

Comparing proportions of men ever married among the skilled or semi-skilled, with the rate for unskilled labourers, it seems that in the in-migrant population, whether or not they came to the town unattached and formed families afterwards between censuses, the nuptiality of skilled and semi-skilled workers tended to be higher than that of the unskilled. Between 1861 and 1871, overall proportions ever married were 47.4% among in-migrant Irish labourers, and 46.7% in the equivalent non-Irish group. For in-migrant skilled and semi-skilled workers, the rate was 57.6%. It could be surmised

---

18 With respect to in- and out-migration in Glamorganshire, 1851 to 1951, see Friedlander and Roshier, 'Study of Internal Migration', pp. 263, 265.

19 Hudson, 'Regional Perspective', p. 22; Pollard, *Peaceful Conquest*, p. 36.

Table 4.8. Marital Status and Relationship to Household Head of In-migrant
Welsh and Irish Puddlers, 1851–71

Marital Status of Welsh Puddlers			*Marital Status of Irish Puddlers*		
Age	*No.*	*%*	*Age*	*No.*	*%*
15–19	–	–	15–19	–	–
20–24	7	17.1	20–24	4	19.0
25–29	19	55.9	25–29	13	32.5
30–34	23	85.2	30–34	15	53.6
35–39	17	100.0	35–39	3	33.3
40–44	14	87.5	40–44	4	36.4
45–49	1	50.0	45–49	4	100.0
50–54	5	83.3	50–54	–	–
55–59	–	–	55–59	1	100.0
60–64	2	100.0	60–64	–	–
Total	88	54.0	Total	44	36.1
Relations to Heads of In-migrant Welsh Puddlers			*Relations to Heads of In-migrant Irish Puddlers*		
Relation	*No.*	*%*	*Relation*	*No.*	*%*
Head	56	50.5	Head	35	28.7
Lodgers and Boarders	33	29.7	Lodgers and Boarders	70	57.4
Others	22	19.8	Others	17	13.9
Total	111	100.0	Total	122	100.0

Source: Record linkage from Middlesbrough Census Enumerators' Books, 1851–61 and 1861–71.

that economic opportunities during the zenith of Cleveland's iron industry were substantial enough that workers, and above all skilled men, would risk moving their entire household. Adult males who migrated alone into the town could similarly afford to form their own household.

The differences in nuptiality between skilled, semi-skilled and unskilled were most marked among younger in-migrants. Table 4.7 shows the proportions ever married in the 20–24 and 25–29 age groups of skilled and semi-skilled workers between 1861 and 1871 as 33.6 and 66.5%, respectively, while those for Irish unskilled labourers were 6.5 and 25.5%. Among non-Irish labourers, rates were 20.0% for those aged 20–24, and 48.4% aged 25–29. Although regional variations in marital practices should be taken into account, it is of interest to note that almost the same pattern of family migration is to be found among upper social classes in mid-nineteenth-century German cities.[20]

The overall proportion ever married of Welsh and Monmouthshire puddlers in the first decade was 54% (see Table 4.8). The proportion ever married among those from Ireland, predominant in the second decade, was

---

[20] Langewiesche and Lenger, 'Internal Migration', pp. 92–3.

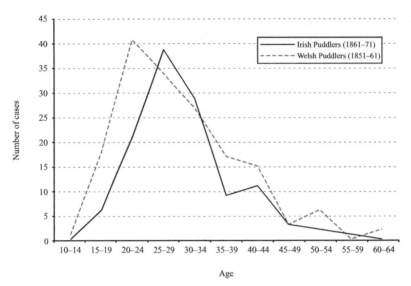

Figure 4.9. Age Structure of In-migrant Welsh and Irish Puddlers, 1851–71

considerably lower, 36%. Many more young and middle-aged Welsh puddlers were married before they came to Middlesbrough, than was the case for the Irish. The married rates among Welsh puddlers were 56% (age 25–29), 85% (30–34) and 100% (35–39), with the corresponding Irish figures 33%, 54% and 33%, respectively.

In 1861, more than one-half of in-migrant Welsh puddlers were recorded as head of their own household, with 30% living as lodgers or boarders. Of all in-migrant Irish puddlers in 1871, as few as 29% were household heads, while the rate of lodgers and boarders was double that of their Welsh equivalents in 1861, at 57%. Although the recent single in-migrant Irish puddlers were more likely to live in Middlesbrough as lodgers, they were also older than their Welsh counterparts, as is shown in Figure 4.9.

A study of the birthplaces of children in families of in-migrant Welsh and Irish puddlers offers some explanation for this last phenomenon. The census records birthplaces of 155 children in 72 families of Welsh or Monmouthshire origin, and 150 children in 60 Irish families. From this we can see that more than one-half, 54.2%, of children of Welsh puddlers who came into the town between 1851 and 1861 had been born in Wales, with 31% born in Middlesbrough and 12% in other English parishes. Of the children born in Wales, many were from Merthyr Tydfil or Dowlais, as presented in Table 4.10.

As few as 7% of the Irish puddlers' offspring, in contrast, were from the same home town or village as their parents. The majority, 46%, were born in Middlesbrough. A further 27% of the children of Irish puddlers were born in other English parishes; of these, more than half (57%) had been born in Co. Durham. A further 17% of the total number of children had been born in

Table 4.10. Birthplaces of Offspring of In-migrant Welsh and
Irish Puddlers, 1851–71

Offspring of In-migrant Welsh Puddlers (1851–61)		*Offspring of In-migrant Irish Puddlers (1861–71)*	
Birthplaces	*No. of Cases*	*Birthplaces*	*No. of Cases*
Middlesbrough	48 (31.0%)	Middlesbrough	69 (46.0%)
Durham (Witton Park, etc.)	8 (5.2%)	Durham (Bury Edge & Darlington, etc.)	23 (15.3%)
Northumberland (Newcastle, etc.)	6	Yorkshire (Sheffield, etc.)	11
Other England	5	Other England	7
England Total excl. Middlesbrough	19 (12.2%)	England Total excl. Middlesbrough	41 (27.4%)
Scotland	2 (1.3%)	Scotland	25 (16.7%)
Merthyr Tydfill	11	Ireland (Westneath, Coulbrig, etc.)	11 (7.3%)
Dowlais	10	Wales	2 (1.3%)
Others	63	Unknown	2 (1.3%)
Wales incl. Monmouthshire	84 (54.2%)	Total	150 (100.0%)
France	2 (1.3%)		
Total	155 (100.0%)		

Source: Record linkage from Middlesbrough Census Enumerators' Books, 1851–61 and 1861–71.

Scotland. In all probability, therefore, many Irish puddlers had left their own birthplace alone, perhaps moving first to other centres of the iron industry, for instance, Co. Durham or Scotland, where they acquired skills in puddling. From these places they would migrate stepwise to Middlesbrough, where many of them formed households. This would explain why they tended to be older than their Welsh counterparts. Conversely, Welsh puddlers were more likely to have trained at home and to migrate directly into Middlesbrough as independent married workers.

Other skilled and semi-skilled workers such as engineers and moulders showed a different migration profile from that of puddlers. Middlesbrough in the mid-nineteenth century recruited more than 80% of its engineers from within England, 64% of the total from the adjacent counties of Durham (36.8%) and Yorkshire (27.5%). Of moulders, 85% were from England, with Durham (35.4%) and Yorkshire (30.4%) providing 66% overall. This tendency was even more pronounced in the next decade. Almost 90% of engineers and moulders arrived from elsewhere in England, 53% of both groups being from Co. Durham or Yorkshire. Among other skilled workers, for example blacksmiths, places of origin were almost the same as those of engineers and moulders. Most, 83% or more, came from places in England, with Durham and Yorkshire again accounting for high proportions, 86%

of the English in-migrant blacksmiths for the first decade and 66% for the second. Short distance migration into Middlesbrough predominated at least until 1861, although after that there was a marked change in the pattern, with much higher proportions recruited from more distant places in South Wales, Staffordshire, and so on.[21]

In total and irrespective of age, the ever-married proportion among in-migrant skilled and semi-skilled workers such as blacksmiths, engineers and moulders, was higher than in the same group within the persistent community. This is shown in Table 4.7, above. It is especially true among younger men, aged 20–29, who came into the town between 1861 and 1871. These were the most migration-prone age groups among the in-migrant population, as we have seen. The proportion ever married among them was 34% (aged 20–24) and 67% (aged 25–29), in contrast to 25% and 44% for those who stayed. Abundant employment and higher wages during the boom in the town's iron industry appear to have attracted many young married couples. The pull of perceived opportunity in Middlesbrough seems to have been strong.

In both decades, 1851–61 and 1861–71, more than one-half of in-migrant blacksmiths, engineers and moulders were married, as opposed to 36% of Irish puddlers who moved into the town between 1861 and 1871. As Pooley suggests, skilled and semi-skilled workers, like the engineers employed in heavy industry, tended to be rather older than the norm and would move usually over very short distances. In their mobility characteristics they were more similar to textile workers than to miners.[22]

Analysis of the birthplaces of unskilled or casual labourers employed in iron and steel, however, show that in the first decade only 41% of such in-migrants originated in England, and 52% during the second period. These figures are markedly lower than the levels of English-born among skilled and semi-skilled in-migrants (see Table 4.5). Almost 60% of these unskilled arrivals in the first decade, and 50% in the second, came from the adjacent English counties of Durham and Yorkshire (see Table 4.6). Most in-migrant unskilled labourers were born in Ireland. The total number of Irish labourers in Middlesbrough's ironworks in the first decade was 397, accounting for 52.1% of all in-migrant labourers, and 251 (43.1%) in the second. Similar variations in birthplace by occupational group were observed in mid-Victorian Liverpool.[23]

Comparing the age structure of male Irish labourers employed at the ironworks with other in-migrant labourers in that industry, the non-Irish group tends to have been older. The age profile of Irish in-migrant labourers between 1851 and 1861 peaked in the age group 20–24. If the next highest age group

21 Redford, *Labour Migration in England*, p. 189. For significant migrations within the county of Yorkshire during the period, see Friedlander and Roshier, 'Study of Internal Migration', p. 257.
22 Pooley and Turnbull, *Migration and Mobility in Britain*, pp. 70, 89.
23 Lawton, 'Mobility in Nineteenth-century British Cities', pp. 212–13.

Table 4.11. Marital Status and Relationship to Household Head of Incoming Irish and Non-Irish Labourers, 1861–71

Proportion Ever Married of In-migrant Irish Labourers			Proportion Ever Married of In-migrant Non-Irish Labourers		
Age	No.	%	Age	No.	%
15–19	–	–	15–19	–	–
20–24	3	6.5	20–24	16	20.0
25–29	14	25.5	25–29	30	48.4
30–34	22	50.0	30–34	26	68.4
35–39	24	77.4	35–39	18	66.7
40–44	17	60.7	40–44	13	76.5
45–49	10	76.9	45–49	19	76.0
50–54	10	90.9	50–54	9	81.8
55–59	6	100.0	55–59	8	80.0
60–64	2	100.0	60–64	8	80.0
65–69	–	–	65–69	–	–
70–	1	100.0	70–	1	100.0
Total	109	47.4	Total	148	46.7

Relations to Head of In-migrant Irish Labourers			Relation to Head of In-migrant Non–Irish Labourers		
Relation	No.	%	Relation	No.	%
Head	94	37.1	Head	113	38.4
Lodgers and Boarders	137	54.2	Lodgers and Boarders	104	35.4
Others	22	8.7	Others	77	26.2
Total	253	100.0	Total	294	100.0

Source: Record linkage from Middlesbrough Census Enumerators' Books, 1861–71.

of 25–29 is added, it can be seen that almost 50% of these Irish labourers who had migrated recently were relatively young, aged 20–29. In the case of non-Irish labourers, the age group 25–29 was predominant.

The difference in age structure between skilled and unskilled labourers can be seen more clearly through a comparison of the age distribution of puddlers with that of non-Irish labourers employed in the iron industry. Puddlers show a clustering in the 20–24 age group which accounts for 27% of all age groups, whereas the peak age group for non-Irish unskilled in-migrants working in the iron industry is in the 25–29 group. The distribution shows more smooth downward lines towards higher age groups than is the case for the puddlers, and with a hump in the age group 35–39.

As regards marital status, Table 4.11 shows that proportions ever married of the in-migrant male Irish labourer group, especially among the younger ones aged 20–29, were lower than those for non-Irish in-migrant labourers. Almost one-half of non-Irish labourers aged 25–29 who came into Middlesbrough between 1861 and 1871 were married or widowed, whereas only 25.5% of in-migrant Irish labourers were married. If we compare the proportions ever married among the in-migrant Irish labourers in those younger age groups, 20–24 and 25–29, with those for the skilled and semi-skilled workers already noted, in both decades many more Irish unskilled labourers employed in the iron industry remained single, than did the skilled and semi-skilled in corresponding age groups.

This tendency was more evident in the second decade, from 1861 to 1871, when as low a proportion as 6.5% of in-migrant Irish labourers in the age group 20–24 were married, while 33.6% of skilled and semi-skilled workers were married at that age. Similarly, 25.5% of Irish labourers aged 25–29 who had migrated into the town in the same period were married or widowed, in contrast to 66.5% of all skilled and semi-skilled in-migrant workers. Unsurprisingly, the proportion of lodgers and boarders among Irish labourers was much higher, 41.1% in the first and 54.2% in the second period, compared with 28.7% and 35.4%, respectively, among non-Irish in-migrant labourers.

Taking into account also the geographical distribution of in-migrants previously examined, it follows that longer distance movement was undertaken mainly by those with higher skills who tended to come from areas where the labour market resembled that of Middlesbrough, as was the case with the Welsh puddlers we have considered. Thus skilled or semi-skilled workers were supplied from certain, limited, areas of the country where a particular industry was located, irrespective of distance, while non-Irish unskilled labourers were recruited from within relatively short-distance areas. Short-distance migrants from the surrounding region closest to Middlesbrough were relatively older than the skilled or semi-skilled ironworkers.

Skill-specific migration, or *niche* migration as some researchers refer to it, appears to have prevailed in this pattern observed in Middlesbrough. Table 4.12 shows the distribution across English and Welsh counties of all Middlesbrough-born people recorded in the 1881 census. The table draws upon information available from the History Data Service at the University of Essex.[24] In all, 10,796 individuals were identified who were born in Middlesbrough and had moved out before 1881 to settle elsewhere in England and Wales. Aside from neighbouring Co. Durham and Yorkshire, almost 50% of the remainder of Middlesbrough-born out-migrants are to be found in Lancashire, Northumberland, Cumberland, Staffordshire, Lincolnshire and Glamorgan. These places, at some distance from Middlesbrough, are counties where iron and steel then predominated.

This distribution matches quite closely the geographic origins of people moving into Middlesbrough between 1851 and 1871, as shown in Table 4.13. The table compares main counties of origin of in-migrants to the town between 1861 and 1871, with the destinations of people moving out from Middlesbrough before the 1881 census. Excepting the nearest counties, Yorkshire and Durham, eight of the 10 highest frequency counties are the

---

[24] History Data Service database (old version).

Table 4.12. Middlesbrough-born Population Living in England and Wales, 1881

County	Born in Middlesbrough	Population[a]	Ratio[b]
Durham	3,221	887,859	362.8
Yorkshire	4,926	2,945,064	167.3
Lancashire	587	3,519,000	16.7
Middlesex	285	2,941,311	9.7
Northumberland	281	439,914	63.9
Surrey	162	1,452,947	11.1
Cumberland	140	254,055	55.1
Staffordshire	138	949,076	14.4
Kent	122	1,019,072	12.0
Lincolnshire	109	477,190	22.8
Norfolk	106	454,941	23.3
Glamorgan (Wales)	60	515,619	11.6
Cheshire	58	654,977	8.9
Warwickshire	55	754,512	7.3
Essex	55	590,092	9.3
Derbyshire	52	468,351	11.1
Hampshire	42	606,455	6.9
Worcestershire	39	386,683	10.1
Nottinghamshire	30	398,389	7.5
Suffolk	29	364,909	7.9
Cambridgeshire	27	188,545	14.3
Gloucestershire	27	583,353	4.6
Sussex	22	501,322	4.4
Monmouthshire	20	214,145	9.3
Berkshire	20	222,152	9.0
Leicestershire	19	328,883	5.8
Devon	17	615,439	2.8
Westmorland	15	64,970	23.1
Wiltshire	15	218,596	6.9
Dorset	12	194,198	6.2
Bedfordshire	10	153,124	6.5
Royal Navy	9	29,747	30.3
Oxfordshire	8	184,521	4.3
Cornwall	8	336,622	2.4
Somerset	8	368,019	2.2
Shropshire	7	256,481	2.7
Flintshire (Wales)	6	81,676	7.3
Carnarvonshire (Wales)	6	120,678	5.0
Herefordshire	6	123,122	4.9
Hertfordshire	6	205,416	2.9
Denbighshire (Wales)	5	117,283	4.3
Huntingdon	5	60,632	8.2
Buckinghamshire	5	179,417	0.6
Breconshire (Wales)	4	59,640	6.7
Anglesey (Wales)	3	52,756	5.7

Continued

Table 4.12. Continued

County	Born in Middlesbrough	Population[a]	Ratio[b]
Pembrokeshire (Wales)	3	94,348	3.2
Carmarthenshire (Wales)	3	126,495	2.4
Rutland	2	21,725	9.2
Merionshire (Wales)	1	54,233	1.8
Cardiganshire (Wales)	0	72,455	0.0
Montgomery (Wales)	0	68,867	0.0
Guernsey	0	34,276	0.0
Isle of Man	0	56,066	0.0
Jersey	0	53,098	0.0
Radnorshire (Wales)	0	24,506	0.0
Miscellaneous	0	1,284	0.0
Total	10,796	26,148,506	41.3

Notes: [a]History Data Service database (old version). [b]Ratio per 100,000 persons (records).
Source: History Data Service database (old version).

Table 4.13. Places of Origin of In-migrants, 1861–71, and Residence of Middlesbrough-born People, 1881

In-migrants (1861–71)		Middlesbrough-born People Recorded in 1881 Census of England & Wales	
Origin		Destination	
Yorkshire	8,023	Yorkshire	4,926
Durham	3,031	Durham	3,221
*Northumberland	598	*Lancashire	587
*Lancashire	441	*Middlesex	285
*Staffordshire	373	*Northumberland	281
*Middlesex	283	Surrey	162
*Cumberland	281	*Cumberland	140
*Lincolnshire	273	*Staffordshire	138
*Norfolk	265	Kent	122
Worcestershire	193	*Lincolnshire	109
*Glamorgan	138	*Norfolk	106
Monmouthshire	121	*Glamorgan	60

Note: *Indicates counties appearing in both columns.
Source: Record linkage from Middlesbrough Census Enumerators' Books, 1861–71; Census Enumerators' Books for England & Wales, 1881.

same in both lists. It appears that an in- and out-migration network operated where labour markets were similar, based on expertise in certain industrial and technological occupations. There was a frequent circulation of labour between these areas at this time, and at least for skilled workers, their migration was apparently well-structured and well-organized, not at all a random outpouring.

Table 4.14. Irish In-migrants, Persistent Population, and Out-migrants, 1851–71

	1851			*1861*	
Out-migrants[a]	Male	150	Persistent	Male	51
	Female	78		Female	36
	Total	228 (72.4%)		Total	87 (4.9%)
Persistent	Male	51	In-migrants	Male	1,056
	Female	36		Female	619
	Total	87 (27.6%)		Total	1,675 (94.7%)
			Children born	Male	1
			After 1851	Female	5
				Total	6 (0.4%)
Total	Male	201	Total	Male	1,108
	Female	114		Female	660
	Total	315 (100.0%)		Total	1,768 (100.0%)
	1861			*1871*	
Out-migrants[a]	Male	878	Persistent	Male	232
	Female	513		Female	150
	Total	1,391 (78.5%)		Total	82 (14.5%)
Persistent	Male	232	In-migrants	Male	1,520
	Female	150		Female	725
	Total	382 (21.5%)		Total	2,245 (85.1%)
			Children born	Male	5
			After 1861	Female	5
				Total	10 (0.4%)
Total	Male	1,110	Total	Male	1,757
	Female	663		Female	880
	Total	1,773 (100.0%)		Total	2,637 (100.0%)

Note: [a]Including those who died between the censuses.

Source: Record Linkage from Middlesbrough Census Enumerators' Books, 1851–61 and 1861–71.

Irish Migrants

As already shown, Irish migrants into Middlesbrough in the late-nineteenth century exhibited distinctive migration patterns compared with the overall migrant population. Table 4.14 breaks down Irish migrants during the periods 1851–61 and 1861–71, into those moving in, those who stayed, and ones who left. Of the total Irish population of 1,768 in 1861, as many as 95% had arrived in the town since 1851, with only 5% present in Middlesbrough 10 years earlier.

Similarly, 85% of the total Irish population of 2,637 in 1871 had come to Middlesbrough during the previous decade, while the group present since before the 1861 census accounted for only 15%, much lower than the settlement ratio for the total population (including Irish-born) in 1871. Thus, both in 1861 and 1871, almost all the Irish residents of Middlesbrough were newcomers who had moved there in the past 10 years. The sex ratio of Irish in-migrants

Table 4.15. Sex Ratio of Irish and Non-Irish In-migrants, 1851–71

| | | In-migrant Irish | | | In-migrant Non-Irish | |
		No.	Ratio		No.	Ratio
1851–61	Male	1,055		Male	6,355	
	Female	619		Female	5,772	
	Total	1,675	171	Total	12,127	110
1861–71	Male	1,520		Male	8,839	
	Female	725		Female	8,151	
	Total	2,245	210	Total	16,990	108

Source: Record linkage from Middlesbrough Census Enumerators' Books, 1851–61 and 1861–71.

Table 4.16. Out-migration Rates of Irish and Non-Irish Populations in Middlesbrough, 1851–61

	1851	Population	Out-migrants[a]	Persistent	Out-migration Rates[a]
Irish	Male	201	150	51	74.6%
	Female	114	78	36	68.4%
	Total	315	228	87	72.4%
Non-Irish	Male	3,580	2,186	1,394	61.1%
	Female	3,495	2,249	1,246	64.3%
	Total	7,075	4,435	2,640	62.7%

Note: [a]Including those who died between the censuses.

Source: Record linkage from Middlesbrough Census Enumerators' Books, 1851–61.

between 1861 and 1871 is remarkable, as high as 210, comparing with a sex ratio among non-Irish migrants in this period of 108 (see Table 4.15).

In both decades, proportions of Irish-born males who left the town or died were significantly higher than those for Middlesbrough's male inhabitants as a whole, by almost 15 points, measuring 75% in the first and 80% in the second decade.[25]

These trends are shown more clearly in Table 4.16, comparing Irish out-migration with rates found in the non-Irish population. Between 1851 and 1861, the out-migration rate (including deaths) for males born in Ireland was 74.6%, as we have seen, whereas the rate for non-Irish was 61.1%. During the second decade, 80% of the Irish left the town or died, while for the non-Irish the figure was 63.4%. The same tendency to high mobility was observed in the Liverpool Irish population in the late-nineteenth century.[26]

These figures are evidence of how a substantial level of Irish immigration turned into an exodus. The number of Irish immigrants who stayed quite briefly in Middlesbrough was large. They did not establish roots in the

25 For the higher mortality among the Irish-born, see Pooley and Turnbull, 'Migration and Urbanization in North-West England', p. 189.
26 Lawton, 'Mobility in Nineteenth-century British Cities', p. 220.

new community. For them, Middlesbrough seems to have been not only a receiving centre, but also a dispatching point from which large numbers were directed to other destinations. It seems likely, as pointed out by Richmond, that Irish migrants did not necessarily mean to settle permanently in their locality, for most of them appeared to have only short-term objectives, and a plan to return to a previous place of residence or to move elsewhere once they had satisfied their immediate aims. So for most Irish migrants, Middlesbrough was not a final destination, marking only a stop on a longer-term tour. Because of the limitations in available source material, tracing both Irish and non-Irish out-migrants to their new abodes is difficult.[27]

The level of persistence found among Middlesbrough's Irish immigrants is not necessarily a pattern replicated everywhere. In the smaller town of Stafford, with quite different industrial and occupational structures, Herson found an Irish population in this same period which was far more settled.[28] The factors determining stability and mobility among Irish and non-Irish groups are still open to question, but one factor promoting settlement may have been family and kin circumstances, irrespective of whether these ties had been formed in Ireland or after a move to England. Of 878 males born in Ireland who formed part of Middlesbrough's persistent population between 1861 and 1871, 64.4% had family commitments, whereas the remainder staying in the town were single men. Of those Irish males who moved out (or died) in the same period, 232 in all, 46.7% were married and 53.3% were single.

Significantly, a relationship which in terms of persistency and transiency between married couples and single people is very similar to that among the Middlesbrough Irish, has been shown in the inhabitants of Graz, Austria, in the late-nineteenth century. There the persistence rate of married couples was 60%, and 38% for single people, between 1857 and 1869. For men, 37% of single and 69% of those married or widowed, stayed in Graz throughout the period between 1857 and 1869. Between 1869 and 1880, 24% of single men and 28% of the married and widowed, remained in the town. At least during this earlier period, 1857 to 1869, Middlesbrough figures for persistence according to marital status are almost identical to those for Graz. Presumably this was because young single people without family or kinship ties could move more readily than older, married people with children or other dependants.[29]

How, then, did migrants find their way into a new community? By and large, initial accommodation could be obtained in lodging houses, but another possibility is that established in-migrant households would act as a reception space for newcomers, providing accommodation for single relatives or those from their home parish. Recent migration studies have suggested the importance of kinship and friendship networks in promoting migration and helping migrants settle in a new environment. It is interesting to consider whether there

27 Richmond, 'Sociology of Migration in Industrial and Post-Industrial Societies', p. 265.
28 Herson, 'Irish Migration and Settlement in Victorian Britain', pp. 90, 102.
29 Hubbard, 'Aspects of Social Mobility in Graz', pp. 6, 18, Table 3.

Table 4.17. Households as Reception Space for Incoming Migrants, 1861–71
(Households with in-migrant single relatives)

Persistent Irish Households		*In-migrant Irish Households*	
Persistent Irish Household Heads (1871–61)	132	In-migrant Irish Household Heads (1861–71)	590
Persistent Irish Households with In-migrant Single Relatives	15	In-migrant Irish Household with In-migrant Single Relatives	48
Proportion of Households Providing Accommodation to the Relatives	11.4%	Proportion of Household Providing Accommodation to the Relatives	8.1%
Persistent Non-Irish Households		*In-migrant Non-Irish Households*	
Persistent Non-Irish Household Heads (1871–61)	1,452	In-migrant Irish Household Heads (1861–71)	2,777
Persistent Non-Irish Households with In-migrant Single Relatives	202	In-migrant Non-Irish Household with In-migrant Single Relatives	404
Proportion of Households Providing Accommodation to the Relatives	13.9%	Proportion of Household Providing Accommodation to the Relatives	14.5%

Source: Record linkage from Middlesbrough Census Enumerators' Books, 1861–71

were differences between Irish and non-Irish households in providing accommodation to relatives. For the in-migrant Irish, Irish household heads already living in the town appear to have been influential in providing channels through which they might sponsor close relatives moving to Middlesbrough.[30]

Table 4.17 demonstrates that the proportion of persistent Irish household heads providing accommodation for single in-migrant relatives was slightly lower, 11.4%, than that of non-Irish household heads (13.9%). Regarding the proportion of in-migrant household heads who had arrived in the town between 1861 and 1871, those born in Ireland were far less likely to accommodate in-migrant single relatives – only 8.1% did so – than their non-Irish equivalents, 14.5% of whom had family members as lodgers.

Table 4.18 indicates the relationships of household heads to their lodgers. Brothers were the largest category in both Irish and non-Irish in-migrant households, whereas among the persistent population, whether Irish or non-Irish, a range of relatives other than brothers was accommodated, such as nephews, nieces or grandchildren. Male siblings would have been most useful in increasing family income of in-migrant households, so that in-migrant

---

[30] Pooley and Turnbull, *Migration and Mobility in Britain*, pp. 67–8 *et passim*; MacRaild, *The Great Famine and Beyond*, pp. 124–30. Regarding the role taken by relatives and friends in migration in nineteenth-century German cities, see Langewiesche and Lenger, 'Internal Migration', p. 97; M. Dupree, 'The Provision of Social Service', p. 356.

Table 4.18. Relationship to Household Heads of Incoming Single Relatives, 1861–71

Persistent Irish Households with In-migrant Single Relatives			In-migrant Irish Households with In-migrant Single Relatives		
Nephew	6	30.0%	Brother	10	16.4%
Niece	4	20.0	Mother	7	11.5
Grandson	3	15.0	Nephew	7	11.5
Granddaughter	2	10.0	Sister	5	8.2
Others	5	25.0	Others	32	52.5
Total	20	100.0%	Total	61	100.0%
Persistent Non-Irish Households with In-migrant Single Relatives			In-migrant Non-Irish Households with In-migrant Single Relatives		
Grandson	60	22.0%	Brother	69	12.9%
Granddaughter	53	19.4	Niece	64	12.0
Niece	52	19.0	Sister	61	11.4
Nephew	31	11.3	Nephew	51	9.6
Sister	16	5.9	Mother	38	7.1
Sister-in-law	7	2.6	Grandson	38	7.1
Mother	7	2.6	Sister-in-law	29	5.4
Others	47	17.2	Others	183	34.3
Total	273	100.0%	Total	533	100.0%

Source: Record linkage from Middlesbrough Census Enumerators' Books, 1861–71.

household heads were likely to take their brothers with them initially, or invite them after settling in the new community.

It is also possible to analyse family and household structures by kin composition, within the context of migration. Table 4.19 compares these structures among the Irish and non-Irish migrants coming into Middlesbrough between 1861 and 1871, based on the Hammel–Laslett household classification scheme for household heads and their co-residential kin. It is evident from this that among the Irish migrants' households, the proportion of extended family units, that is, conjugal family units which included kin-linked relatives, and multiple-family households composed of two or more kin-linked conjugal family units, are much lower than those for the non-Irish migrant households. Extended and multiple-family units as a proportion show an incidence in the Irish households which is half that found in the non-Irish.[31]

Conversely, the proportion of solitary migrant households among the Irish, as high as 5%, besides the no-family households where there are co-residents but no conjugal family unit can be discerned, which account for almost 3%, is markedly higher than those for non-Irish migrants. Similarly the Irish migrants' households which stayed at least for a decade between 1861 and 1871 have a much lower proportion of extended family units and a higher ratio of solitaries, than do those observed among non-Irish households. For

---

[31] Laslett, 'Family and Household', pp. 516–23.

Table 4.19. Household and Family Structure of In-migrant Irish and Non-Irish Populations in Middlesbrough, 1861–71

	Irish In-migrants		Non-Irish In-migrants	
	No.	%	No.	%
Solitaries	30	5.1	25	0.9
No-family households	16	2.7	51	1.8
Simple-family households	466	79.0	2,008	72.3
Extended-family units	60	10.1	576	20.8
Multiple-family households	14	2.4	117	4.2
Indeterminate	4	0.7	0	0.0
Total	590	100.0	2,777	100.0

Source: Record linkage from Middlesbrough Census Enumerators' Books, 1861–71.

Table 4.20. Out-migration Rates of Irish and Non-Irish Iron-workers from Middlesbrough, 1851–71

		No. of cases	Out-migrants[a]	Out-migration Rates (%)[a]
1851–61				
Irish	Skilled	11	10	90.9
	Unskilled	127	100	78.7
	Total	138	110	79.7
Non-Irish	Skilled	271	174	64.2
	Unskilled	230	150	65.2
	Total	501	324	64.7
1861–71				
Irish	Skilled	110	99	90.9
	Unskilled	752	605	80.5
	Total	862	704	81.7
Non-Irish	Skilled	1,063	779	73.3
	Unskilled	821	608	74.4
	Total	1,884	1,387	73.6

Note: [a]Including those who died between the censuses.

Source: Record linkage from Middlesbrough Census Enumerators' Books, 1851–61 and 1861–71.

both in-migrant and persistent households, the Irish show significantly higher proportion of solitaries and no-family households as well as simple-family households. An explanation most likely lies in their available living space or their inherent family structure.[32]

If the persistence rates of Irish ironworkers are compared to those for non-Irish workers, a very marked difference is discernible, shown in Table 4.20. Almost 80% of Irish ironworkers, skilled and unskilled, have been identified by record linkage as having left the town (or died) between 1851 and 1861,

---

[32] For kinship composition of households observed in Elmdon, Essex, in 1861, see Laslett, 'Family and Household', pp. 518–19.

Table 4.21. Out-migration Rates by Occupation of Irish and Non-Irish
Populations from Middlesbrough, 1861–71

Occupation	1861 Population		Out-migrants[a]		Out-migration Rates (%)[a]	
	Irish	Non-Irish	Irish	Non-Irish	Irish	Non-Irish
Puddler	66	332	60	283	90.9	85.2
Furnaceman[b]	16	78	16	60	100.0	76.9
Engineer	6	274	6	192	100.0	70.1
Moulder	3	259	2	151	66.7	58.3
Roller	10	73	8	59	80.0	80.8
Shingle	7	5	6	5	85.7	100.0
Iron founder	2	26	1	14	50.0	53.8
Forgeman	0	16	0	15	–	93.8
Ironworks lab.	567	578	444	414	78.3	71.6
Other lab.	185	243	161	194	87.0	79.8
Total	862	1,884	704	1,387	81.7	73.6

Notes: [a]Including those who died between censuses. [b]Blastfurnaceman, furnaceman and mill furnaceman.

Source: Record linkage from Middlesbrough Census Enumerators' Books, 1861–71.

and more than 80% between 1861 and 1871. In both periods, the variation in rates between Irish and non-Irish is much more remarkable for skilled workers.

Between 1851 and 1861, albeit from a small sample, more than 90% of Irish skilled ironworkers left the town or died, compared with only 64% of their non-Irish equivalents. Similarly in the second decade, between 1861 and 1871, 90% of the Irish skilled ironworkers left the town or died, while the rate among the non-Irish was 73%. Of the skilled workers, Irish puddlers' out-migration rates are conspicuously high in both decades, reaching 91% between 1861 and 1871, as shown in Table 4.21. It is not certain whether the high mobility of Irish ironworkers, irrespective of their level of skill, was drifting or purposeful, driven by the loss of employment or by the offer of better wages elsewhere.

It is worthy of note that at least as far as the Irish migrants were concerned, skilled or semi-skilled workers appear to have been more likely to leave than were unskilled labourers. A very similar tendency has been found in Graz, Austria, between 1857 and 1869, with 25% of skilled workers remaining, compared with 42% among the unskilled. For the non-Irish workers of Middlesbrough, difference in out-migration rates between the skilled and unskilled is not so obvious. Albeit only by a little, out-migration rates of non-Irish unskilled labourers are higher than those of skilled workers. Interestingly, among unskilled labourers employed in the ironworks, the difference in out-migration rates between Irish and non-Irish workers is not so marked as that seen among skilled ironworkers. In the second decade, of the unskilled labourers in Middlesbrough, 80% of the Irish and 74% of the non-Irish left the town or died.[33]

---

[33] Hubbard, 'Aspects of Social Mobility in Graz', p. 8.

Table 4.22. Life-course Changes in Occupation of Persistent Irish and
Non-Irish Labourers, 1861–71

Occupation in 1861	No. of Cases	Occupation in 1871	No. of Cases	%
Irish Persistent Labourers				
Labourers	182	Labourers	155	85.2
		Puddlers	4	2.2
		Ironworkers	3	1.6
		Shinglers	2	1.1
		Contractors	2	1.1
		Others	16	8.5
Total	182	Total	182	100.0
Non-Irish Persistent Labourers				
Labourers	264	Labourers	128	48.5
		Puddlers	8	3.0
		Ironworkers	4	1.5
		Moulders	4	1.5
		Engine fitters	4	1.5
		Engine men	4	1.5
		Others	112	42.4
Total	264		264	100.0

Source: Record linkage from Middlesbrough Census Enumerators' Books, 1861–71.

One factor associated with persistence seems to have been adaptability
to shifts in the local labour market. This suggests the possibility that the
rapid industrial expansion in iron and steel enabled Irish labourers to be
elevated to the ranks of the skilled or semi-skilled, moving into occupations such as puddlers, rollers, shinglers and moulders, which were learned
by on-site experience rather than through a conventional apprenticeship.
It seems, though, that Irish migrants into late nineteenth-century Middlesbrough were offered little opportunity for promotion. Table 4.22 attempts
to measure this. Although the Middlesbrough Irish did not tend to cluster in
particular geographical locations within the town, the possibilities the town
afforded Irish in-migrants for individual advancement seem to have been few.

Table 4.22 makes plain the differences in upward movement between Irish
and other labourers. Although more than half of non-Irish unskilled labourers
who can be identified in both the 1861 and 1871 Middlesbrough censuses
changed occupation during this period, as many as 85% of labourers born
in Ireland remained in the same type of work. It may be surmised that Irish
unskilled labourers did not have the same opportunity as the non-Irish to
make their way up through the social and occupational hierarchy to become
skilled, semi-skilled, independent craftsmen or self-employed. Economic
prospects for first-generation Irish labourers in Middlesbrough seem not to
have been as bright as for their non-Irish counterparts.

While as few as 15% of Irish manual workers in Middlesbrough experienced any upward shift in status between 1861 and 1871, American cities

saw higher rates of upward career mobility for manual workers, irrespective of their ethnic origins. In Boston, for example, before the middle of the nineteenth century only about 10% of the city's manual labourers could expect upward career mobility, whereas after 1850 this restriction relaxed. In post-1850 America, the same trend was seen in other cities, with widening scope for career mobility among the lower ranks of workers, irrespective of city size or population growth rates. It should also be noted that the non-Irish labourers of Middlesbrough, with an upward mobility rate of 51.5%, enjoyed better opportunities than manual labourers in certain urban communities in the United States. Between 1850 and 1860, 18% of manual labourers in Boston and 17% of those in Poughkeepsie experienced upward career mobility. The figure for the latter town between 1860 and 1870 was 18%. Atlanta registered 19% upward mobility between 1870 and 1880.[34]

If there were upward occupational mobility for Irish migrants into Middlesbrough, it seems to have been a protracted inter-generational process. Like the north-eastern Germans, and unskilled or semi-skilled ironworkers in the town of Bochum in the Ruhr, the Irish migrants in Middlesbrough apparently had little hope of being anything more than low-skilled manual workers. Although in general there was a fairly extensive job ladder up which not a few unskilled factory workers could expect to rise, the Irish labourers perhaps saw no future prospects in Middlesbrough, a plight they shared with their counterparts in America before 1850, after which restrictions on upward mobility there were relaxed. Throughout the United States, Irish immigrants 'were strongly clustered in low-skilled labouring jobs and unusually slow to climb out of them over time'.[35]

Trade Union-related Mobility

Skilled workers such as engineers, iron founders, steam engine-makers and boiler-makers showed high mobility in the nineteenth century, as Southall has shown.[36] Aided by elaborate systems of trade union benefits covering unemployment, sickness, superannuation, funeral and especially travel costs, skilled workers, often with a travelling card or certificate for finding work, moved around the branch network. Trade union funds paid a travelling benefit to itinerant members in search of work. This kind of migration was not drifting, but purposeful, organized and structured. Union members moved around in order to escape unemployment and poor working conditions in their home branches, and would seek job opportunities elsewhere using information from the union head office about the state of trade in every region

---

34 Thernstrom, *The Other Bostonians*, pp. 232–5.
35 Crew, *Town in the Ruhr*, pp. 71, 78–9; Thernstrom, *The Other Bostonians*, pp. 253–4. For social immobility experienced by Polish coal miners who had immigrated to the Ruhr district, see Klessmann, 'Long-distance Migration, Integration and Segregation', p. 106. For social mobility seen in Graz, Austria, see Hubbard, 'Aspects of Social Mobility in Graz', pp. 11–14.
36 Southall, 'Mobility, the Artisan Community and Popular Politics', p. 105; Hobsbawm, *Labouring Men*, pp. 34–54; Southall, 'The Tramping Artisan Revisits', pp. 281–3.

where there was a branch. The system facilitated the movement of unionized skilled workers by making travel arrangements and paying railway fares to destinations where the union found that employment was available.

We can infer from the workings of a similar system which existed in Germany and Austria from the early modern period that these British union members would have moved within dense and widespread branch networks. They would be provided with accommodation in receiving branches, with travel allowances and be helped to find the workplaces. Although the German and Austrian tramping system satisfied the needs of guild masters, political authorities, and of the journeymen themselves, in one main objective, especially in the nineteenth century, it differed in nature from the British one. In Germany and Austria the practice represented a means of social control by the state, a tight network of police control over the movement of migrant journeymen. In Britain, the scheme through which trade unions supported their members was based on voluntary self-help, a mutual aid principle among workers.[37]

It is not certain whether the system of travel benefits offered by trade unions in nineteenth-century Britain served to regulate the labour supply and exert control over the labour market in the way that it did in Germany. There 'it was in the context of industrial disputes that travelling as a means of influencing labour market conditions in favour of the workers was important' and 'it was used as a means of threatening employers with the withdrawal of the workforce'.[38] However it was unquestionable that this organized travel benefit system became a generally approved form of self-help against unemployment and contributed to creating a fluid and flexible labour market in Britain. If migration is defined broadly as a permanent or semi-permanent change of residence, labour mobility supported by trade unions is one type of migration. The kind of movement observed in particular among itinerant engineers, however, is a type of mobility different from the usual geographical migration involving a change of address.

A further exercise in record linkage provides information on trade union-based short-term mobility, and confirms the high mobility levels of skilled workers in Britain before the 1870s. The information was collected from monthly reports of the Amalgamated Society of Engineers (ASE) in 1868. The ASE was the largest trade union at this time, established in 1851 and embracing a membership of nearly 11,000. In 1868 it had a total of 313 branches covering England and Wales, Scotland, Ireland, Australia, New Zealand, Queensland, Canada, Malta, Turkey, America and France. The reports enable calculations of the number of mobile artisans, engineers in this case, to and from branches all over the country, and the average duration of jobs.[39]

---

37 For details of the German and Austrian systems of providing benefits through guilds and trade associations, see Ehmer, 'Tramping Artisans in Nineteenth-century Vienna', pp. 164–84.

38 Rössler, 'Travelling Workers and the German Labour Movement', p. 135.

39 Modern Records Centre, Univ. of Warwick, MSS 259/4/14/1-107; MSS 259, 63, 65-76, 104; Chase, *Early Trade Unionism*, p. 219. A significant mutual self-help system at work during the

In 1868, of 32,186 engineers who were members within the 287 United Kingdom branches of the ASE, the total number who can be categorized as mobile amounted to 14,433. Most of these belonged in the younger age group, from 21–29. The largest number moving in search of employment were aged 23, a total of 1,434 times in a year, with the second highest level of movement in engineers aged 24, 1,418 in all. Significant numbers of middle-aged engineers, aged 30–47, took advantage of the travel benefits. This suggests that the situation differed from that in Germany, where the benefits were criticized for meeting 'only the needs of the young and mobile members, many of whom ceased paying their dues and left the organization once they had been successful in finding a job or after they had completed their travelling years and got settled'. In Britain, not only young unmarried engineers but also those with families were eligible for travel benefits.[40]

Table 4.23 compares the branches of origin of migrant members of the ASE with the main destinations of those engineers. The Sheffield branch was the largest single source, with a total of 360 instances of members being dispatched elsewhere during the year, while Manchester Office was the largest recipient, accepting 733 engineers from other branches. The distribution of branches of origin followed a very similar geography to that of destinations. Thirteen of the 30 highest frequency branches in both categories are the same. It would appear that in-and-out short period mobility networks operated between these localities, like the pattern of short-term mobility observed in German and Austrian tramping journeymen in the same period.[41] Nominal record linkage of the ASE documents makes clear that among the engineers with a high propensity to move, there are examples of men who moved more than 50 times in a year between branches for employment (see Table 4.24). Their average length of stay was less than a week.

Two remarkable cases are those of engine fitters, James Alexander who was 40 years of age, and Richard Schofield, aged 33. As Table 4.25 illustrates, Alexander, a member of Lincoln branch at the beginning of the year, changed branch twice that year, from Lincoln to Ripley in Derbyshire, and from Ripley to Sunderland. He moved as many as 67 times in total in a year from his base branches, including two journeys to Middlesbrough, in September and October. The length of time employed away from his home branch totalled 242 days, accounting for more than 77% of his working days in 1868.

From his branch in Lincoln, Alexander travelled to Ripley at the end of January 1868, settling there until August. From that time he based himself in the Sunderland branch. While based at Ripley, he was travelled to 38 different branches, mainly in Northern England and Scotland. The longest stay in a branch was for 12 days, but most were for less than a week.

---

same period among German nascent trade unions, the Workers' Brotherhood, is described by Rössler, 'Travelling Workers and the German Labour Movement', pp. 127–32, *et passim*.
[40] Rössler, 'Travelling Workers and the German Labour Movement', p. 140.
[41] Ehmer, 'Tramping Artisans in Nineteenth-century Vienna', pp. 174–5.

Table 4.23. Origins and Destinations of Migrant Engineers, 1868

Origins	No. of Cases	Destinations	No. of Cases
Sheffield	360	Manchester Office	733
Wolverton	346	Liverpool	279
Lincoln	260	Sheffield	243
Worcester	235	Derby	220
Birmingham 2nd	217	Wolverhampton	217
Halifax	206	Halifax	209
Heywood	198	Nottingham	203
Belfast 2nd	187	Crewe	196
Crewe 2nd	184	Liverpool 4th	188
Manchester 4th	183	Worcester	179
Birkenhead	177	Birmingham	176
Manchester 5th	167	Lincoln	169
Derby	163	Birmingham 2nd	155
Rotherham	163	Chester	155
Newry	163	London South	152
Crewe	161	Sheffield 2nd	149
Dublin	156	Hull	148
Liverpool	153	Swindon	146
Belfast	149	Southampton	143
Manchester 3rd	149	York	138
Leigh	147	Sunderland	138
Bury	144	Wolverton	137
Hull	141	Birkenhead	136
Burnley	139	Northampton	130
Plymouth	134	Coventry	128
Ashton	133	Doncaster	128
Birmingham	130	Dublin	128
Manchester East	128	Warrington	122
Liverpool 4th	127	Bristol 2nd	120
Peterborough	127	Gloucester	120
Other Branches	9,106	Other Branches	8,975
Total	14,433	Total	14,433

Source: Modern Records Centre, Univ. of Warwick, MSS 259/4/14/1-107.

Richard Schofield, as demonstrated in Table 4.26, also changed his base branch twice in a year, from Heywood, Lancashire, to Newry in Ireland, and then to Tredegar in Monmouthshire. From each base branch, he travelled around mainly Midland branches, and into Wales and Ireland. He visited 39 different branches, and stayed at each branch for about 4 days on average, including longer stays in Manchester, for 19 days, and Birmingham and Belfast for 16 days.

While he was a member of the Tredegar branch, Schofield received benefit of 4s 8d to weather a period of unemployment. He worked away from his home branches for 164 days, more than half of his total working days in that year.

Table 4.24. Migrant Engineers, 1868

Name	Surname	Age	Trade	Origins (Branch)	Mobility	Average Staying Days
James P.	Alexander	40/42	Fitter	Lincoln	3	3.0
				Ripley	41	3.5
				Sunderland	23	3.9
Robert	Wilson	43/44	Millwright	Colne	55	2.7
James	Peach	23/24	Fitter	Plymouth	55	4.8
Clement	Gregory	28/29	Fitter	Openshaw	53	5.7
Denis	Mills	29/30	Smith	Heywood	5	2.8
				Colne	43	2.7
Armitage	Mortimer	28	Turner	Oldham 1st	48	3.2
Samuel	Stansfield	31/32	Turner	Heywood	44	2.9
John	Baxendale	46/47	Turner	Sheffield	44	6.3
Richard	Schofield	33/34	Fitter	Heywood	18	5.0
				Newry	5	3.2
				Tredegar	17	3.4
John	Jones	49/50	Smith	Stoke-on-Trent	2	7.0
				Ripley	40	5.0

Source: Modern Records Centre, Univ. of Warwick, MSS 259/4/14/1–107.

Table 4.25. Mobility Pattern of James Alexander, 1868

Month	Origins (Branches)	Card No.	Destinations (Branches)	Days Paid	£	s	d
Jan.	Lincoln	4745	Birmingham 2nd	5		8	4
	Lincoln	4745	Derby	2		3	4
	Lincoln	4745	Rugeley	2		3	4
Feb.	Ripley	4949	Huddersfield	1		1	8
	Ripley	4949	Liverpool 4th	4		6	8
	Ripley	4949	Marsden	1		1	8
	Ripley	4949	Oldham 4th	7		11	8
	Ripley	4949	Penistone	2		3	4
	Ripley	4949	Sheffield 2nd	4		6	8
	Ripley	4949	Sutton	2		3	8
	Ripley	4949	Warrington	2		3	4
Mar.	Ripley	4949	Accrington	2		3	4
	Ripley	4949	Bolton 1st	4		6	8
	Ripley	4949	Burnley	2		3	4
	Ripley	4949	Bury 2nd	2		3	4
	Ripley	4949	Dewsbury	1		1	8
	Ripley	4949	Hurtlepool	2		2	4
	Ripley	4949	Manchester 1st	3		5	0
	Ripley	4949	Middlesbro'	4		4	8
	Ripley	4949	Preston	2		3	4
	Ripley	4949	Todmorden	1		1	8
	Ripley	4949	York	4		4	8

Continued

Table 4.25. Continued

Month	Origins (Branches)	Card No.	Destinations (Branches)	Days Paid	£	s	d
Apr.	Ripley	4949	Jarrow-on-Tyne	7		8	2
	Ripley	4949	Gatestead	12		14	0
	Ripley	4949	Newcastle 2nd	2		2	4
	Ripley	4949	South Shields	2		2	4
	Ripley	4949	Sunderland	2		2	4
May	Rugby	4949	South Shields	1		1	2
	Ripley	4949	Dumfries	2		2	4
	Ripley	4949	Glasgow 2nd	12		14	0
	Ripley	4949	Greencek	3		3	6
	Ripley	4949	Port Glasgow	2		2	4
	Ripley	4949	Renfrew	2		2	4
June	Ripley	4949	Glasgow	7		8	2
	Ripley	4949	Greenock	2		2	4
July	Ripley	4949	Coatbridge	2		2	4
	Ripley	4949	Edinburgh	7		8	2
	Ripley	4949	Glasgow	8		9	4
	Ripley	4949	Leith	3		3	6
	Ripley	4949	Paisley	3		3	6
	Ripley	4949	Uddingston	2		2	4
Aug.	Ripley	4949	Jarrow	2		2	4
	Ripley	4949	North Shields	3		3	6
	Ripley	4949	Sunderland	7		8	2
Sept.	Sunderland	6328	Hartlepool	4		4	8
	Sunderland	6328	Middlesbro'	3		3	6
	Sunderland	6328	Stockton-on-Tees	4		4	8
Oct.	Sunderland	6328	Hartlepool	7		3	2
	Sunderland	6328	Jarrow	2		2	4
	Sunderland	6328	Middlesbro'	4		4	8
	Sunderland	6328	Gateshead	5		5	10
	Sunderland	6328	North Shields	4		4	8
	Sunderland	6328	Stockton-on-Tess	6		7	0
	Sunderland	6328	Sunderland	3		3	6
	Sunderland	6328	York	2		2	4
Nov.	Sunderland	6328	Doncaster	2		2	4
	Sunderland	6328	Gainsborough	2		2	4
	Sunderland	6328	Leeds North	4		4	8
	Sunderland	6328	Lincoln	10		11	8
	Sunderland	6328	Newark	2		2	4
	Sunderland	6328	Northampton	5		5	10
Dec.	Sunderland	6328	Banbury	2		2	4
	Sunderland	6328	Bath	2		2	4
	Sunderland	6328	Chippenham	5		5	10
	Sunderland	6328	Devizes	2		2	4
	Sunderland	6328	Oxford	2		2	4
	Sunderland	6328	Southhanpton	8		8	2

Source: Modern Records Centre, Univ. of Warwick, MSS 259/4/14/1–107.

Table 4.26. Mobility Pattern of Richard Schofield, 1868

Month	Origins (Branches)	Card No.	Destinations (Branches)	Days Paid	£	s	d
Jan.	Heywood	4713	Shrewsbury	3		5	0
Feb.	Heywood	4926	Birmingham 2nd	16	1	0	2
	Heywood	4926	Birmingham 3rd	3		5	0
	Heywood	4713	Coventry	4		6	8
	Heywood	4926	Stafford	2		3	4
	Heywood	4926	Stockport	3		5	0
Mar.	Heywood	4926	Chester	3		3	6
	Heywood	4926	Oswestry	5		5	10
	Heywood	4926	Warrington	2		2	4
Apr.	Heywood	4926	Bolton 2nd	2		2	4
	Heywood	4926	Liverpool	2		2	4
	Heywood	4926	Liverpool 4th	1		1	2
	Heywood	4926	St. Helen's	3		3	6
	Heywood	4926	Manchester Office	19	1	2	2
May	Heywood	4926	Birkenhead	2		2	4
	Heywood	4926	Belfast	16		18	8
	Heywood	4926	Lisburn	2		2	4
	Heywood	4926	Newry	2		2	4
June	Newry	5802	Holyhead	2		2	4
July	Newry	5802	Llanelly	7		8	2
	Newry	5802	Neath	2		2	4
	Newry	5802	Pont-y-Pridd	3		3	6
	Newry	5802	Tredegar	2		2	4
Oct.	Tredegar	6635	Shrewsbury	8		9	4
	Tredegar	6635	Tredegar	4		4	8
Nov.	Tredegar	6635	Chepstow	6		7	0
	Tredegar	6635	Gloucester	2		2	4
	Tredegar	6635	Hereford	3		3	6
	Tredegar	6635	Kidderminster	2		2	4
	Tredegar	6635	Newport	7		8	2
	Tredegar	6635	Shrewsbury	2		2	4
	Tredegar	6635	Worcester	2		2	4
Dec.	Tredegar	6635	Burton-on-Trent	2		2	4
	Tredegar	6635	Chesterfield	2		2	4
	Tredegar	6635	Derby	2		2	4
	Tredegar	6635	Huddersfield	2		2	4
	Tredegar	6635	Kidderminster	4		4	8
	Tredegar	6635	Rugeley	2		2	4
	Tredegar	6635	Sheffield 2nd	6		7	0
	Tredegar	6635	Walsall	2		2	4

Source: Modern Records Centre, Univ. of Warwick, MSS 259/4/14/1–107.

Table 4.27. Mobility Pattern of Charles Mordue,
Middlesbrough Engine-smith, 1866–67

		Destinations	*Staying Days*
1866	Sep.	Leeds 5th	6
	Oct.	Huddersfield	1
		Leeds 5th	1
		Middlesbrough	15
		York	1
		Manchester Office	5
	Nov.	Hartlepool	2
		Jarrow	2
		Gateshead	9
		Newcastle-upon-Tyne	1
		Sunderland	1
	Dec.	Jarrow	2
		Middlesbrough	24
		Stock-on-Trent	3
1867	Jan.	Middlesbrough	30
	Feb.	Middlesbrough	28
	Mar.	Middlesbrough	14
	Apr.	Middlesbrough	30
	May	Hartlepool	4
		Jarrow-on-Tyne	1
		Middlesbrough	8
		Gateshead	3
		Newcastle-upon-Tyne 2nd	1
		Stockton-on-Trent	2
	Jun.	Middlesbrough	24
	Jul.	Middlesbrough	24

Source: Modern Records Centre, Univ. of Warwick, MSS 259/4/14/1-107.

Trade union-aided, short-term mobility can be shown more vividly through an individual case study worked out by linking the ASE records to census enumerators' books. Charles Mordue was born in Middlesbrough in 1844, possibly the eldest son of William, an anchor smith originally from Northumberland, and Mary Mordue, from Cumberland. In 1861, when Charles was 17 years of age, he was recorded in the census as a blacksmith. His brother William, then 15, was also a blacksmith, and a younger brother John, at the age of 13 too young to have yet started his apprenticeship, was noted as a labourer.[42]

At the age of 21 in 1865, Charles Mordue became a member of the Middlesbrough branch of the ASE, on completion of his indentures as an engine smith. In 1867 at the age of 23 he was ousted from the union on account of 'acting contrary to Society's interest'. Immediately after being expelled, Mordue married a woman called Eleanor from Yarm, and they had

---

[42] National Archives, RG 9/3687 (1861).

Table 4.28. Origins and Destinations of Migrant Engineers of ASE
Middlesbrough Branch, 1865–72

| *From the Middlesbrough Branch* | | *To the Middlesbrough Branch* | |
Destination	*Total No.*	*Origin*	*Total No.*
Darlington	6	Bolton	6
Halifax	6	Bradford	7
Hartlepool	11	Carlisle	8
Huddersfield	5	Darlington	7
Hull	13	Halifax	5
Jarrow	8	Hartlepool	10
Lambeth	8	Hull	21
Leeds	13	Leeds	20
London	6	London	5
Manchester	10	Manchester	15
Middlesbrough	20	Middlesbrough	20
Newcastle	11	Newcastle	9
Stockton	6	Oldham	5
Sunderland	8	Sheffield	11
York	9	Sunderland	17
Other 99 branches	116	Swindon	5
		Wolverton	5
		Other 99 branches	114
Total	256	Total	290

Source: Amalgamated Society of Engineers, Monthly Reports, Modern Records Centre, Univ. of Warwick, MSS 259/4/14/1-107.

three sons together. He remained in Middlesbrough at least until he was 37 years of age in 1881, when recorded as a blacksmith in an ironworks. Ten years earlier he had been described as an engine smith. From 1866 to 1867, while still a member of the union, Mordue moved frequently around the branch network in Yorkshire and Lancashire, as shown in Table 4.27. Most of his movements were between branches in the North East. The average length of stay in a branch was less than a week, except in Middlesbrough where he was perhaps paid benefit or found work, and stayed for much longer periods of time, from 14 to 30 days.[43]

Records of the Middlesbrough branch of the Amalgamated Society of Engineers are investigated in Table 4.28 for information about the mobility patterns of its members. During the period between 1865 and 1872, a total of 256 engineers from the Middlesbrough branch transferred to 114 branches across the country in pursuit of work. Most went to nearby branches in Co. Durham, Yorkshire and Lancashire. The number of engineers moving into Middlesbrough from other branches for employment during the period totalled 290.[44]

---

[43] Modern Records Centre, Univ. of Warwick, MSS 259/2/1/15; National Archives, HO 107/2383 (1851), RG 9/3687 (1861), RG 10/4893 (1871), RG 11/4851 (1881).
[44] Modern Records Centre, Univ. of Warwick, MSS 259/4/14/3, 2–14.

Like those moving out of Middlesbrough, in many cases the in-migrant engineers came from branches in adjacent counties, roughly the same group of places as with those moving away. It appears from this that trade unions encouraged the development of short-distance mobility, and of wider migration networks in which skilled workers such as engineers frequently moved between branches, seen here as most often including Middlesbrough, Leeds, Manchester, Hull, Hartlepool and Sunderland. On the question of whether migratory skilled workers supported by trade unions actually changed residence and lived with their family in the area of their new branch, the trade union records provide no answers. Married workmen would in some cases leave their family behind, sending money and returning home at intervals. This enabled a frequent exchange of labour between these areas, and at least as far as skilled workers were concerned, migration or mobility seems to have been well-structured, and generally not occurring ad hoc.[45]

It remains unclear whether or not the mobility patterns of James Alexander, Richard Schofield, Charles Mordue and other engineers described above were typical of those of many other engineers and other skilled workers organized by trade unions. Yet the development of a railway network which covered almost the whole country by the 1860s, accompanied by a decrease in transportation costs relative to average income, diminished one of the major intervening obstacles, that of distance, and an increase in the volume of migration across the whole group of engineers resulted.[46]

Under-developed Indigenous Labour Market: a Hypothesis

For Middlesbrough's iron and steel industry to maintain a sustained growth, one of the most urgent problems to confront was workforce recruitment, especially of skilled and semi-skilled workers. The town could not as yet sufficiently produce them. As Sidney Pollard has pointed out, the environment in Middlesbrough was not ripe to generate the home-grown flexible labour supply which older-established industrial towns such as Manchester, Liverpool, Birmingham and Leeds could offer. Apart from these recruitment difficulties, the staple industries of iron and steel enjoyed other comparative advantages, and were competitive enough with home and overseas rivals to enable the Middlesbrough ironmasters to pay higher wages (see Tables 4.29 and 4.30). These advantages, of abundant opportunities for employment and higher earnings, gave impetus to the remarkable labour migration described above.[47]

As it was, Middlesbrough relied to a great extent on ready-made exogenous skilled and semi-skilled workers, trained elsewhere before they came

---

[45] Pooley and Turnbull, *Migration and Mobility in Britain*, p. 16.

[46] Lee, 'A Theory of Migration', pp. 287, 291; Pollard, *Peaceful Conquest*, p. 23.

[47] Pollard,'Labour in Great Britain', p. 118; *The Times*, 25 Sep. 1866 and 27 Dec. 1866; *Middlesbrough Weekly News and Cleveland Advertiser*, 3 Aug. 1866.

Table 4.29. Wage Rates in Cleveland District, Staffordshire and Wales, 1866

Blast Furnace Workers	Cleveland Districts	Staffordshire	Wales
Wage Rates per Day			
Keepers	8s 4d–9s 8d	5s 4d–6s 9d	5s 4d
Chargers	6s 7d–7s 6d	4s 5d–5s 10d	4s 5d
Slaggers	4s 9d–6s 3d	4s 0d–4s 9d	3s 2d
Labourers	3s 0d–5s 0d	2s 8d–2s 10d	1s 8d
Wage Differentials between Cleveland Districts, Staffordshire and Wales			
Keepers	156–181	100–127	100
Chargers	149–170	100–132	100
Slaggers	150–197	126–150	100
Labourers	180–300	160–170	100

Source: *Middlesbrough News and Cleveland Advertiser*, 3 Aug. 1866.

Table 4.30. Wage Rates in the North of England and Belgium in 1866

Forge Workers	In the North	English Average	Belgium
Wage Rates per Day			
Puddlers	10s 3d	7s 6d–7s 10d	4s 2d–5s 0d
Puddler underhands	7s 2d	2s 6d–2s 11d	2s 3d–3s 1d
Shinglers	19s 4d–35s 2d	9s 0d–15s 0d	–
Forge rollers	20s 8d–27s 7d	9s 0d–15s 0d	4s 2d–5s 10d
Shearers	28s 0d–31s 0d	–	1s 10d–2s 6d
Labourers	–	2s 8d–3s 4d	1s 5d–2s 1d

Source: *The Times*, 25 Sept. 1866, 27 Dec. 1866.

to the town. It would seem serendipitous that the town industrialized before the 1870s, in an age of labour surplus when British labour markets were loose and mobile in terms of both geographical and inter-occupational, inter-disciplinary cross-over. It proved relatively easy for Middlesbrough to recruit exogenous skilled and semi-skilled workers at low cost.

As this ready-made exogenous labour force was readily available, employers could dispense with training those native youths who perhaps had a family or trade union connection with certain trades, and who might have taken the chance, if it had been offered, to learn skills within the town's staple industries. Because Middlesbrough could take advantage of such an externally available labour force, its own educational and training facilities seem not to have developed adequately. Tables 4.31 and 4.32 reveal the limitations in training up indigenous skilled and semi-skilled workers. Of all skilled and semi-skilled workers such as blacksmiths, moulders, puddlers, engineers and blast furnacemen who have been identified as staying in the town in the two decades, 1851–61 and 1861–71, as few as 45% in the first period and 36% in the second appear to have been trained within the town during this time.

Table 4.31. Formation of Indigenous Labour Market in Middlesbrough
Persistent Skilled and Semi-skilled Workers, 1851–61

Occupations in 1861	No. of Cases	Previous Occupations recorded in 1851	No. of Cases	Recruitment of Indigenous Labour Force
Blacksmiths	62	Scholars or no occupations	26	41.9%
		Blacksmiths	22	
		Others	14	
Moulders	83	Scholars or no occupations	33	39.8%
		Moulders	31	
		Labourers	4	
		Others	15	
Puddlers	23	Scholars or no occupations	9	39.2%
		Puddlers	4	
		Labourers	3	
		Others	7	
Engineers[a]	72	Scholars or no occupations	39	54.2%
		Engineers	14	
		Others	19	
Total	240	Scholars or no occupations	107	44.6%

Note: [a]Including boilermakers.

Source: Record linkage from Middlesbrough Census Enumerators' Books, 1851–61.

This group was the main element in the industry's 'labour aristocracy', and indispensable to the town's development.[48]

So, for example, of the 93 workers recorded as puddlers in 1871 who have been identified by record linkage as present in the town since 1861, 43 were recorded as 'scholars' or of 'no occupation' 10 years earlier. Of the remaining 50 workers, 33 were already puddlers before 1861, 11 had been labourers, and six had been engaged in an occupation other than puddler. Of 152 moulders staying in the town throughout the period between 1861 and 1871, 49 of them, accounting for only 32.2%, had been scholars or of 'no occupation' in 1861. There were 82 others recorded as working as moulders before 1861. Some of these would have been trained in the skill of iron moulding outside the town and entered as skilled workers before 1861.

Viewed from a different perspective, another illustration of Middlesbrough's under-developed indigenous labour market is given in Table 4.33. This shows the proportions of indigenous and exogenous labour making up the

---

[48]   Cf. Crew, *Town in the Ruhr*, p. 77.

Table 4.32. Formation of Indigenous Labour Market in Middlesbrough
Persistent Skilled and Semi-skilled Workers, 1861–71

Occupations in 1871	No. of Cases	Previous Occupations recorded in 1861	No. of Cases	Recruitment of Indigenous Labour Force
Blacksmiths	86	Scholars or no occupations	26	30.2%
		Blacksmiths	46	
		Others	14	
Blastfurnacemen	21	Scholars or no occupations	1	14.3%
		Blastfurnacemen	7	
		Puddlers	3	
		Labourers	7	
		Others	3	
Moulders	152	Scholars or no occupations	49	32.2%
		Moulders	82	
		Iron founders	9	
		Iabourers	4	
		Others	8	
Puddlers	93	Scholars or no occupations	43	46.2%
		Puddlers	33	
		Labourers	11	
		Others	6	
Engineers[a]	184	Scholars or no occupations	75	40.8%
		Engineers	56	
		Blacksmiths	8	
		Labourers	11	
		Others	34	
Total	536	Scholars or no occupations	194	36.2%

Note: [a]Including boilermakers.

Source: Record linkage from Middlesbrough Census Enumerators' Books, 1861–71.

total skilled and semi-skilled workforce of its iron and steel industry in 1861 and 1871. In 1861, of 1,240 skilled and semi-skilled workers, 249 of them, as few as 20%, have been identified as present in the town from 1851. The remaining 991 workers, that is, 80% of all skilled and semi-skilled workers there in 1861, had in-migrated to the town during the previous decade.

Strikingly, of the 402 puddlers recorded in 1861, only 23 have been identified as resident since 1851, the remaining 379 having migrated from elsewhere. Though in 1871 the proportion of indigenous men among the skilled labour force increased from 20 to 30%, exogenous workers still predominated.

Table 4.33. Indigenous and Exogenous Labour Market in Middlesbrough, 1861 and 1871

Occupation	Indigenous Persistent 1851–61	Exogenous In-migrant 1851–61	Total in 1861	Indigenous Persistent 1861–71	Exogenous In-migrant 1861–71	Total in 1871
Blacksmiths	62 (37.3%)	104 (62.7%)	166 (100.0%)	87 (35.8%)	156 (64.2%)	243 (100.0%)
Moulders	84 (30.7%)	190 (69.3%)	274 (100.0%)	151 (41.1%)	216 (58.9%)	367 (100.0%)
Puddlers	23 (5.7%)	379 (94.3%)	402 (100.0%)	93 (22.4%)	323 (77.6%)	416 (100.0%)
Engineers	72 (23.6%)	233 (76.4%)	305 (100.0%)	87 (30.5%)	427 (69.5%)	614 (100.0%)
Blastfurnacemen	8 (8.6%)	85 (91.4%)	93 (100.0%)	21 (22.3%)	73 (77.7%)	94 (100.0%)
Total	249 (20.0%)	991 (80.0%)	1,240 (100.0%)	593 (31.1%)	1,195 (68.9%)	1,734 (100.0%)

Source: Record linkage from Middlesbrough Census Enumerators' Books, 1851-61 and 1861–71.

Table 4.34. Indigenous Labour Market in Middlesbrough, 1851–1861–1871

Occupation	No. of Persistent Workers in 1851	Total No. of Workers in 1851	%	No. of Persistent Workers in 1861	Total No. of Workers in 1861	%	No. of Persistent Workers in 1871	Total No. of Workers in 1871	%
Blacksmiths	21	103	20.4	35	166	21.1	33	250	13.2
Moulders	21	103	20.4	47	269	17.5	54	379	14.2
Puddlers	3	26	11.5	11	402	2.7	14	417	3.4
Engineers	8	81	9.8	29	305	9.5	45	615	7.3
Total	53	313	16.9	122	1,142	10.7	146	1,661	8.8

Source: Record linkage from Middlesbrough Census Enumerators' Books, 1851-61 and 1861–71.

Table 4.35. Out-migration Rates of Skilled and Semi-skilled Workers, 1851–71

Occupations	No. of cases	Out-migrating[a] between 1851 and 1861	Out-migration Rates (%)[a]
1851			
Blacksmiths	103	70	68.0
Moulders	103	60	58.3
Engineers	81	57	70.4
Puddlers	26	19	73.1
Total	313	206	65.8
1861			
Blacksmiths	166	82	49.4
Moulders	269	138	51.3
Engineers	305	188	61.6
Puddlers	402	313	77.9
Blastfurnacemen	66	46	69.7
Total	1,208	767	63.5

Note: [a]Including those who died between the censuses.

Source: Record linkage from Middlesbrough Census Enumerators' Books, 1851–61 and 1861–71.

Over 70% of the skilled ironworkers needed by the expanding town's industries consisted of newcomers.[49]

Table 4.34 shows the level of local recruitment of skilled and semi-skilled workers. It presents the proportion of those who stayed in the town throughout the two consecutive decades from 1851 to 1861 and from 1861 to 1871, of the total skilled and semi-skilled labour force recorded at the end of each period. If we consider the making of an indigenous labour market between 1851 and 1871 based on these figures, it seems incontrovertible that Middlesbrough was heavily dependent on exogenous labour. For example, in 1871, there were in total 1,661 skilled and semi-skilled ironworkers, of whom just 146, comprising 8.8%, had lived in the town through the two decades from 1851 to 1871. The great majority, more than 90% of those engaged in the iron and steel industry in 1871, were from outside. Indeed almost 97% of puddlers had been recruited from outside the town.

A final body of evidence is available to support the hypothesis that efforts to create an indigenous labour market were insufficient. The out-migration rates among skilled and semi-skilled workers, seen in Table 4.35, add weight to the idea that a large indigenous labour force could not have accumulated in the town. In the first decade, 65.8% of skilled and semi-skilled workers are found to have left, while 63.5% departed during the second phase, 1861–71.

Even taking account of the number who died between censuses, out-migration rates were high enough to work against the establishment of a skilled

---

[49] For the proportion of in-migrant skilled artisans to total workforce needed by the local economy in Duisburg in the late nineteenth century, see Jackson, *Migration and Urbanization in the Ruhr Valley*, pp. 229–30.

and semi-skilled labour force of sufficient size. If the town's staple industries had indeed increased the numbers of trainees among the local workforce, as suggested by figures from the second decade, they were likely to lose most of it. This is true for the whole labour force, indigenous or exogenous, and can be observed in the case of puddlers and blast furnacemen, of whom almost 78% and 70%, respectively, left the town (or died) between censuses.

It is important to note how far this differed from conditions prevailing elsewhere, for example, in Bochum in the Ruhr, where factory apprenticeship usually to a skilled metal trade was most common in the second half of the nineteenth century. By the middle of the 1860s, the apprenticeship system had already disappeared from process work in the Cleveland iron and steel industry. As John Kane, who consolidated in 1868 three separate trade unions for skilled ironworkers into the National Amalgamated Association of Malleable and Other Iron-workers, testified to the Royal Commission on Trades Unions in 1868: 'There is no apprenticeship system in connection with the iron trade at the present time; there was formerly, but there is not now.'[50]

At the time, the breakdown of the apprenticeship system aroused considerable public discussion. In 1890, Alfred Marshall pointed out that 'the old apprenticeship system is not exactly suited to modern conditions and it has fallen into disuse; but a substitute for it is wanted'. He also suggested that 'it does not seem impracticable to revive the apprenticeship system in a modern form'. Yet in the Cleveland iron and steel industry in the nineteenth century, technological education was charged with particular difficulties.[51]

As early as 1844, when the town's population was still between about 5,000 and 6,000, and before a full-fledged development of the Cleveland iron industry had begun, the Middlesbrough Mechanics' Institute was founded with 104 members. Eligible to become members were people aged 12 years and upwards, including apprentices and females. In late nineteenth-century Middlesbrough, virtually all the technical education available was provided through this voluntary organization, the mechanics' institute. Up to the middle of the nineteenth century, the institute's main objective seems to have been teaching a basic knowledge of science. It appears to have been most effective in providing a broad general education rather than specific scientific instruction. The institute's rules stated its object as 'to promote the diffusion of useful knowledge among the working classes, by the establishment of a library and reading room, by occasional lectures on various subjects of popular interest, and by instruction, in classes of the members, in the practical branches of science'.[52]

---

[50] For implications of apprenticeship for intergenerational social mobility in Bochum, see Crew, *Town in the Ruhr*, pp. 89–90; PP, 1867-68 [3980-I] XXXIX, q. 8472, p. 17.

[51] Marshall, *Principles of Economics*, p. 267.

[52] Butterworth, 'Development of Technical Education in Middlesbrough', p. 27; Middlesbrough Central Lib., MMI 374, pp. 1, 2, 4.

As a result of support from Middlesbrough's leading industrialists, for example, Bolckow, Vaughan and Samuelson, who made frequent donations, the institute continued to be a centre for scientific education throughout the period. Yet until the beginning of the 1860s, there were no classes in science there. By the mid-nineteenth century, as Britain's economic position was under challenge from foreign competition, central government and industry leaders began to pay attention to the importance of technical education and to promote a national provision of facilities. The Department of Science and Art was founded in 1856 to provide technical education for the working class.[53]

In Middlesbrough, as in Staffordshire, Warwickshire and South Wales, classes in chemistry and metallurgy began to be offered. With government aid, Middlesbrough Mechanics' Institute started in 1861 a first venture in technical education, while the newly built Middlesbrough School of Science held classes in chemistry and other subjects. Towards the end of the 1860s, efforts were made to revive the system of apprenticeship by running day-release classes in mathematics for local apprentices, but this failed on account of employers' unwillingness to support the project. Local enterprise did not step in to supply the working class with technical education, since skilled workers were relatively easily available without training them at their own cost.[54]

In fact, the attempt to start day-release classes for Middlesbrough apprentices was opposed by employers on the grounds that 'the classes would not be valued as much as if the apprentices had to attend in their spare time'. When steel production was launched in the late 1870s, using Cleveland iron ore and the Gilchrist-Thomas process, the demand for trained chemists increased, and an enlarged chemistry school was established. The iron and steel companies, however, made little progress with their own specialized education and training before 1902, when in Middlesbrough a class was started at the high school, held in employers' time and catering for boys of 16 and upwards, who were paid as though at work.[55]

Other than this general description of the development of technical education in late nineteenth-century Middlesbrough, little is known about how skilled ironworkers underwent their practical training. The engineers who worked in maintenance and repair, or those engaged in work on production processes that required higher technological training, for example, steam-engine makers, served apprenticeships for seven years. Yet in the late-nineteenth century iron industry itself, especially before the introduction of the Gilchrist-Thomas steel-making process, whole sectors of production had dispensed with formal apprenticeship for many workers who were classed as skilled. In most cases it appears that operatives received technical training

53 Butterworth, 'Development of Technical Education in Middlesbrough', p. 27; Musgrave, *Technical Change, the Labour Force and Education*, p. 266.
54 Musgrave, *Technical Change, the Labour Force and Education*, p. 37; Butterworth, 'Development of Technical Education in Middlesbrough', p. 29.
55 Musgrave, *Technical Change, the Labour Force and Education*, pp. 89, 92; Butterworth, 'Development of Technical Education in Middlesbrough', p. 29.

on-the-job from master workers to their under-hands on the shop floors, or from other skilled workers.[56]

From the 1880s, Middlesbrough faced severe domestic and foreign competition in the iron and steel trades. At the same time, the British labour market gradually reduced its mobility and became less fluid. To cope with this situation, the town's employers, instead of continuing to depend on ready-made exogenous labour, should have ensured a supply of lower-cost indigenous workers. Especially after the late 1870s, when Middlesbrough's staple industry shifted towards steel production, the town seems to have found difficulty in adapting itself to new circumstances by developing institutions to provide the local population with relevant technical training. It appears that industrial and institutional arrangements were not flexible enough to allow re-structuring of the old system. Arguably the inadequate supply of skilled and semi-skilled workers from among the local population was one reason why Middlesbrough's prosperity was so short-lived.

As a final overview, the labour market in the late nineteenth-century Cleveland iron and steel industry might be summarized as follows. First of all, before the time when an internal labour market in iron and steel came to predominate, the labour market covering a much wider area functioned effectively. This was highly fluid, with few barriers to check the free movement of workers.

Employers, organized into various voluntary groupings such as the Cleveland Ironmasters' Association and the North of England Iron Manufacturers' Association, thereby jointly exploited their labour force, for instance accommodating each other with operatives when any firm suffered from a shortage of labour. This is indicated in the minutes of the Board of Arbitration and Conciliation for the North of England Manufactured Iron Trade. The rules of this body also remark that ironworkers in the North East were dealt with not 'as groups separated into as many bodies as there are employers, but as a *class*'. Employer organizations had agreements to control outputs of pig and wrought iron, as well as the wage rates paid to their members' workmen.[57]

The pig-iron makers of the North Riding of Yorkshire, Co. Durham and Northumberland organized in the Cleveland Ironmasters' Association in 1866, had as a shared objective 'the interchange of information on all subjects affecting the interest of the trade; securing united action and mutual support for the general welfare'.[58] The region's ironmasters who were engaged in converting pig iron into rolled or manufactured iron in its various forms, of rails, plates, angles, bars, and so on, who were united into the North of England Iron Manufacturers' Association in 1865, had more precise and detailed rules than the Ironmasters' Association. These ranged from general quorum and membership

---

[56] Musgrave, *Technical Change, the Labour Force and Education*, p. 91.
[57] Modern Records Centre, Univ. of Warwick, MSS 365/BAC, Rules, p. 5; Minute Book, Vol. 1, original emphasis.
[58] Modern Records Centre, Univ. of Warwick, MSS 365/CIA, ff. 30–2, 1866–76.

requirements, to crucial matters such as the current selling prices of products, labour relations and wage rates paid to workers in the member firms. Members were expected to take united action on wage reductions.

Their rules suggest that they were greatly concerned about wage rates, selling prices and the strikes staged in pursuit of higher wages and other concessions. The association agreed to 'abide by the decision of the majority on any question of proposed united action in the reduction of wages or otherwise'. As a result of such agreements, among about 28 wrought-iron makers in the North East, 'these piece work of tonnage prices are, with very slight exceptions, the same at all the establishments in the north of England, and whenever the state of trade justifies an increase or a reduction, such change is made almost simultaneously at the various establishments'. There was even provision to give an allowance from association funds to firms which experienced strikes, according to the number and the size of furnaces put out of operation during stoppages.[59]

These rules were essentially gentlemen's agreements, although some of them were rather more binding. Especially in relation to outputs of pig iron and the wage rates paid to their workers, both the Cleveland Ironmasters' Association and the North of England Iron Manufacturers' Association closely regulated members' decision-making. From remarks in the minutes, referring frequently to wage rates and the selling prices of pig and wrought iron and finished iron products, it would seem that their agreements were effectively carried out. The tone of the rules suggests that the associations were something like cartels, in a nascent stage.

Conversely, ironworkers, especially skilled ones, tend to have moved relatively freely, taking advantage of lower costs of migration resulting from the development of a national railway network. Mobility was also encouraged by the trade unions' supporting system of paying fares to travel in search of opportunities for employment around the branch network. This system relieved employers of the costs of migration, as trade union funds bore the expense.[60] Those British trade unions that organized for particular trades, distinct from the enterprise-based unions, were also likely to have brought about a less segmented and thus more homogeneous labour market. Moreover the establishment of the Board of Arbitration and Conciliation for the North of England Manufactured Iron Trade in 1869, which afterwards achieved the formation of sliding scale rules in fixing wage rates, facilitated the development of a flexible, wide-ranging and unified labour market.

Thus we may speculate that the institutional framework within which both employers and employees conducted themselves, contributed to a great extent to the making of a more mobile labour market in iron and steel. Certainly such a mobile and unified market was created in the Cleveland industry at

---

[59] Modern Records Centre, Univ. of Warwick, MSS 365/NEI, pp. 1–14; MSS 365/BAC, Rules, p. 5.

[60] Pollard, 'Labour in Great Britain', p. 152.

this time. Yet this in turn had the result of inhibiting training and educational facilities in the region. The cost to Cleveland industrialists of training labour at their own expense was higher than recruiting ready-made skilled workers from outside, even though in-migrant workers demanded higher wages. As Musgrave has pointed out, Middlesbrough lacked educational facilities even though they could easily have been provided in such a heavily concentrated industrial area. As a result, maintaining the town's early lead proved more difficult than it might have been. When Middlesbrough's economic and geographic advantages had lessened, the superior educational provision in other places stood industries there in good stead.[61]

---

[61] Musgrave, *Technical Change, the Labour Force and Education*, p. 253.

5

Welfare Provision in Mid-Victorian Middlesbrough

We have long and earnestly desired to see an hospital established, in the benefits of which the suffering and afflicted could participate, without having first to pass through the portals of pauperism; and such the Cottage Hospital is; for there the patients, who are admitted without ticket, can be attended by their own club doctors, and thus be spared the humiliating feeling that they are dependent upon others for medical assistance ... Would it not be a grand and honourable thing, if the working-men of Middlesbro' could point to such an institution, and say, that is maintained by *us*![1]

The Cottage Hospital as Safety Net for Middlesbrough Workers

Health care in Britain during this period came in many guises and was offered through a multiplicity of institutions. Recent investigations in medical history suggest that a complex network of overlapping systems insured against health risks, ranging from membership of mutual friendly societies, to contractual medical aid companies. As Paul Johnson has pointed out, any simple assertions about the development of British medical welfare, for instance from private to public, or local to national, will be erroneous. A wide variety of welfare instruments prevailed in Britain before, and even after, Beveridge.[2]

This chapter presents a study of medical services available to victims of industrial accidents in a late nineteenth-century voluntary hospital, North Ormesby Hospital, on the eastern outskirts of Middlesbrough, then in the North Riding of Yorkshire. We are primarily concerned with the type of medical care offered by the hospital, the context within which it worked, and the complex structure of welfare through which the working population acquired their safety net, given that the hospital was supported largely by subscriptions from industrial workers throughout this period. The hospital looked after Middlesbrough residents, especially workers employed in the iron and steel, railways and chemical industries, those most vulnerable to the risk of an industrial accident. From its foundation, this hospital was organized on a funding model markedly different from the voluntary principles of eighteenth-century philanthropic and charitable institutions.[3]

---

[1] *Middlesbrough Times*, 15 Sep. 1860, original emphasis.
[2] See for example Cherry, *Medical Services and Hospitals in Britain*, pp. 30, 41–53; Dupree, 'Provision of Social Service', p.351; Johnson, 'Risk, Redistribution and Social Welfare', p. 246; Harris, 'Did British Workers Want the Welfare State?', pp. 210–11.
[3] Doyle, 'Voluntary Hospitals in Edwardian Middlesbrough', p. 9.

Plate 5.1. North Ormesby Hospital, c.1900

North Ormesby Hospital's fund-raising was based on collecting subscriptions and donations from workers in the region, as shown in a local newspaper article: 'We have provided the means of support for it; and should any accident befall us, we shall not require to go a begging for a ticket of admission from some of our wealthy neighbours to the hospital.'[4] This point will be examined later in more detail.

The relationship between the medical establishment, the town's staple iron, steel and railway industries, and their workforces, is analysed here from the hospital's council minute books, 1867–1907. Case books from 1861 to 1870 and 1883 to 1908, along with the hospital's annual reports, have made it possible to construct a profile of the age-, sex- and occupation-specific morbidity of its patients, and to identify trends in the sources of hospital income. The case books offer a relative wealth of epidemiological evidence, allowing us to gauge the morbidity prevailing in mid-Victorian Middlesbrough.[5]

Rates of Morbidity

Overall morbidity has been calculated from hospital records over two periods: from soon after the hospital's opening, from 1861 to 1870; and from 1883 to 1908. Throughout, there were more male than female in-patients, though the proportion fell slightly in the later period, males accounting for 67% of the total 15,137 in-patients as compared to 72% of the total 1,454 in the earlier phase.[6]

---

4   *Middlesbrough Times*, 15 Sep. 1860.
5   Teesside Archives, H/NOR 1/1; H/NOR 10/1–3; 1st to 59th annual reports of the Cottage Hospital, North Ormesby, 1859–1917. For detail of medical treatment in the hospital at this period, see Croker, 'Early Hospital Provision in Middlesbrough', pp. 49–73.
6   Calculated from North Ormesby Hospital case books, 1861–70, 1883–8, 1885–1908: Teesside

Figure 5.1 charts the numbers of in- and out-patients over more than half a century, and the composition of surgical and medical cases.[7] From the opening of the hospital, out-patients outnumbered in-patients, which can be explained by the limited accommodation available, and expense of nursing care, for in-patients.

On average, the number of out-patients was virtually twice that of in-patients, and at the beginning of the twentieth century, the gap between the two groups became much wider still. Except for a very short period in the late 1860s, the hospital accommodated many more surgical in-patients than ones suffering from medical illnesses. This reflects the fact that Middlesbrough inhabitants in the late-nineteenth century, particularly if they were male, were far more likely to need surgical treatment for traumatic injury suffered in industrial accidents, rather than be hospitalized because of illness.

Presented in Figure 5.2 are sex- and age-specific distributions of in-patients that show noticeable changes in age structure between the two periods. In the first series, the highest numbers of males appear among the 20–24 age group, and then the group aged 25–29, whereas in the second a peak appears in a younger group, aged 15–19, with older ages from 20 upwards showing higher levels throughout. Another marked change is in the numbers of infant and child in-patients, especially in the male age group under the age of four, which by the second period have become significant.[8]

It is likely that changes in the age structure of Middlesbrough's population from the 1880s onwards account for this, in part at least, for at this time the town's iron and steel industry no longer attracted in-migrants from the 20–24 and 25–29 age groups in anything like the numbers of the previous decades.[9] It is also significant that towards the end of the nineteenth century, in-patient care provided by the hospital was extended beyond adult males, to include their wives and children. A separate ward for sick children was established in 1866. These developments suggest that the hospital altered its fund-raising practices over the period. For instance, the changing profile of in-patients could have resulted from hospital efforts to increase contributors by providing greater access to care for their dependants.[10]

Diseases and symptoms recorded in the case books through both periods

Archives, H/NOR 10/1-3.

[7] Calculated from 1st to 59th annual reports of the Cottage Hospital, North Ormesby, 1859–1917.

[8] Males aged 0–4 comprise 8.9%, females of the same age group 11.3%, of the total 10,068 male and 4,807 female in-patients.

[9] Based on record linkage from Middlesbrough census enumerators' books, 1851–61 and 1861–71, and the enumerators' books for 1881: National Archives, HO 107/2383, RG 9/3685-3689, RG 10/4893, RG 11/4851. For the development of the iron and steel industry in Middlesbrough during this period, see for example, Birch, *The Economic History of the British Iron and Steel Industry*, p. 333; Bullock, 'The Origins of Economic Growth on Teesside', pp. 85–96; Lillie, *History of Middlesbrough*, pp. 96–109; Taylor, 'Infant Hercules and Augean Stables', pp. 53–80.

[10] 8th annual report of the Cottage Hospital, North Ormesby, p. 3; for changes in age structure of patients in North Ormesby Hospital in the early-twentieth century, see Doyle, 'Competition and Cooperation', pp. 344–5; see also Cherry, 'Beyond National Health Insurance', p. 480.

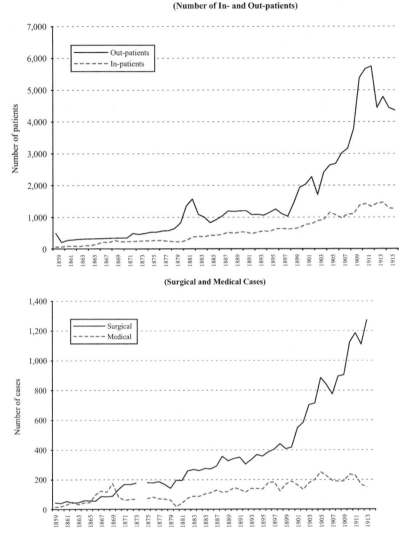

Figure 5.1. Number of Patients in North Ormesby Hospital

range from medical conditions such as those of the cardiovascular, gastro-enterological and respiratory systems, some requiring surgical treatment, and dermatological and ophthalmological ailments, to illnesses classified as gynaecological, proctological, urological, dental and so on. In some cases the affected parts were not specified, and symptoms or states were recorded rather than the names of diseases.

Given the contemporary state of pathology and nosology (the classification of diseases), and an associated lack of accurate diagnosis during the period, some of the diseases and symptoms recorded in these documents cannot be

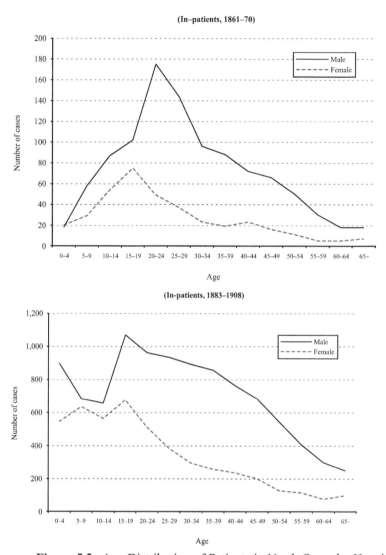

Figure 5.2. Age Distribution of Patients in North Ormesby Hospital

confidently identified in present-day terms. Yet many conditions treated at the hospital are easily recognizable, for example many of the disorders treated by surgery, as well as dermatological complaints, burns and scalds, scrofula, hernias, cataracts, abscesses, ophthalmic problems, conjunctivitis, rheumatism, bronchitis, pneumonia, and skin inflammation and ulcers. The hospital records do therefore present sufficient evidence for us to gauge fairly accurately the nature and incidence of ailments from which patients suffered.

The most common reason for males to be admitted to the hospital during the first period was, as shown in Table 5.3, because they had suffered an acci-

Table 5.3. Morbidity Rates from Hospital Records, 1861–70 and 1883–1908

Male		Female	
1861–70			
Injury	191	Rheumatism	28
Burn & scald	125	Abscess	27
Fracture	122	Debility	26
Rheumatism	82	Ulcerated legs, etc.	24
Abscess	49	Burn	20
Ulcerated legs, etc.	47	Injury	14
Crushed legs, etc.	35	Conjunctivitis	13
Bronchitis	29	Bronchitis	12
Conjunctivitis	21	Chorea	11
Phthisis	20	Synovitis	11
Others	255	Others	165
Total	976	Total	351
1883–1908			
Fracture	1,082	Ulcer	253
Burn & scald	689	Chorea	193
Bruise	502	Anaemia	177
Contusion	327	Tonsil and adenoid	177
Ulcer	304	Tuberculosis	169
Inguinal & other hernia	234	Abscess	149
Abscess	223	Gastric ulcer	135
Tuberculosis	223	Burn & scald	114
Crush	210	Eczema	92
Rheumatism	206	Necrosis	92
Laceration	204	Rheumatism	90
Pneumonia	150	Carcinoma & cancer	82
Bronchitis	141	Fractures	79
Sprain	131	Keratitis	70
Necrosis	127	Dyspepsia	63
Others	5,315	Others	2,872
Total	10,068	Total	4,807

Source: Teesside Archives, H/NOR 10/1–3.

dental injury such as a burn or fracture. Women were mainly admitted for medical conditions such as rheumatism, an abscess or debility. In the second period, the picture is almost the same. For men, surgical cases predominated, frequently involving compound and simple fractures, burns, bruises and contusions. Females more typically presented with ulcers, chorea, anaemia, tonsil and adenoid problems, and tuberculosis, all of these medical illnesses. Newly arrived in-migrants, whether labourers from the surrounding agricultural areas seeking simple jobs requiring physical strength rather than skill and training, or more highly qualified individuals, were perhaps more susceptible to industrial accidents when working in unfamiliar industrial surroundings.

Table 5.4 shows age- and sex-specific morbidity. Almost 40% of male in-patients aged 15–34, from the young and middle-aged working popula-

Table 5.4. Age-specific Morbidity Rates, 1883–1908

Age Group	Male	No. of Cases	Female	No. of Cases
0–4	Phimosis	105 (11.7)	Burn & scald	37 (6.8)
	Inguinal hernia	80 (8.9)	Nevus	33 (6.1)
	Burn & scald	67 (7.5)	Tonsil & adenoid	31 (5.7)
	Tuberculous diseases	46 (5.1)	Eczema	28 (5.1)
	Others	599 (66.8)	Others	415 (76.3)
	Total	897 (100.0)	Total	544 (100.0)
5–14	Fracture (comp. & simple)	99 (7.4)	Chorea	151 (12.6)
	Tuberculous diseases	88 (6.6)	Tonsil & adenoid	134 (11.2)
	Tonsil & adenoid	79 (5.9)	Tuberculous diseases	105 (8.8)
	Burn & scald	59 (4.4)	Necrosis	42 (3.5)
	Others	1,014 (75.7)	Others	765 (63.9)
	Total	1,339 (100.0)	Total	1,197 (100.0)
15–34	Fracture (comp. & simple)	441 (11.4)	Anemia	171 (9.2)
	Bruise & contusion	439 (11.4)	Gastric ulcer	119 (6.4)
	Burn & scald	341 (8.8)	Bursitis patella	71 (3.8)
	Incised wounds, etc.	156 (4.0)	Tuberculosis & phthisis	69 (3.7)
	Others	2,480 (64.4)	Others	1,432 (76.9)
	Total	3,857 (100.0)	Total	1,862 (100.0)
35–49	Fracture (comp. & simple)	305 (13.2)	Ulcer of foot, etc.	59 (8.6)
	Bruise & contusion	236 (10.3)	Carcinoma of breast, etc.	54 (7.8)
	Burn & scald	144 (6.3)	Rheumatism	22 (3.2)
	Ulcer of leg, etc. & varicose vein	120 (5.2)	Tuberculosis & phthisis	17 (2.5)
	Others	1,497 (65.0)	Others	537 (77.9)
	Total	2,302 (100.0)	Total	639 (100.0)
50+	Fracture (comp. & simple)	170 (11.4)	Ulcer of leg, etc.	59 (14.4)
	Bruise & contusion	107 (7.2)	Carcinoma of breast, etc.	48 (11.7)
	Ulcer of leg, etc. & varicose vein	97 (6.5)	Fracture (comp. & simple)	18 (4.4)
	Burn & scald	51 (3.4)	Strangulated hernia	11 (2.7)
	Others	1,068 (71.5)	Others	275 (66.8)
	Total	1,493 (100.0)	Total	411 (100.0)

Note: Percentages in parentheses.

Source: Teesside Archives, H/NOR 10/1–3.

tion, were admitted to the hospital as casualties of accidents. Among the age groups 35–49, and from 50 years of age upwards, geriatric conditions such as leg ulcers, varicose veins, rheumatism, bronchitis, sciatica and cardiac disease account for a considerable proportion of in-patient admissions.

Table 5.5. Causes of Death in North Ormesby Hospital

(1860–70)		(1883–1908)	
Male			
Compound & simple fractures	15 (26.3)	Compound & simple fractures	90 (15.8)
Injury	7 (12.3)	Pneumonia	52 (9.2)
Burn & scald	6 (10.5)	Burn & scald	37 (6.5)
Phthisis	6 (10.5)	Phthisis & tuberculosis	25 (4.4)
Abscess	4 (7.0)	Strangulated hernia	12 (2.1)
Bronchitis	3 (5.3)	Bronchitis	12 (2.1)
Others	16 (28.1)	Others	340 (59.9)
Total	57 (100.0)	Total	568 (100.0)
Female			
Phthisis	2 (25.0)	Tuberculosis	16 (7.0)
Burn & scald	1 (12.5)	Burn & scald	15 (6.5)
Others	5 (62.5)	Cardiac diseases	9 (4.0)
		Strangulated hernia	9 (4.0)
		Cancer	7 (3.0)
		Others	173 (75.5)
Total	8 (100.0)	Total	229 (100.0)

Note: Figures in parentheses are proportion of total case as a percentage.

Source: Teesside Archives, H/NOR 10/1–3.

Female participation rates in the iron and steel and railways labour force were so low that women were almost free from industrial accidents. Duration of in-patient treatments for females in the later period, 34.4 days on average, was slightly longer than that for males, 31.1 days on average, which appears to reflect a lower incidence of acute sickness for women.[11]

Among the accident cases, injuries to feet, legs, ankles and backs predominated. Many of these were due to incidents in workplaces, especially in ironworks and on the railways. As those who compiled the hospital's annual reports during the period often lamented, burns were of the most appalling kind, chiefly from molten iron.[12]

Compound and simple fractures, together with burns and other injuries, account for almost half the deaths occurring in the hospital during the first period analysed, while in the second period the most frequent causes of death were accidental fractures and burns, comprising 22% of the total 568 deaths shown in Table 5.5.

Hospital mortality averaged over 5% throughout the period, with male mortality more than 6%, as shown in Figure 5.6.[13] This was substantially higher than the death rate observed in other voluntary hospitals, for instance,

[11] For the national average length of stay in voluntary hospitals during the period, see Pinker, *English Hospital Statistics*, p. 111; for length of stay and causes of admission to North Ormesby Hospital in the early-twentieth century, see Doyle, 'Competition and Cooperation', p. 345.

[12] See for example, annual report of the Cottage Hospital, North Ormesby, for 1862, p. 2.

[13] Calculated from 1st to 59th annual reports of the Cottage Hospital, North Ormesby, 1859–1917.

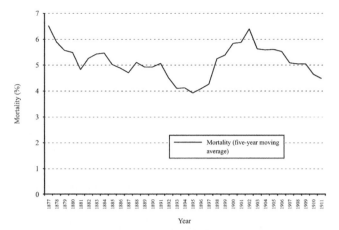

Figure 5.6. Mortality in North Ormesby Hospital

that of 3.1% for male in-patients in the Leeds General Infirmary at the beginning of the nineteenth century.[14] The epidemiological evidence drawn from North Ormesby Hospital's late nineteenth-century case books shows the main consumers of medical services to have been male manual workers employed in heavy industries and living in a physically hazardous environment. In consequence the hospital came to specialize in treating male workers who had suffered serious industrial accidents, a focus on severe surgical cases which perhaps explains the hospital's high rate of mortality.

Fund-raising

Figure 5.7 indicates the proportion of subscriptions and donations contributed by employees of various firms in the Middlesbrough area in relation to the total amount of such payments received by the hospital.[15] Workers' contributions to the hospital fund were impressively high throughout the period. Their donations accounted on average for more than half of the hospital's funds. Towards the end of the nineteenth century, the share of the hospital's ordinary income which derived from workers' subscriptions rose rapidly to more than 60%. At the beginning of the twentieth century, the hospital was run almost entirely from workers' subscriptions. It can safely be said that throughout its history from 1859, this hospital was heavily dependent on workers' support for its funding.[16]

This same pattern of reliance on workers' donations was seen elsewhere

---

[14] Hospital mortality in the Leeds General Infirmary has been calculated from admission and discharge registers, 1815–17: West Yorkshire Archive Service, Leeds. Causes of death and hospital mortality at North Ormesby Hospital have been established from hospital case books, 1861–70, 1883–8, 1885–1908: Teesside Archives, H/NOR 10/1-3; 1st to 59th annual reports of the Cottage Hospital, North Ormesby, 1859–1917.

[15] Calculated from 1st to 59th annual reports of the Cottage Hospital, North Ormesby, 1859–1917.

[16] For hospital fund-raising in the twentieth century, see Lewis et al., *Health Services in Middlesbrough*, pp. 9–16; Doyle and Nixon, 'Voluntary Hospital Finance', pp. 8–14.

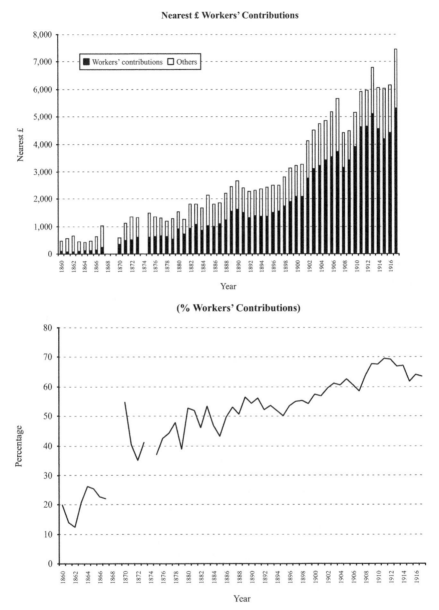

Figure 5.7. Workers' Contributions to North Ormesby Hospital

in hospitals in areas of heavy industry, such as Glasgow, Sheffield, Sunderland, Newcastle or Swansea, where accidents, emergencies and environmental diseases were prevalent. Even among these institutions, though, North Ormesby

Table 5.8. Hospital Fund-raising (North Ormesby Hospital and Leeds General Infirmary)

North Ormesby Hospital (1876)			General Infirmary at Leeds (1857)		
Subscribers	No. of Cases	Amount (£)	Subscribers	No. of Cases	Amount (£)
Companies	10	53.4 (5.5)	Companies	174	482.5 (20.8)
Friendly Societies	3	12.6 (1.3)	Friendly societies	9	29.4 (1.3)
Poor Law Unions	2	12.6 (1.3)	Poor Law Unions	7	45.2 (2.0)
Overseers of the Poor	–	–	Overseers of the Poor	11	45.2 (2.0)
Other Organizations	3	4.4 (0.4)	Other Organizations	4	40.3 (1.7)
Individuals			Individuals		
Aristocrats	3	17.1 (1.8)	Aristocrats	23	123.4 (5.3)
Gentry	19	68.1 (7.0)	Gentry	119	390.3 (16.8)
Ecclesiastical	7	12.6 (1.3)	Ecclesiastical	45	110.5 (4.8)
Lay Mr	18	23.3 (2.4)	Lay Mr	396	761.3 (32.9)
Mrs	10	13.6 (1.4)	Mrs	93	202.4 (8.7)
Miss	9	7.8 (0.8)	Miss	40	86.1 (3.7)
Workers at Various Co.	–	631.8 (65.0)			
Hospital Sat. & Sun. Fund	–	114.5 (11.8)			
Total	–	971.8 (100.0)	Total	921	2,316.6 (100.0)

Source: 18th Annual Report of North Ormesby, Middlesbrough, 1876, pp. 10–13; Annual Report of the State of the General Infirmary at Leeds, 1856–7.

Hospital was exceptional in that so much of its finance came from workers in heavy industry, to a degree rare among British hospitals of this era.[17]

The differences between how this institution was financed, and the funding of other hospitals, are worth noting. Table 5.8 compares the subscribers for North Ormesby Hospital in 1876 to those for the General Infirmary at Leeds in 1857. The proportion collected from employees in the Middlesbrough area accounted for as much as 65% of all subscriptions, whereas that from local companies amounted to less than 10% of workers' contributions, that is only 5.5%. As for individuals, the amounts from the peerage and gentry comprised 9%, while ordinary lay people contributed 4%.

In contrast, Leeds General Infirmary experienced a more even distribution in the sources of its subscriptions. The infirmary had not adopted a formal contributory scheme, so did not receive contributions from workmen as a

---

[17] Cherry, 'Before the National Health Service', pp. 318, 324; for working men's contributions and participation in managing voluntary hospitals in Lancashire, see Dupree, 'Provision of Social Service', p. 362; for workmen's contributions in selected London and provincial voluntary hospitals, see Pinker, *English Hospital Statistics*, pp. 152–4.

Table 5.9. Company and Employee Contributions to North Ormesby
Hospital, 1860–81

Name of Company	Company Contributions (£)	Employees Contributions (£)	Total Amount (£)
Cochrane & Co.	9 (5.6)	152 (94.4)	161 (100.0)
Bell Brothers	14 (23.0)	47 (77.0)	61 (100.0)
Gilkes, Wilson, Pease & Co.	10 (25.0)	30 (75.0)	40 (100.0)
Clay Lane & South Bank Iron Works	0 (0.0)	55 (100.0)	55 (100.0)
Gjers, Mills and Co.	0 (0.0)	15 (100.0)	15 (100.0)
Samuelson & Co.	5 (100.0)	0 (0.0)	5 (100.0)
North Eastern Railway	10 (28.6)	25 (71.4)	35 (100.0)
Total	48 (12.9)	324 (87.1)	372 (100.0)

Notes: Average annual contributions over the period. Figures in parentheses are percentages within companies.

Source: Annual Reports, North Ormesby Hospital, Middlesbrough, 1860–81.

body. Instead it relied much more on wealthy landed interests in the West Riding of Yorkshire. The peerage and gentry contributed 22% of all subscriptions to the Infirmary. The Leeds General Infirmary was also supported to a significant degree by a rising bourgeoisie of manufacturers and merchants, the petite bourgeoisie consisting of shopkeepers and professionals, as well as other middle-class people. The same situation was to be found in Bristol, where in terms of funding and time dedicated to welfare provision, voluntary hospitals relied on the middle class. Contributions from these lay individuals to the Leeds General Infirmary were of fundamental importance, amounting to 45% of hospital income. These middle-class supporters gained stature from their work with the voluntary hospital system, enjoying respectability and cachet in return for their support of improved medical facilities. In addition, donations from industrial concerns, mainly textile companies based around Leeds, accounted for 21% of total subscriptions.[18]

In Middlesbrough, with the exception of Snowden and Hopkins' ironworks, which subscribed a total of £5, no company made any contribution to the hospital in 1860.[19] So in fact North Ormesby Hospital was originally financed by the workers themselves. The relative importance of companies and their employees in supporting the hospital between 1860 and 1881 is shown in Table 5.9.

Throughout this period, the totals donated by six major ironworks and the local railway company amounted to less than one-seventh the total contributions from their employees. Among the businesses, Clay Lane and South

---

[18] Doyle, 'Competition and Cooperation', p. 345; for urban morbidity and fund-raising at Leeds General Infirmary at the beginning of the nineteenth century, see Yasumoto, *Industrialisation, Urbanisation, and Demographic Change*, pp. 113–56.

[19] Annual report of the Cottage Hospital, North Ormesby, 1860, p. 3.

Bank Ironworks and Gjers, Mills and Co. made no contributions at all, whereas their workers gave an annual average totalling £55 and £15, respectively. This is quite striking, considering how many patients were referred to the hospital by these companies.

Of the companies referring employees and their families to the hospital, Cochrane and Co. sent the highest number, as many as 30% of all male surgical cases, and 17% of men referred for medical reasons, 1860–71. They were responsible for 13% of male and 9% of female in-patients in the 1883–1908 period, as Tables 5.10 and 5.11 illustrate. However, this company contributed a total of only £9 on average per annum throughout the period. By contrast, their employees' subscriptions averaged £152 yearly. The hospital's minute books often remarked on this fact: 'The council would contrast the sum contributed by the working men with the small sum which has been contributed by the employers of labour'; 'working men who have so nobly assisted themselves deserve a little more encouragement at the hands of those who are owners of capital'; and noting 'the owners of works whose subscriptions have not covered the cost of patients sent in by them'. Although it looks as though ironmasters and the railway company began to support joint contributory schemes, companies' contributions were clearly minimal compared with the level of support offered by their workers.[20]

Hospital Management

The North Ormesby Hospital was founded in 1859 as the Middlesbrough Cottage Hospital by Sister Mary of the Anglican Christ Church Sisterhood, out of a deep concern about the lack of nursing care available for those injured by a boiler explosion the previous year at Snowden, Hopkins and Co.'s Middlesbrough ironworks. While the hospital retained its religious and charitable influences, very soon after it was built, as we have seen, it came to rely on money raised from workers in the iron and steel and railway companies.[21] With this background in mind, we turn to consider the hospital's internal organization and running.

At the outset, the hospital promoters tried to remain neutral in their dealings with opposing interests, diligently pursuing their own aim to establish an independent medical institution. They not only organized a workers' association in the hospital, named the Working Men's Committee, for the purpose of having workers cooperate formally in fund-raising, but also asked the area's employers to arrange for their workforce to contribute small regular payments to the hospital. The promoters visited the ironworks themselves to encourage these weekly contributions from workers. They urged the local

[20] 15th annual report of the Cottage Hospital, North Ormesby, 1873, p. 7; Teesside Archives, H/NOR 1/1, hospital council minutes 8 Oct. 1879. For employers' contributions to voluntary hospital contributory schemes in East Anglia in the early-twentieth century, see Cherry, 'Beyond National Health Insurance', pp. 478–9.

[21] Stout, *History of North Ormesby Hospital*, pp. 5, 48–85.

Table 5.10. Referrals by Companies to North Ormesby Hospital, 1860–71

Companies			Diseases	
Male surgical cases				
Cochrane & Co.	Ironworks	163 (30.9)	Injury	135
Bell & Brothers Co.	Ironworks	36	Burn & scald	97
Gilkes, Wilson & Co.	Ironworks	22	Fracture	82
Hopkins & Co.	Ironworks	22	Crush	29
Backhouse, Dixon & Co.	Shipbuilding	20	Contusion	7
Bolckow, Vaughan & Co.	Ironworks	16	Wounds	6
Stockton & Darlington Railway Co.		15	Others	18
Jones, Dunning & Co.	Engineering	12		
Other Companies		58		
Total		372 (69.9)		374
Others		33 (6.2)		
No recommendations		127 (23.9)		
Total		532 (100.0)		
Male medical cases				
Cochrane & Co.	Ironworks	75 (17.0)	Rheumatism	40
Gilkes, Wilson & Co.	Ironworks	19	Ulcerated leg, etc.	27
Bolckow, Vaughan & Co.	Ironworks	14	Abscess	19
Bell & Brothers Co.	Ironworks	13	Bronchitis	11
Backhouse, Dixon & Co.	Shipbuilding	11	Phthisis	6
Hopkins & Co.	Ironworks	11	Pneumonia	6
Other Companies		30	Diseases	6
			Inflammation	6
			Others	53
Total		173 (39.0)		174
Others		73 (16.4)		
No recommendations		198 (44.6)		
Total		444 (100.0)		

Note: Percentages in parentheses.

Source: Teesside Archives, H/NOR 10/1.

ecclesiastical community to contribute, setting up various schemes including medical charities such as the Hospital Saturday and Sunday Funds.[22]

In spite of these efforts to broaden the base of support, increasingly in both contributions to fund-raising and numbers of patients admitted, North Ormesby Hospital came to function substantially as a worker's medical centre to treat the accidents that were an almost daily occurrence in this dangerous industrial environment. Immediately after its erection in 1859, and before the formation of the hospital council in 1866, workers employed by four of

---

[22] Teesside Archives, H/NOR 1/1, hospital council minutes 1 July 1868, 2 Aug. 1871, 27 Aug. 1867; Middlesbrough-On-Tees Medical Charities, Hospital Sunday programme, 1872, pp. 1–16. For Scottish voluntary hospitals supported by workers' donations organized within the workplace, see Dupree, 'Provision of Social Service', p. 364.

Table 5.11. Referrals to North Ormesby Hospital, 1883–1908

Companies, etc.	Number of Patients Admitted	%
Male		
Cochrane & Co.	1,277	12.7
Emergency	539	5.4
Raylton Dixon & Co.	477	4.7
Cargo Fleet Iron Works	410	4.1
North Eastern Railway	357	3.5
Wilson, Pease & Co.	344	3.4
Bolckow & Vaughan Co.	285	2.8
Sadler & Co.	269	2.7
Anderston Foundry	239	2.4
Normanby Iron Works	237	2.3
Dorman Long & Co.	208	2.1
Bell Brothers	186	1.8
Clay Lane Iron Works	126	1.3
Accident	86	0.9
Others	5,028	49.9
Total	10,068	100.0
Female		
Cochrane & Co.	428	8.9
Emergency	204	4.2
Bolckow & Vaughan Co.	180	3.7
Dorman Long & Co.	178	3.7
North Eastern Railway	162	3.4
Cargo Fleet & Co.	129	2.7
Anderston Foundry	118	2.5
Wilson, Pease & Co.	101	2.1
Sadler & Co.	99	2.1
Raylton Dixon & Co.	77	1.6
Normanby Iron Works	77	1.6
Bell Brothers	73	1.5
Clay Lane Iron Works	34	0.7
Accident	8	0.2
Others	2,939	61.1
Total	4,807	100.0

Source: Teesside Archives, H/NOR 10/2–3.

the major iron companies in the region, Cochrane, Bolckow and Vaughan, Samuelson, and Snowden, contributed £110, accounting for as much as 23% of the hospital's ordinary income.[23]

From the hospital's foundation, workers employed in heavy industry evidently took an initiative in organizing a system to collect subscriptions. The hospital council minutes reported that a deputation from their Working Men's Committee 'made some suggestions as to improved organization for

---

[23] Annual report of the Cottage Hospital, North Ormesby, 1860, p. 3.

collecting subscriptions and for attending to other matters affecting the interests of the hospital'. A sub-committee was then appointed to consider issues which the workmen's deputation had brought to the council meeting, the result of which was the formation of the House Committee in 1870.[24]

It seems likely that the Working Men's Committee formed in 1867 ceased to be active at the beginning of the 1870s, after fulfilling its role of trustee to enable the region's workers to form a close relationship with the hospital and to support it with substantial contributions. The House Committee, a decision-making agency responsible for the hospital fabric and admissions, was made up of 20 to 36 individuals representing iron and steel, shipbuilding, railways and chemical companies, and friendly societies. The vast majority of committee members were workers. According to the hospital's annual report for 1878, the committee consisted of 28 people, 13 members representing the local area and 15 from the firms. Of the latter, nine were from the main Cleveland ironworks, one from the forge, two from chemical firms, two from the railways and one from shipbuilding.[25]

This arrangement apparently provided a better-organized structure than the provisional association of the Working Men's Committee. At this time the system of collecting workers' contributions became more systematic and structured, with the share of the hospital's ordinary income derived from workers' contributions rising to more than 60%, as we have already observed. The Middlesbrough working class tended to regard this hospital as especially their own, and to give it their united and consistent support, presumably seeing it as the most important safety net available. The hospital's council thought highly of the fact that the workers were assisting themselves and promoting self-help.[26]

Self-help, Patronage or Contributory Insurance?

It appears that the new system, of employers deducting contributions from their workers' wages, replaced an earlier arrangement by which the hospital's Working Men's Committee or Working Men's Meeting had recruited subscribers and received contributions for the hospital. The wage books of Bell Brothers, one of the region's major ironworks, shows that the company's employees in the late 1860s, across the spectrum of skilled, semi-skilled and unskilled, spent approximately 5% of their weekly or fortnightly wages on forms of insurance against emergencies.[27]

Bell Brothers made deductions from their workers' pay for house-rent,

[24] Teesside Archives, H/NOR 1/1, hospital council minutes 8 Oct. 1869, 13 Nov. 1869.

[25] Doyle, 'Power and Accountability', p. 217; 20th annual report of the Cottage Hospital, North Ormesby, 1879, p. 4.

[26] For house committees in voluntary hospitals, see Berridge, 'Health and Medicine', p. 207; for the North Ormesby Hospital house committee, see Doyle, 'Voluntary Hospitals in Edwardian Middlesbrough', pp. 13–20; 9th annual report of the Cottage Hospital, North Ormesby, 1867, p. 6; 10th annual report of the Cottage Hospital, North Ormesby, 1868, p. 2.

[27] British Lib. Polit. and Econ. Science, Coll Misc 0003; for sick clubs in Middlesbrough in the early-twentieth century, see Bell, At the Works, pp. 118–25; for workers' administration of funds collected in companies, see Fitzgerald, British Labour Management, p. 86.

doctor's fees contracted through the company, payments to a sick club and to the 'Roman Catholic Fund'. From their fortnightly wages, 4d or 6d was deducted to pay for the doctor, together with 1s 4d for the sick fund, and 2d as contribution to the North Ormesby Hospital. Workers employed at all Middlesbrough companies had been encouraged to subscribe to the hospital at the time of its opening, when a local newspaper issued the plea: 'Suppose that in the town and neighbourhood there are 20,000 workmen, and that each of them was to subscribe 1d per week, the sum realized by this means would be £82 6s 8d, or £4,281 6s 8d per annum.'[28]

A local newspaper report in 1861 emphasized the benefits of having medical help on hand:

> A somewhat curious and at the same time dangerous accident occurred at the Port Clarence iron works, on Friday last week. A person named John Garvey was engaged in the act of sprigging a wagon, when, through some misapplication of the cumbrous lump of wood, it flew out of the wheel and hit him upon the mouth, cutting his cheek severely, and driving the whole of his front teeth out. A portion of the tongue about three quarters of an inch in length was also taken off. Dr. Young was speedily in attendance and did all that he could to alleviate the poor man's sufferings. The portion of his tongue has been replaced, and the sufferer is progressing as favourably as could be expected under the circumstances.[29]

Guidance for ironmasters across the region on how to make deductions from workers' wages for medical service expenses, industrial physicians' fees, or to support medical institutions, was available from the North of England Iron Manufacturers' Association. An Association meeting in Darlington in 1871 modified the rules in line with alterations suggested by workmen. With the proviso that 'Rules 14 and 15 to be optional according to circumstances of various firms', the following were agreed:

> 14: Every workmen to pay from out of his wages a sum of one penny per week for a doctor, and in consideration of such payment to be entitled, in case of sickness or accident whilst in the service of the firm, to receive medical and surgical attendance without further charge, and a further sum of one halfpenny per week as a subscription to the funds of the .... Infirmary or Hospital. The tickets of admission, &c., received by the firm in exchange for such subscription, will be applied for the use and benefit of workmen requiring the same.

> 15: Any married workman may at his option pay an additional one penny per week, and thereby become entitled to have medical and surgical attendance provided for his wife and family in case of sickness or acci-

[28] *Middlesbrough Times*, 15 Sep. 1860.
[29] *Middlesbrough Weekly News and Cleveland Advertiser*, 11 May 1861.

dent, whilst such workman is in the service of the firm; but this is not to extend to medical attendance for his wife on her confinement.[30]

So at least as far as iron workers employed by members of the North of England Iron Manufacturers' Association were concerned, an agreement between the trade unions and the employers' association containing an element of compulsion relating to medical and surgical insurance was in force in the 1870s.

This evidence suggests that sickness benefit services in the period were independently organized at individual works. It also indicates that within companies, besides the usual sickness schemes which offered compensation for loss of income during illness, or which paid the fees of doctors contracted by the firms, all of these benefits financed by contributions deducted from wages, there was a membership sick club especially designed to send injured employees to North Ormesby Hospital.[31]

In times of sickness, scheme members could call upon this benevolent fund to which they contributed only a minimal amount of money, perhaps a farthing or a penny each week. If dependants of contributory scheme members needed hospital treatment, they could also apply to the fund. It is not entirely clear exactly how the system worked. Most likely the contributing member and their dependants enjoyed free hospital treatment in return for the weekly subscription deducted from wages. Members may have had to be referred for hospitalization by company doctors.[32]

Some of the other channels available in this period to help the working class support themselves in times of hospitalization and other misfortune appear in Table 5.12. The table shows levels of fund-raising and expenditure undertaken by the Middlesbrough branches of the Amalgamated Society of Engineers and the Steam Engine Makers' Society in 1876, with figures for the hospital that same year provided for comparison.

Unionized workers could expect a good return in medical care in exchange for their union subscriptions, with as much as 29% of union funds spent on members' health needs by the Steam Engine Makers' Society and 9% by the Amalgamated Society of Engineers. Even those workers who were not organized into formal associations such as trade unions, friendly societies or other benevolent alliances, could nevertheless qualify for medical care by subscribing to a self-supporting sick and accident fund based on voluntary mutual aid, provided by North Ormesby Hospital. Labourers who were not union members could obtain medical benefits by subscribing 2d a week, deducted from wages by Bell Brothers and other employers.

It was in employers' interests, especially in the iron and steel industry,

30 Univ. of Warwick, Modern Records Centre, MSS 365/NEI.

31 For similar company-based sick benefit services, see for example, Seth-Smith, *200 Years of Richard Johnson & Nephew*, p. 124, and Fitzgerald, *British Labour Management*, pp. 84–92.

32 For subscriptions and hospitalization practices in early twentieth-century voluntary hospitals on contributory schemes, see Cherry, 'Beyond National Health Insurance', p. 467.

to support a wide variety of welfare services for their workers, and it seems that many companies did so. Relying upon export markets, iron and steel manufacturers were forced to be highly competitive and were susceptible to trade cycles. Company-based or company-specific labour management and industrial welfare were important means of cultivating a loyal workforce.[33]

Labour shortages and high turnover were very serious problems in a newly-built, isolated, industrial community heavily dependent upon the staple industries of iron and steel and railways. As Robert Fitzgerald has pointed out, in such circumstances employers tried to create an internal labour market within their firms, not only through improved security of employment but also by providing welfare benefits. In an industry as competitive as iron and steel, with small- and medium-scale firms predominant, this tendency was quite remarkable.[34]

From the employers' viewpoint it was sensible to combine this policy with paternalism, particularly towards non-unionized labour in the small- and medium-sized iron and steel businesses prevalent at this time. For instance, Bell Brothers, which hired many unskilled Irish labourers to work on their furnaces, used company welfare as an important tool of labour management. With a generally paternalistic attitude, they attempted to appease the non-unionized members of their workforce by offering company-based private welfare schemes to persuade workers not to act against them during industrial disputes.[35]

Another factor explains the unusual welfare system prevailing in Middlesbrough and its neighbourhood during this period. As noted earlier, a rapidly expanding iron and steel sector, offering increasing employment for both skilled and unskilled labour, and combined with higher productivity achieved with the Cleveland Practice of iron-making developed in the late 1860s and early 1870s, brought higher wages. It was these high levels of pay that made possible workers' healthcare security based on self-help principles, and its fairly smooth introduction into the Middlesbrough area.[36]

Not only in pig iron but also in wrought-iron making, wage levels in Middlesbrough iron and steel were remarkable, by far the highest reached by Welsh and other British counterparts, for example, those in Staffordshire or even in Belgium. A letter sent in 1864 from the General Manager's office of Bolckow, Vaughan and Co. Ltd to William Menelaus, general manager of Dowlais Ironworks in Merthyr Tydfil, confirms the wage differential between Witton Park Mill employees and their Welsh equivalents: 'All men helping to charge and draw as well as the [?watchers], are paid day work by the

---

[33] Fitzgerald, *British Labour Management*, p. 77.

[34] Fitzgerald, *British Labour Management*, p. 3.

[35] Fitzgerald, *British Labour Management*, pp. 84–7; Chase, '"Dangerous People"?', pp. 33–5.

[36] Bell, *Manufacture of Iron and Steel*, pp. 562–7; Landes, *Unbound Prometheus*, pp. 219, 228, 268–9; Harrison, 'Development of a Distinctive Cleveland Blast Furnace Practice', pp. 57–64, 74–9, 84–9; *John Gjers: Ironmaster*, pp. 10–11, 27, 60, 81; Jeans, *Notes on Northern Industries*, p. 65; Gjers, 'President's Address', pp. 30–54, Appendix Tables B, C.; Gjers, 'Description of the Ayresome Ironworks, pp. 202–17.

Table 5.12. Fund-raising and Expenditure of Middlesbrough Associations, 1876

	Amalgamated Society of Engineers (No. of Branch Members: 228)			Steam Engine Makers Society (No. of Branch Members: 15)			North Ormesby Hospital		
	£	s	d	£	s	d	£	s	d
Income									
Contributions, etc.	515	11	8	21	16	7	Subscriptions — 230	6	6
Received from other branches	110	0	0	36	2	0	Subscriptions from Workmen — 646	15	11
Others	36	3	3	3	9	7	Donations — 611	5	9
Total	661	14	11	61	8	2	Total — 1,488	8	2
Balance, Dec., 1875	1,269	18	5	21	11	8	Balance, Dec., 1875 — 426	8	4
Grand Total	1,931	13	4	82	19	10	Grand Total — 1,914	16	6
Expenditure									
Travelling	391	4	10	2	8	7.5	House-keeping Acc. — 1,447	14	11
Unemployed	–	–	–	13	10	0	Medical & Surgical Acc. — 87	4	1
Sick	169	5	4	23	16	4	Furnishing & Repair Acc. — 89	14	1
Funerals	12	0	0	5	0	0	Establishment Acc. — 284	5	0
Superannuation	4	8	0	–	–	–	–	–	–
Others	39	12	11	9	3	3.5	Others — 5	18	5
Total	616	11	1	53	18	3	Total — 1,914	16	6
Balance, Dec., 1876	1,315	2	3	29	19	10	Balance, Dec., 1876 — –	–	–
Grand Total	1,931	13	4	82	19	10	Grand Total — 1,914	16	6

Source: Univ. of Warwick, Modern Records Centre, MSS 259/2/1/1; Annual Report of the Income and Expenditure of the Steam Engine Makers' Society, 1876, p. 198.

company at rates 30 per cent or so higher than men of the same class are paid with you ... This is, I fancy, much above what you have to pay.'[37]

From the late 1860s to 1874, real wages of wrought iron workers in the Cleveland region were also steadily rising. After that, during the depression from 1875 until 1879, there was a decreasing trend in wages. While employment opportunities remained abundant, though, and wages and living standards relatively high, the Middlesbrough working class could afford to give money to hospital-building and had the resolve to participate in managing their own medical institution. This relative affluence enjoyed by the working population in mid-Victorian Middlesbrough fostered respect for independence and self-help as well as the determination to establish their own safety net.[38]

Apart from company-based private welfare provision, evidently rather unsystematic and limited at this stage, Middlesbrough's own economic structure, that is, a newly founded town whose economy was extremely concentrated on iron and steel and the railways, gave rise to the unusual welfare system described here. A mono-industrial structure, with most employees experiencing very similar working conditions, presented workers with obvious interests in common. Besides this, the heavy influx of young population within a short period, and resultant increased density of population, heightened not only the *densité matériale* but also intensified the sphere of human relations, *densité morale, densité dynamique* or *densité sociale* as Durkheim asserted.[39]

Banks also noticed this feature of the local mid-Victorian urban community, remarking that 'in so far as a town like Middlesbrough could be shown to display characteristics of "moral density" distinct from what obtained generally, and more like what was typical of the American frontier, added emphasis would be given to the analysis of urban life in Durkheimian terms'.[40] Thus the medical care prevailing there, provided by a voluntary hospital based on contributory schemes rather than on an old subscription-recommendation system, could be said to be a quasi-public model of social security.

Lastly, let us consider the foundations and character of such a voluntary hospital, based on this study of the early stages of a hospital system that was built on nascent contributory schemes. Middlesbrough workers were inclined to be heavily involved in a range of collective self-help organizations, such as friendly societies, trade unions or other benevolent societies, as Asa Briggs noted. This was presumably a consequence of Middlesbrough's being an entirely new town, planted as late as 1830, without the fixed or disposable old endowments and legacies available elsewhere, as in London, Bristol, Birmingham, Liverpool, Sheffield, Leeds, Glasgow or other long-established centres. So Middlesbrough's

---

[37] *Middlesbrough Weekly News and Cleveland Advertiser*, 3 Aug. 1866; 17 Aug. 1866; *The Times*, 25 and 27 Sep. 1866; Glamorgan R.O., D/D G/C5/11/19.

[38] Porter, 'David Dale and Conciliation', p. 171; *The Times*, 25 Sep. and 27 Dec. 1866; cf. Doyle, 'Power and Accountability', p. 212; for the argument that relatively high wages allowed Lancashire workers to afford contributions, see Dupree, 'Provision of Social Service', p. 359.

[39] Durkheim, *De la Division du Travail Social*, p. 257.

[40] Banks, 'The Contagion of Numbers', pp. 116–17.

working class had to strive to cater for their own needs, which was likely to have strengthened among the workers a grassroots solidarity, or a shared sense of collective identity with other inhabitants. A wide variety of other voluntary associations, as noted in Chapter 3, also helped this process of integration.[41]

Strictly speaking, the system on which the management, finance and fund-raising of the local voluntary hospital were all based, cannot be said to have originated from this working-class grassroots principle *per se*. A remark in North Ormesby Hospital council minutes in 1867 suggests that iron companies 'issue notices to their workmen recommending them to contribute a farthing each man weekly to the hospital'. The workers appear initially to have been rather passive in following a pattern established by hospital promoters and local employers in terms of managerial, financial and fund-raising mechanisms for the new medical institution.[42]

Nevertheless, once the system was in place and workers could identify the hospital as promoting their interests, they came to participate actively. The contributory principle allowing for a certain degree of democratic grassroots involvement was welcomed, encouraging as it did a working-class tradition of self-help, as Harris identified. Working-class people regarded this hospital as particularly their own, and continued to give it their united and systematic support to ensure that it remained a reliable safety net. Having such a medical institution in the vicinity lessened the fear surrounding the ever-present threat of severe industrial accidents in this hazardous physical environment.[43]

Conversely, by maintaining and promoting a voluntary hospital specializing in the treatment of industrial accidents and emergency cases, employers gained tangible advantages, a means of meeting the needs of their workforces, upon which efficient production depended. Thus the origin of medical welfare provision in Middlesbrough was a mixture of indirect company involvement and the encouragement of working-class self-help.

This is the so-called 'mixed economy' where medical service provision with a charitable principle co-exists with a sort of contributory quasi-insurance arrangement supported both by industrial and labour interests. So what we see is a composite system, self-help promoted among the working population, patronage or paternalism of management towards their workforce with the intention of securing a robust and efficient labour force, and an early form of contributory insurance.[44]

The North Riding Infirmary, Regional Governance and Cleveland Elites

Immediately after the Middlesbrough Cottage Hospital opened, and before it moved from the town centre to a healthier site in North Ormesby in

---

[41] Briggs, *Victorian Cities*, p. 246; Turner, 'The Frontier Revisited', pp. 98–9. For the collective identity among workers seen in Bochum in the Ruhr, see Crew, *Town in the Ruhr*, p. 101.

[42] Teesside Archives, H/NOR 1/1, hospital council minutes 27 Aug. 1867.

[43] cf. Harris, "Did British Workers Want the Welfare State?', p. 200. Regarding initiatives taken by workers in other industrial areas, see Weindling, 'Linking Self Help and Medical Science', p. 17.

[44] See Cherry, *Medical Services and Hospitals in Britain*, p. 72.

1861, there were moves to found another voluntary hospital in the town. The body responsible for this scheme included most of the ironmasters in the region together with local authorities, mayor, aldermen, councillors and town clerks. The motivation seems to have been partly a rivalry with the more spontaneous and smaller-scale cottage hospital, in which the Anglican Order of Holyrood played a prominent part, and which gradually came to devote itself exclusively to the relief of the local working class. But another possible explanation for the initiative is that the Cleveland ironmasters, railway companies, local dynasties such as the Pease family, landlords, magistrates and influential members of local authorities saw a new medical institution as another means of asserting themselves in regional governance. These local élites sought to promote paternalistic social welfare with the kind of medical care for industrial accidents provided by North Ormesby Hospital, within a larger-scale medical institution under their own leadership.[45]

It seems clear that the new hospital was intended to extend élite governance, including the role of local authorities, in rivalry with the older establishment supported and managed predominantly by the working class. It was an attempt to enhance the political and social status of the élite by providing medical care for inhabitants of Middlesbrough and the wider region.

Paternalistic welfare provision by the Cleveland local élite extended beyond medical services. Henry Bolckow founded the Albert Park in 1866, which cost him as much as £30,000, and made gifts of £7,000 towards new schools in the town in 1869, 1873 and 1874. Isaac Wilson and William Taylor established and managed the Middlesbrough Mechanics' Institute in 1840. As Pat Hudson points out:

> The new entrepreneurial classes, prominent ironmasters and other industrialists, came to dominate the municipal administrations, charities, and social and cultural lives of most industrial cities. Participation in local government or charities and civic duties raised the profile and respectability of businessmen whilst creating opportunities for regular meetings and ceremonies which enhanced the integration and legitimacy of local commercial élites.

Likewise the network which promoted and managed the North Riding Infirmary consisted of ironmasters, railway owners, clergymen, landed interests, local statesmen and municipal authorities.[46]

It is remarkable that this group thought of entirely replacing the North Ormesby Hospital with their own new medical institution. Edward Gilkes, owner of an important engine works in Middlesbrough and a promoter of the

---

[45] *Middlesbrough Weekly News and Cleveland Advertiser*, 11 Feb. 1860.
[46] Gott, *Henry Bolckow*, pp. 88–9; Lillie, *History of Middlesbrough*, pp. 110–11, 176; Hudson, 'Industrial Organization and Structure', p. 50; for nineteenth-century local élites in Britain see Goldsmith and Garrard, 'Urban Governance', pp. 17–18.

Plate 5.2. North Riding Infirmary

new hospital, made this clear at a meeting in December 1859: 'The present institution', that is the North Ormesby Hospital, he said, 'would have to be supported for the next two years' and he repeated that 'the present hospital would have to be supported in the meantime'.[47]

The new hospital was intended to encompass the whole of the Cleveland district, with the proposed title the Cleveland District Infirmary. Isaac Wilson MP, a partner in the Gilkes Wilson engine works, suggested that 'something more than a small hospital, like the present, was needed, and anything established to succeed must embrace the whole of the Cleveland district'. When this hospital was officially opened in 1864, the proud local view that Middlesbrough was the most populous centre of the North Riding of Yorkshire became enshrined in its new title, the North Riding Infirmary. The towns of Darlington, Stockton and other municipalities in South Durham were also invited to be involved.[48]

In the early stages of its foundation, many prominent ironmasters, and the Pease family for the railway company, as well as the region's landed interests, donated liberally to the project, a total of £3,435 (see Table 5.13). The municipal authority also supported the North Riding Infirmary with annual subscriptions, shown in Table 5.14. The Catholic Church expressed opinions on management of the planned hospital, and offered objections to certain rules about religious provision for patients. As Goldsmith and Garrard point out, local and urban governance in this period involved 'a wider range of actors in the business of governing the local community, and the development of partnerships and joint ventures by the local authority with other public, private, voluntary and grassroots organizations'. It included 'a whole

---

47 *Middlesbrough Weekly News and Cleveland Advertiser*, 3 Dec. 1859.
48 *Middlesbrough Weekly News and Cleveland Advertiser*, 3 Dec. 1859; 9 Sep. 1866; 11 Feb. 1860.

Table 5.13. Donations Promised to North Riding Infirmary, 1860

Donors	£	s	d
The Right Honorable Earl of Zetland	200	0	0
The Right Honorable Lord Feversham	50	0	0
The Stockton Darlington Railway Company	500	0	0
Messrs. Bolckow and Vaughan	500	0	0
Total	1,250	0	0
Joseph Pease, Esq.	150	0	0
John Pease, Esq.	50	0	0
Henry Pease, Esq., MP	50	0	0
Joseph Whitwell Pease, Esq.	50	0	0
Henry Fell Pease, Esq.	50	0	0
Edward Pease, Esq.	50	0	0
Arthur Pease, Esq.	50	0	0
Gurney Pease, Esq.	50	0	0
Total	500	0	0
Messrs Gilkes, Wilson & Co.	100	0	0
Messrs Gilkes, Wilson, Pease & Co.	100	0	0
Total	200	0	0
Messrs Snowden & Hopkins	200	0	0
Messrs Bell Brothers	200	0	0
Bernard Samuelson, Esq.	100	0	0
The National Provincial Bank of England	100	0	0
Messrs. J. Backhouse & Co.	100	0	0
Thomas Light Elwon, Esq.	100	0	0
John Beaumont Pease, Esq.	50	0	0
The Honorable W.E. Duncombe, MP	25	0	0
John Castell Hopkins, Esq.	25	0	0
Messrs. Fossick & Hackworth	20	0	0
Messrs. Richardson, Duck & Co.	20	0	0
Joseph Taylor	10	0	0
Henry Thompson, Esq.	10	0	0
Joseph Firmstone, Esq.	10	0	0
Messrs. Anthony Harris & Co.	5	0	0
Messrs. Warner, Lucas & Barret	5	0	0
Messrs. Newsom & Brewster	5	0	0
Total	985	0	0
Grand total	2,935	0	0

Source: *Middlesbrough Weekly News and Cleveland Advertiser*, 18 Feb. 1860.

series of joint ventures, coalitions, and building networks and partnerships with other organizations, many of which are often orchestrated by the local authority'. The men of influence in the region all played a significant role in the birth of the North Riding Infirmary.[49]

---

[49] *Middlesbrough Weekly News and Cleveland Advertiser*, 18 Feb. 1860; 11 Feb. 1860; Teesside Archives, CB/M/T, General District Revenue, etc., 1866–74; Goldsmith and Garrard, 'Urban Governance', p. 16.

From the outset, the role of directing the hospital was firmly assigned to the local élite. Four noblemen, the Earl of Zetland, Lord Feversham, Lord De L'isle and Dudley and Lord Teignmouth were appointed as presidents, and there were as many as 45 vice-presidents, all of them men of influence in the North East: members of parliament, clergymen, mayors, ironmasters, representatives of the Pease family and the owner of the *North Eastern Daily Gazette*, which covered an area far beyond Middlesbrough, including Darlington, Stockton and Richmond. Seven prominent ironmasters and Pease family members became the trustees. The manager of the Middlesbrough branch of the National Provincial Bank was appointed hospital treasurer, while the mayor, aldermen and council of Middlesbrough, along with ironmasters and Joseph Pease, formed a committee to purchase land for a site for the proposed infirmary.[50]

It seems that the Cleveland élite achieved their objective with the newly built medical institution, for as Table 5.15 shows, the number of in-patients, diseases treated and level of hospital mortality were almost the same as those at North Ormesby Hospital. The two cases described below, one treated at North Ormesby Hospital and the other at the North Riding Infirmary, are similar enough to suggest that both medical institutions would deal with industrial accidents and traumatic injuries. North Ormesby Hospital treated this serious scalding injury in 1860:

> A serious accident occurred at the works of Messrs. Bolckow and Vaughan ... to a poor lad some 13 years of age, named Joseph Brittain ... The injured lad was attending to his duty, being at the time of the accident engaged in lifting a bar of iron, when his foot accidentally slipped, and he was thrown helpless into a slag bogie full of furnace refuse in a state of fusion close by. He was drawn out instantly but his right leg was frightfully scalded by the metal. On the same evening he was taken to the Cottage Hospital, where he at present lies under the care of the doctors of that institution and the worthy lady superintendent. Probably the leg will have to be amputated.[51]

The second case was dealt with by the North Riding Infirmary immediately after it opened in 1864:

> A serious accident occurred at the works of Messrs Bell, Brothers, Port Clarence, to a labourer named Peter Trotter, 31 years of age. A little after 10 o'clock, Trotter, in attending to his regular duties, was riding on the wagons of a mineral train, when he, by some mishap or other fell off on to the line below, and two of the wagons laden with iron stone, passed over his right leg, severing it completely from the body. The poor fellow was at once taken to the North Riding Infirmary, when Dr. Craster cut away the lacerated portions of his leg, and performed amputation.[52]

---

[50] *Middlesbrough Weekly News and Cleveland Advertiser*, 11 Feb. 1860.
[51] *Middlesbrough Weekly News and Cleveland Advertiser*, 21 Jul. 1860.
[52] *Middlesbrough Weekly News and Cleveland Advertiser*, 24 Jun. 1864.

Table 5.14. Subscriptions by the Borough of Middlesbrough to the North Riding Infirmary, 1866–74

Year	Subscription	
1866–7	£10	
1867–8	£10	
1868–9	£35	Includes subscriptions to the Reformatories and Industrial School
1869–70	£40 10s	Includes subscriptions to the Reformatories and Industrial School
1870–1	£45 10s	Includes subscriptions to the Reformatories and Industrial School and Hull Training Ship, etc.
1872–3	£35 10s	Includes subscriptions to the Reformatories and Industrial School and Hull Training Ship, etc.
1873–4	£35 10s	Includes subscriptions to the Reformatories and Industrial School and Hull Training Ship, etc.

Source: Teesside Archives, CB/M/T, General District Revenue, etc., 1866–74.

Table 5.15. Number of In- and Out-patients, 1873–94

	North Ormesby Hospital			North Riding Infirmary		
Year	In-patients	Out-patients	Mortality (%)	In-patients	Out-patients	Mortality (%)
1873	240	450	2.9	378	556	6.3
1874	245	480	–	394	451	9.1
1890	521	1,186	6.1	683	2,110	4.1
1891	517	1,193	4.6	611	2,044	6.7
1892	469	1,069	4.5	472	1,809	6.1
1893	517	1,075	4.4	513	2,077	3.7
1894	552	1,047	2.9	666	2,263	6.5

Source: Teesside Archives, H/MI 2/1/4, ff. 3–256; H/MI 2/1/5, ff. 1–348; 1st to 59th Annual Report of the Cottage Hospital, North Ormesby, 1859–1917.

In the 1860s and 1870s, Middlesbrough experienced a boom in hospital-building. Some, as we have seen, was prompted by local initiative, but other ventures resulted from a series of Acts imposing sanitary inspectors and a uniform system of sanitary districts. On the same day that the Cottage Hospital moved from the town centre to the suburban parish of North Ormesby, an auxiliary institution for convalescent in-patients, Coatham Convalescent Home, was opened. Besides the North Riding Infirmary, West Lane Isolation Hospital for infectious diseases, mainly caring for smallpox and typhoid fever cases, opened in 1872. It came under the control of the borough Medical Officer of Health. It was followed, in 1878, by the Middlesbrough Workhouse, with a separate infirmary treating the sick poor.[53]

---

[53] Doyle, 'Changing Functions of Government', pp. 290–1; *Stockton Gazette and Middlesbrough Times*, 24 May 1861.

Towards the end of the nineteenth century came another wave of hospital foundations. Three new medical institutions, Broomlands Children's Hospital under the control of the Poor Law Board of Guardians, Hemlington Smallpox Hospital, and Cleveland Asylum for those suffering mental illness, were added. Middlesbrough's escalation in hospital-building coincided with a rapid expansion of the Cleveland iron and steel industry, which accelerated industrial clustering during the 1860s, and made necessary improvements in urban physical as well as social infrastructure.[54]

Of the Middlesbrough medical institutions which existed in the late-nineteenth century, North Ormesby Hospital and the North Riding Infirmary were organized on principles of voluntarism, whereas five others were funded either by local authorities or through the poor rate, reflecting the so-called mixed economy of welfare schemes. Although the early-twentieth century saw an altered nuance in this relationship of competition and cooperation, between voluntary and municipal, or private and public sectors, throughout the late-nineteenth century the town's two main hospitals, which handled acute, emergency, surgical and industrial accident cases, were based on voluntarism.[55]

Although operating on a code of voluntarism and mutual aid within the local community, as we have observed above, the North Ormesby Hospital was based not on philanthropy and charity dispensed by the middle class, but on the principles of cooperative or friendly societies more often found in Yorkshire woollen mills or Lancashire cotton-spinning factories. Fund-raising and management were under the control of artisans and the working class. Their pride in providing a reliable level of healthcare security for workers exposed daily to severe dangers, is evident from the hospital's House Committee records.[56]

The status of House Committee members at the North Riding Infirmary from 1872 to 1875, shown in Table 5.16, is clear indication of the differences between Middlesbrough's two main medical institutions at that time. In the early-twentieth century, the infirmary's House Committee became increasingly worker dominated. Yet in day-to-day hospital running and important administrative decision making, this committee was far less powerful than its equivalent body at the North Ormesby Hospital, reflecting the influence of the local élite from the time of the infirmary's establishment.[57]

Fund-raising and management of the purpose-built North Riding Infirmary were more systematic and formalized than at the North Ormesby Hospital, with

54 Doyle, *History of Hospitals in Middlesbrough*, pp. 10–11.
55 Doyle, 'Competition and Cooperation', pp. 355–6.
56 Hudson, *Genesis of Industrial Capital*, pp. 21, 76–81; Morris, 'Clubs, Societies and Associations', p. 40; Pickstone, *Medicine and Society'*, p. 11; 20th annual report of the Cottage Hospital, North Ormesby, 1879, p. 4.
57 Doyle, 'Power and Accountability', p. 221.

its cottage hospital origins and working-class leadership. The infirmary's fund-raising was a mixture of eighteenth-century voluntarism based on philanthropy and charity, and the type of contributory scheme procedures adopted by North Ormesby. Thus:

> Subscribers of one guinea per annum have the privilege of recommending one out-patient, of two guineas, two out-patients, or one in-patient; and subscribers of larger sums in the same proportion, during the time of their subscription. Benefactors who have at one time given £10 to the charity have the same privileges during their lives as annual subscribers of one guinea, and so in proportion for greater benefactions.

Among the subscribers was the Independent Order of Oddfellows based in Middlesbrough, which resolved in 1866 that 'the district subscribe £10 10s automatically to the North Riding Infirmary'.[58]

Every subscriber of two guineas or more to the infirmary became a governor, who was:

> Entitled to recommend at any time any additional number of in-patients, on the payment of two guineas for each; and the minister of any church or chapel making a collection has power to recommend one in or two out-patients for every amount of £10 10s. during one year after the payment of such collection, and for £20 shall be a governor for 10 years. Religious or civil institutions, mercantile or other firms giving benefactions of £20 or upwards, may nominate one of their body to whom the privilege shall be limited. Any person bequeathing a legacy of £50 or upwards may by his or her will or codicil nominate a life governor.[59]

The system based on subscribers recommending in- and out-patients was similar in principle to that adopted by the Leeds General Infirmary, and by most voluntary hospitals established in the eighteenth century. Yet at the same time the North Riding Infirmary depended for its running costs on the same method of working-class subscriptions and contributions employed by North Ormesby Hospital. The Infirmary House Committee's minutes in 1873 show how the system worked. Andrew Brown was reported as referring to his workmen's contributory scheme: 'My men have been paying 1d per week per man ... I have now in hand I think about 11 weeks' contributions and intend sending them to the committee at the infirmary next week'.[60]

Soon after the infirmary's foundation, in 1866, its governors had to appeal in the local newspaper for more support:

58   *Middlesbrough Weekly News and Cleveland Advertiser*, 28 Sep. 1866; Teesside Archives, U/OD 1/1.
59   *Middlesbrough Weekly News and Cleveland Advertiser*, 28 Sep. 1866.
60   Pickstone, *Medicine and Society*, p. 11; Sigsworth, 'Gateways to Death?', pp. 99–100; Yasumoto, *Industrialisation, Urbanisation, and Demographic Change*, pp. 113–56; *Middlesbrough Weekly News and Cleveland Advertiser*, 3 Dec. 1859; Teesside Archives, H/MI/2/1/4, f. 58.

Table 5.16. North Riding Infirmary House Committee Members, 1872–5

Carl F.H. Bolckow (ironmaster, nephew of Henry Bolckow)
John Gjers (ironmaster)
Isaac Sharp (accountant, gasworks-manager, agent to the Owners of the
    Middlesbrough Estate, the first improvement commissioner)
Edgar Gilkes (ironmaster, town councillor, mayor)
John Beaumont Pease (woollen manufacture, ironmaster, alderman)
John Dunning (surveyor, inspector, etc., agent to the Owners of the Middlesbrough
    Estate, ironmaster, town councillor, alderman, mayor)
H.G. Reid (owner of the North Eastern Daily Gazette)
Rev. Canon George Austin (clergyman)
Robert Stephenson (town councillor, alderman, mayor)
John Imeson (theatre owner, town councillor, alderman, mayor)
John Hunter (theatre owner, town councillor)
Thomas Brentnall (grocer, town councillor, alderman, mayor)
Henry Thompson (chemist's shop owner, town councillor, alderman, mayor)
Thomas Dalkin (town councillor, alderman, mayor)
David Buckney (town councillor)
Thomas George Robinson (town councillor)
James Jennings (town councillor)
John Hunter (town councillor)
George Hearse (town councillor)
John Frederick Wilson (ironmaster, town councillor, alderman)
Joseph Hutchinson (town councillor)
John Rushford (town councillor)

Sources: Teesside Archives, H/MI/2/1/4, ff. 3–256; Lillie, *History of Middlesbrough*, pp. 467–72 *et passim*; Orde, *Religion, Business and Society*, pp. 2, 4, 33, 64, *et passim*; Tomlin and Williams, *Who was Who*, pp. 7–48; Gott, *Henry Bolckow*, p. 99.

> Very many of the working men of the neighbourhood and sailors visiting the port have shewn their appreciation of the value of the infirmary by contributing nearly £800 in small sums weekly… [but] expenses are of necessity very heavy, especially at the outset… [and] at least £1,000 a year is required to uphold the institution and provide for even the present average of patients, from 20 to 30 in number.[61]

During the infirmary's early years in operation, it often had deficits, which were covered by the National Provincial Bank in Middlesbrough and the region's ironmasters. A shortfall of £697 in 1873 was paid off by Bolckow and Vaughan. As the infirmary had its foundations in voluntarism, its aim was essentially to 'benefit the community without financial gain to itself', including self-help or mutual aid 'whose object was the well-being of the individual or group choosing to take part in it'.[62]

---

61 *Middlesbrough Weekly News and Cleveland Advertiser*, 28 Sep. 1866.
62 Teesside Archives, H/MI/2/1/4, ff. 3–256; Lillie, *History of Middlesbrough*, p. 176; Dupree, 'Provision of Social Service', p. 356.

From the standpoint of the Cleveland élite, North Ormesby's position as the only hospital available to the region's inhabitants was not acceptable. The medical care practised at North Ormesby, under working-class control, was apparently successful, and it seems that this was a source of frustration and a challenge to the economic, political, social and religious élites centred upon the Cleveland heavy industries. That a monopoly of local medical care was enjoyed by North Ormesby Hospital, they perhaps saw as an evasion of their own responsibility for regional governance.

The movement to improve welfare provision intensified against a background of the great strike and lockout of 1866. A new prominence was given to enhancing the town's physical and social infrastructure, further developing the North Riding Infirmary and other medical institutions, providing public spaces such as Albert Park, and extending local authority powers to upgrade the urban environment through an Improvement Act in 1866, the fourth since 1841. Not a few remarkable historical events in Middlesbrough and the Cleveland region during this period should be understood in the context of a local élite intent on avoiding severe class conflict, and trying to mitigate a serious antagonism between labour and capital.[63]

This chapter has illustrated how welfare provision in mid-Victorian Middlesbrough developed from a 'minimal' or 'minimalistic' state, working through a mixed transitional stage, before a shift to more uniform and higher minimum standards of provision by central government and commercial insurance companies. Welfare provision here was profoundly influenced by the town's unique trajectory of urban development and by the economic, social and political environments which it shaped. North Ormesby Hospital continued to be predominantly based on the voluntarism of the working class, while the North Riding Infirmary, initiated as a means through which the Cleveland local élite might extend its role in regional governance, was based on voluntarism and local authority support. Other medical institutions established in Middlesbrough in the late-nineteenth century were managed with funds either from local authorities or from poor rates.[64]

At the beginning of the twentieth century, both North Ormesby Hospital and the North Riding Infirmary became 'genuinely pan-class organizations in which middle- and working-class groups shared responsibility and management functions'. Yet the pattern of voluntarism and mutual aid organized by the workers of mid-Victorian Middlesbrough remained in the mainstream of welfare provision. In the history of British medical welfare provision before the National Health Service was established, Middlesbrough's hospital development was an unusual case in which, as Doyle has suggested, 'workers were not only consumers but also producers of hospital services'.[65]

---

63 Gott, *Henry Bolckow*, pp. 88–9.
64 Thane, 'Government and Society', pp. 31–3, 37; Matthew, *Gladstone*, p. 169; Dupree, 'Provision of Social Service', pp. 393–4; Doyle, 'Power and Accountability', p. 209.
65 Doyle, 'Power and Accountability', pp. 218, 224.

6

Conclusion

In mid-Victorian economic and social history, Middlesbrough holds a unique position. It made a substantial contribution to establishing institutions of historical importance: an industrial clustering based on Britain's leading industrial sector at that time; a system of labour relations founded in conciliation and arbitration; and associations delivering welfare provision on the principle of working-class self-help. Middlesbrough also offers a remarkable case study of a rapidly forming urban identity, as well as an example of transient prosperity. Within a relatively short period, the town experienced the full life-cycle of an industrial district, from critical mass to take-off, peak entry to saturation.[1]

The Board of Arbitration and Conciliation for the North of England Manufactured Iron Trade in particular was a pioneering episode in British labour history. Its aim was to centralize negotiations between employers and employed about wages and working conditions, by establishing a representative body of conciliation that bargained on behalf of the whole industry across the region. The board afterwards drew up rules for a sliding scale to fix wage rates, thus avoiding any severe conflict between capital and labour, and securing stable development for the industry. This was significant in facilitating a sustained growth in Cleveland iron and steel, for a time at least.[2] It was the first such attempt in a key British industry, and contributed largely to establishing an efficient and peaceful system of agreeing pay rates, in a highly competitive trade susceptible to sharp business fluctuations. In a region where a single industry dominated the local economy, this institution had a decisive impact on the regional economy.

The Great Strike and lockout in 1865 and 1866 had a deep effect on industrial relations in Cleveland iron and steel.[3] The latter half of the 1860s heralded a period of peaceful solution to industrial disputes, with terms of employment and wage levels set by the newly established Board of Arbitration and Conciliation from 1869. Before the arbitration and conciliation system became institutionalized thus, employers associated within the North of England Iron Manufacturers' Association in 1865, and the Cleveland Ironmasters' Association in 1866. Workers were represented by a national trade

---

1   Wilson and Popp, *Industrial Clusters and Regional Business Networks*, p. 7.
2   *Ironworkers Journal*, 1 June 1870.
3   For labour disputes in Cleveland 1864–6, see Tholfsen, *Working Class Radicalism*, pp. 183–4; Gott, *Henry Bolckow*, p. 45; Howard, 'Strikes and Lockouts in the Iron Industry', p. 419; Cockcroft, 'Great Strike', pp. 4–5; Chase, *Early Trade Unionism*, pp. 230–1.

union, the National Amalgamated Association of Malleable and Other Iron-workers, from 1868. The fact that these institutions based on mutual coopera-tion, speaking for both employer and employed, already existed in the region, made possible the arbitration and conciliation system and made it so effective in establishing peaceful relationships.

After the Great Strike in 1866, in which the National Association of Puddlers, Shinglers, Rollers, Millmen and Others was defeated decisively though not completely broken, the first institutionalized collective bargaining in the iron and steel industry was launched. One of its most active promoters, David Dale, director of the Consett Iron Company,[4] who would become the Board's first president, later described the impetus behind this initiative:

> It was the feeling that there was needed some organization by which the bargain between the two classes could be brought about. It was felt that though a bargain had to be made between the two parties, there was no agency or machinery by which the class bargain could be entered into; and it was that which first led to the desire to establish some sort of representative body, by which that class bargain could be effected.[5]

David Dale had persuaded the ironworkers to inspect the Board of Hosiery and Glove Trades of Nottingham, which had been established by A. J. Mundella, while as chairman of the North of England Iron Manufac-turers' Association, he had asked his members to consider 'the establishment of a local committee of employers and employed'. An association meeting resolved 'that a committee considering of the two joint standing commit-tees be appointed to prepare a draft scheme' in 1868. The next year, the association agreed to adopt a plan to establish the board, 'should the men be favourable to the experiment'. In the meantime, before any final decision by the association, the ironworkers signalled their acceptance of the machinery of conciliation, as their official organ, the *Ironworkers Journal*, reported in detail. As an influential trade union leader, and later arbitrator on the board, John Kane, testified to the parliamentary committee, one main reason why the conciliation system was set up at this time was that the trade union was exhausted after the unsuccessful strikes of 1866.[6]

Establishing formal arbitration procedures was a sign of improved class relations, and testimonies confirm the conciliation board's success. Henry Crompton, a referee for the Board of Arbitration and Conciliation for the Lace Trade in Nottingham, used his own experience to assess the perform-ance of the North of England body. In 1869, he noted, the board represented

---

4   Warren, *Consett Iron*, pp. 23, 25, 81.
5   *Trans. National Assoc. Promotion of Soc. Science* (Newcastle upon Tyne, 1870), pp. 476–7.
6   Modern Records Centre, Univ. of Warwick, MSS.365/NEI, pp. 163–4, 167-70, 176; Porter, 'Wage Bargaining under Conciliation Agreements', p. 462; Odber, 'Origins of Industrial Peace', p. 209; Hicks, 'Early History of Industrial Conciliation', p. 36; *Ironworkers Journal*, 15 Mar. 1869; PP, 1868-9 [4123-I] XXXI, qu. 8329-79.

35 ironworks and about 13,000 workers. Each works sent two delegates, an employer and an operative. A large proportion of the region's companies was represented on the board, which was made up of firms running 1,913 puddling furnaces, of a total 2,136.[7]

Crompton reported that 'since the board has been in existence there have been six arbitrations on the general question of wages: three before Mr. Thomas Hughes, two before Mr. Kettle, and one recently before two arbitrators, Mr. Williams and Mr. Mundella, who agreed without reference to the umpire fixed upon'. Between 1869 and 1875, wages were settled without resort to strikes or lockouts, and in 1875 the board's committee adjudicated on more than 40 disputes, with its decisions generally accepted and any appeal exceptional.[8]

Crompton believed that the achievements of the North of England body could be attributed to the breadth of representation on its board. Its equivalent for the South Staffordshire iron trade, which was less successful according to Crompton, was composed of two ironmasters' associations along with the trade union, while in northern England the organization consisted 'simply of 12 masters and 12 operatives, but every works joining the board shall if possible have a representative of the employers and a representative of the operatives'. In South Staffordshire, there had been 'no attempt to include those who were outsiders and not unionists'. In a period when unions did not yet represent a majority of workers in the region, the method of representation adopted by the board in Cleveland, with membership based on the works, not the union, seems to have been the key to a more effective means of conciliation.[9]

More pertinent to the northern board's success, in Crompton's view, was that it was 'adapted to all industries in which the employments are not too varied, and which are grouped into large aggregates, as distinguished from those trades which are scattered all over the kingdom'. The industrial agglomeration established in Cleveland by the latter half of the 1860s enabled the board's formation, and ensured its smooth running. According to Porter, between 1865 and 1896 there were 34 wage arbitration awards by the iron industry board, of which the advanced, reduced and unchanged awards account for 26.5%, 41.2% and 32.5%, respectively. Contrast this with the coal industry, where there were no advanced awards at all, while reduced awards made up 90.5%, and unchanged ones 9.5%.

From the late 1860s to the end of the nineteenth century, the existence of the conciliation board and its introduction of the sliding scale to fix wage rates, appear to have worked to the advantage of Cleveland ironworkers, compared with their equivalents in other regions and industries. In 1869, its first verdict was to raise wages from 8s to 8s 6d per ton. In 1872 came an

7   Crompton, *Industrial Conciliation*, pp. 56–7.
8   Crompton, *Industrial Conciliation*, pp. 58–9.
9   Crompton, *Industrial Conciliation*, pp. 64–5; Odber, 'Origins of Industrial Peace', pp. 213–15.

increase in puddlers' wages of one shilling a ton, followed by a further rise of 2s, bringing the puddlers' pay to 12s 6d a ton. The following year they had a further 9d. While these improvements in pay did not proportionally match the ironmasters' increases in profits, and of course there were intermittent falls, the institution's effectiveness in raising wage levels should not be lightly dismissed. Between 1870 and 1880, above all in the first half of the 1870s, there was in fact a sharp rise in ironworkers' pay and in real earnings on Teesside.[10]

Despite the improving class relations and general up-turn of the iron trade since 1869, the Middlesbrough industry's decline was already setting in when the town celebrated its jubilee in 1881. The region responded to the situation following the 1873 depression partly by developing a steel industry based on the Thomas-Gilchrist process. However the steel industry in Middlesbrough never enjoyed a prosperity to compare with that experienced during the heyday of iron production. Cleveland pig-iron making began to suffer from a comparative disadvantage as demand for steel overtook that for iron, both at home and abroad. Furthermore, as the high phosphorous Cleveland iron ores were unsuitable for high-grade steel, the local steel plants were obliged to import raw materials from Bilbao in Spain, or from Cumberland.[11]

The apogee of the Cleveland iron and steel industry fell in the latter half of the 1860s and 1870s. From the beginning of the 1880s, its rivals, Germany and the United States, were catching up fast. The British iron and steel industry as a whole was already encountering severe competition from Germany in European markets during the slump from the 1870s and throughout the 1880s. Between 1885 and 1889, Germany's exports of pig iron and steel were equivalent to 28% of the total exported from Britain, 1.16 million tons compared with Britain's 3.76 million tons. One of the largest German iron companies, Bochumer Verein in the Ruhr, exported more than half of its total production in 1887 and 1888.[12]

Towards the end of the nineteenth century, German iron and steel companies moved to overcome their relative disadvantages compared with Britain, by engaging in vertical integration. Meanwhile an import-substituting industrialization proceeded rapidly in the United States, where imports of pig iron declined from 1,282,000 tons in 1872, to 578,000 tons in 1885. Meanwhile, home production grew from 2.55 million tons to 4.04 million tons in this same period. In 1890, America finally surpassed Britain in pig iron production, with 9.2 million tons as against 7.9 million tons.[13]

Moreover, at the end of the nineteenth and the beginning of the twentieth centuries, German producers began to overcome labour cost disadvantages

---

[10] Crompton, *Industrial Conciliation*, pp. 67, 60; Porter, 'Wage Bargaining under Conciliation Agreements', p. 475; Hall, 'Wages, Earnings and Real Earnings', pp. 205, 215–17.

[11] Gott, *Henry Bolckow*, p. 47.

[12] Burnham and Hoskins, *Iron and Steel in Britain*, p. 277; Crew, *Town in the Ruhr*, pp. 36–7.

[13] Crew, *Town in the Ruhr*, p. 39; Burnham and Hoskins, *Iron and Steel in Britain*, p. 272.

by mechanizing production processes and by adopting American technology, for example by electrifying all production processes.[14] Both German and American achievements in raising productivity around the turn of the century were the result of specific efforts to save on labour costs.

The German increase in productivity was such that output per worker, measured in tons per blast furnace employee, expanded by almost 60%, from 187.49 tons in 1890, to 299.44 tons in 1909. In the United States the success was even more remarkable. Between 1890 and 1910, output per worker in blast furnaces there nearly tripled, and in steel plants the output per worker doubled. During the same period, labour costs in American steel making reduced from 22.5% to 16.5%. As stated by Brody, 'labour savings were in fact the nub of the American accomplishment'.[15]

Concomitantly, technological improvement had its effect on labour productivity. Both in pig and wrought iron making, the mechanization of materials handling, the integration of production stages, and introduction of continuous rolling methods, all raised efficiency. In 1890, Sir Lowthian Bell was shocked to discover that Pittsburg blast furnaces smelted six times the quantity of iron as those of his own works at Clarence.[16]

In terms of plant size and integration too, Britain lagged behind Germany and the United States. At the beginning of the twentieth century, the median size of plants belonging to the German steel cartel was four times that of the median for British iron firms, and more than twice that in the Cleveland area. We should beware overstating the extent of these developments and of the decline of British iron and steel, for up to the beginning of the twentieth century the British industry continued to dominate the world market. Yet the point of divergence in Britain's global hegemony in iron and steel can probably be located at the beginning of the twentieth century for pig iron, and 1893 for steel.[17]

The international context – the rapid growth of the American and German iron industries as they developed technologies and improved productivity at the turn of the century – was the most powerful underlying cause of Cleveland's transient prosperity in iron and steel. Yet the economic, social, political, geographical and even cultural structure of Middlesbrough itself must also be considered. Distinct from other Victorian industrial towns, it enjoyed initial good fortune in its natural endowments, reaping a comparative advantage which, however, from the end of the nineteenth century acted as a restraint on further sustainable development.

The cumulative effects of changes experienced in the town from the middle of the nineteenth century brought about idiosyncrasies in industrial, urban and demographic structures. There was an over-reliance upon the iron and steel

---

14 Crew, *Town in the Ruhr*, p. 40.
15 Crew, *Town in the Ruhr*, p. 233; Brody, *Steelworkers in America*, pp. 40, 27–8.
16 Brody, *Steelworkers in America*, pp. 17, 29.
17 Landes, *Unbound Prometheus*, pp. 263, 269.

industry, in terms of industrial make-up, the labour market, entrepreneurial resources and technology. The urban infrastructure was inadequate, and the age and gender profile of the population extraordinary. Towards the end of the nineteenth century, when Middlesbrough iron and steel faced serious competition both at home and abroad, the town found difficulty adapting to changing circumstances, with industry lacking the necessary flexibility to reorganize.[18]

The iron and steel trade was particularly dependent on natural resources, iron ore and coal as well as efficient, low cost transport facilities to carry heavy and bulky materials, needs which tended to determine its location in unusual places. The industry was often to be found close to under-developed colliery or ironstone mining areas, apart from old-established settlements. Such new communities, built largely on iron and steel, generally lacked an economic structure rooted deeply within their surrounding region. Thus the industrial profile of most locations specializing in iron and steel was not sufficiently diversified, as it lacked the broader economic and social bases which should have built cumulatively over a long period. There were obvious exceptional cases with a more varied industrial foundation, for instance the German iron-producing town of Duisburg in the Ruhr valley, which was not overshadowed by any one large company or industry.[19]

A mono-industry structure, with over-concentration upon one staple industry and little diversification into other sectors, tended to lead to inflex-ibility in adapting to changing circumstances. The iron industry, producing capital rather than consumer goods, was particularly susceptible to business fluctuations. Prices of pig iron and finished products were prone to consider-able fluctuation. British iron and steel also had a high degree of dependence on exports throughout the period, so that exogenous factors tended to control the market and demand was unstable. Because initial levels of capital invest-ment were relatively low, the industry was very competitive and carried high risk, especially during the boom period of the late 1860s and 1870s, with the entry of many speculative firms without substantial reserves.[20]

Marshall contrasted a region of diverse economic structure, with one reliant on a mono-industry. He pointed out that 'a district which is dependent chiefly on one industry is liable to extreme depression, in case of a falling off in the demand for its produce, or of a failure in the supply of the raw material which it uses'. Furthermore, 'in those iron districts in which there are no textile or other factories to give employment to women and children, wages are high and the cost of labour dear to the employer, while the average money earnings of each family are low'. He suggested that 'the remedy for

[18] Hudson, 'Institutional Change', pp. 206, 209–10; for features of social class, population change and living conditions in mid-twentieth century Middlesbrough compared with other British urban centres, see Moser and Scott, *British Towns*, pp. 17, 20–4, 92, 146–7

[19] Jackson, *Migration and Urbanization in the Ruhr Valley*, p. 11.

[20] Hicks, 'Early History of Industrial Conciliation', pp. 35–7, 28; PP, 1851 [1691-I] LXXXVIII, Part I, p. cclxxix; Fitzgerald, *British Labour Management*, pp. 3, 77, 84–7.

this evil is obvious, and is found in the growth in the same neighbourhood of industries of a supplementary character. Thus textile industries are constantly found congregated in the neighbourhood of mining and engineering industries, in some cases having been attracted by almost imperceptible steps.'[21]

Compared to nearby Darlington, Middlesbrough is a negative example in terms of the role a town might play within its regional economy. By the eighteenth century, Darlington was established as a thriving market town and regional centre, a hub for distributing agricultural produce from surrounding areas. Accumulated capital generated by the bustling mercantile activity was re-invested to improve the urban infrastructure. From the eighteenth century, consumer goods industries such as foods and textiles developed, while financial facilities necessary for a well-balanced growth of the local economy were established.[22]

Thus Darlington possessed a more diversified economic structure than Middlesbrough, and its consumer goods industries and commerce helped build an organic relationship between the town and its hinterland, as well as with other urban centres. In consequence the town was incorporated within and rooted deeply into the regional economy. The iron and engineering industries developed in Darlington from the mid-nineteenth century were grafted on to an urban economy already matured as the cohesive centre of its region, and they further diversified the town's economic structure. In contrast, Middlesbrough's relationship with surrounding rural areas was of a very limited nature, except in the market for unskilled labour.

From a technological point of view, Middlesbrough was disadvantaged. The effect of the growing iron industry on the town's economy overall seems to have been restricted. Just as Habakkuk has identified with the British textile industry, Middlesbrough did not advance over a wider industrial front, even as the iron industry grew to a considerable size, because its interrelations with other local industries were not of a nature which would automatically stimulate expansion within these other trades. Moreover, technical improvements achieved in iron manufacture could not generally be applied far outside the industries in which they had been made.[23]

Even where there was innovation within a staple industry, because it was limited to one sector it could not be expected to have effects across the wider economy during a severe recession, for as Habakkuk suggests, it is only where resources are stretched that innovation is likely to reverberate in that way. Habakkuk's proposition about cross-fertilization of techniques between different industries, that many later technical innovations consisted of applying the techniques of one industry to another, again highlights

---

[21] Marshall, *Principles of Economics*, pp. 333–4.

[22] Cookson, *Victoria History*, pp. 29–51; *Townscape of Darlington*, pp. 40–102; Banham, *Backhouses' Bank*, pp. 6–35.

[23] Habakkuk, *American and British Technology*, p.181.

Middlesbrough's disadvantage, since its economic base was narrow and less diverse than many other places.[24]

Social structure partly determined the town's pathway in the late-nineteenth century. Middle-class inhabitants were thinly spread, with as much as 85% of the working population engaged in manufacturing, and only 10% in the commercial sector. This brought about an unusual pattern in consumption. Apart from the necessities of daily life – food, drink and clothing – there was little spending on intermediate- and high-quality articles, so that Middlesbrough's economy was caught up in a vicious circle leading to a thinner tertiary sector. The urban upper middle class, chiefly consisting of ironmasters, ceased to live in town, choosing to move to the country. This urban exodus advanced further towards the end of the nineteenth century, when the second generation of these families followed suit. A working-class culture dominated social life in the town.[25]

Environmental factors that adversely affected living conditions were a further influence on the sustainability of this urban community. The original urban settlement of Middlesbrough was planted on land reclaimed from a salt marsh alongside the River Tees. This arrangement was unhealthy from the outset, and subsequently deteriorated because of overcrowding and unplanned insanitary building within the old town. In town-making here, economics counted for more, and desirable urban amenities such as health, good housing or pleasant outlook, for less. The 'shopocracy', which had risen to power in the late-nineteenth century, was specifically responsible for this environmental predicament. Once in control of municipal affairs, the lower middle-class small tradesmen in foodstuffs, clothes and accommodation, aimed above all to keep the cost of local public services to a minimum.

The infant mortality rate (IMR), the number of infants born alive but dying within 12 months, expressed per thousand live births, is stark illustration of urban amenity, environmental and health standards prevailing towards the end of the nineteenth century. The IMR for Middlesbrough was 195 in 1898, 183 in 1899 and 198 in 1900. Compare these with an average IMR in England and Wales of 132 in 1903, and an average for other urban areas of 144.[26]

The stillbirth ratios (SBR) are similarly informative. Stillbirth rates, the number of late foetal deaths calculated per thousand live births, reflect maternal health and are therefore indicative of social, medical and environmental factors.[27] Compared with the overall SBRs for mid- or late-nine-

---

[24] Habakkuk, *American and British Technology*, pp. 185, 193.

[25] Briggs, *Victorian Cities*, pp. 257–8; Harrison, 'Ironmasters and Ironworkers', pp. 234–5; for provision of infrastructure by ironmasters, see McCord and Rowe, 'Industrialization and Urban Growth in North-East England', pp. 34, 49–51, 62–3; Bell, *At the Works*, pp. 127–41, 246–72.

[26] Teesside Archives, CB/M/H2, 1898, p. 4; 1899, pp. 3,8; 1900, p. 10; Davies, 'Maternal Mismanagement or Environmental Factors?', p. 40; regarding low standards of public health in Middlesbrough, see for example Ranger, *Report to the General Board of Health*, pp. 8, 16; National Archives, MH/113/4, pp. 1–2, 4.

[27] Pressat, *Dictionary of Demography*, pp. 84, 214–15; Mooney, 'Stillbirths and the Measurement of Urban Infant Mortality Rates', pp. 42–52.

Table 6.1. Dependency Ratio among the Middlesbrough
Population, 1851–81

Year	Male	Female	Total
1851	679[a]	730	703
1861	632	741	681
1871	574	807	672
1881	665	804	728

Notes: [a]Proportions of the child (0–14) and the elderly (60+)
populations to the working (15–60) population as shown per 1,000
population.

Sources: National Archives, Census Enumerators' Books, HO 107
2383 (1851), RG 9 3685-3689 (1861), RG 10 4889-4895 (1871), C
RG 11/4852 (1881).

teenth-century England, those for Middlesbrough were markedly high. SBRs
in Middlesbrough in 1881, 1898, 1899, 1900 and 1901 measured 68.8, 47.5,
53.7, 54.1 and 59.5, respectively (and see Appendix 4). As these Middlesbrough calculations exclude stillbirth burials at the Roman Catholic graveyard, actual SBRs for the town were higher still.[28]

Between 1840 and 1859, SBRs in England as a whole, estimated by
various methods, ranged from 30 to 44. At the end of the nineteenth
century, the average SBR in England was somewhere around 40; for the
Royal Maternity Charity in London in 1857–61, 34. Liverpool work-
house recorded an exceptionally high SBR of 135, 1868–70 and Glasgow
Maternity Hospital a rate of 150 in 1897. The SBR figure for the Glasgow
Hospital domiciliary service that same year was 83, and 43 in the Glasgow
West End branch.[29]

There are further indicators of deficient standards of public health in
Middlesbrough. In 1887 and 1888, the town experienced an outbreak of infectious disease with pneumonia-like symptoms and an extremely high mortality
rate. In this period, every winter brought a further outbreak of this unidentified infection, and it continued to carry off many victims. The disease, which
infected 369 inhabitants in 1888, differed in many respects from classic pneumonia. In terms of acuteness and high mortality, it was diagnosed neither as
pneumonia nor as tuberculosis, and there was no consensus among patholo-
gists and bacteriologists. Some regarded it as *Yersinia pestis*, others as a
kind of *Bacillus coli communis*, but eventually it was named *Middlesbrough
pleuropneumonia bacillus*.[30] The fact that the infectious disease broke out
frequently, was not identified elsewhere, but was seemingly endemic to
Middlesbrough, seems to indicate worsening living conditions in the town.

---

[28] Calculated from National Archives, RG 11/4852 (1881); Teesside Archives, PR/ACK; CB/M/H2,
      1902, p. 16; 1900, pp. 4, 10, 13.
[29] Woods, *Death before Birth*, pp. 96, 92, 196; *The Demography of Victorian England and Wales*,
      p. 257, fn.
[30] Stout, 'The 1888 Pneumonia in Middlesbrough', pp. 664–8.

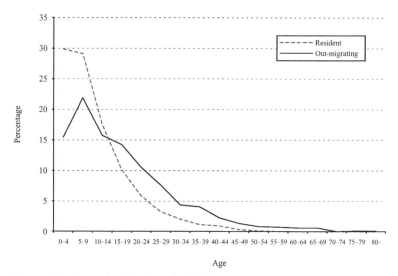

Figure 6.2. Age Distribution of Middlesbrough-born Males (Resident and Out-migrating) in 1881

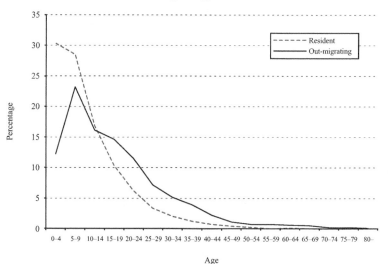

Figure 6.3. Age Distribution of Middlesbrough-born Females (Resident and Out-migrating) in 1881

By the beginning of the 1880s, signs of slack were already starting to appear in the town's economy. The dependency ratio as illustrated in Table 6.1, that is the proportion of child (0–14) and elderly (60+) population to workers aged 15 to 60, shown per 1,000 population, suggests a cloud already hanging over the town's economy in the 1880s. In 1861 and 1871, when business prospects were burgeoning, the dependency rates were 681 and

Table 6.4. Labour Force Participation Rates of Three Different
Middlesbrough Populations aged 15–64, 1881

	Male	*Female*
Middlesbrough Population Enumerated in the 1881 Census	95.5% (17,769)[a]	23.6% (14,958)
Middlesbrough-born Population Resident in Middlesbrough	91.6% (2,016)	33.3% (772)
Middlesbrough-born population Outgoing		
Yorkshire	91.2% (1,001)	41.8% (507)
Durham	94.8% (772)	33.7% (283)
Other 37 Counties & Wales	93.3% (601)	41.6% (232)
Total	92.8% (2,324)	39.2% (1,022)

Note: [a]Working population.

Sources: National Archives, Census Enumerators' Books, RG 11/4852.

672. In 1881, the ratio rose to 728, an increasing proportion of economically dependent to productive inhabitants.

Further evidence from the 1881 census enumerators' books suggests the difficulties facing the town. Data gathered by searching the census across England and Wales for Middlesbrough-born residents shows that, for both males and females and especially among the younger age groups from 15 to 39, far fewer people had stayed in their birthplace than had moved to settle elsewhere (see Figures 6.2 and 6.3). Table 6.4 illustrates that labour force participation rates for females who left the town before 1881 are higher (39.2%) than among those who were born in the town and remained there until 1881 (33.3%), and higher than among all resident females (23.6%).

As Table 6.5 illustrates, there are clear differences in labour force participation rates between the out-migrating and resident population. The rate for out-going young females aged 15 to 19 was over 60%, as against 46.6% for resident females. The next age group, 20 to 24, shows the same trend, 45.5% for out-going as opposed to 34.4% for resident. It suggests that by the 1880s, as Middlesbrough's economy began to falter, employment prospects for the town's working-age population, especially younger females, were less favourable, and that they were likely to have had to leave the town to seek employment elsewhere.

Middlesbrough was evidently some way ahead of many other British urban and industrial centres in seeking solutions to its problems through the self-help principle. There were established, for instance, amicable industrial relations through the conciliation board, a medical institution based on working-class mutual aid and collaborative technical innovations in iron-making encouraged among the Cleveland ironmasters. Yet in spite of the leading role assumed by mid-Victorian Middlesbrough and its region in British industrial and labour history, the town has not yet succeeded in replacing those old industries with new ones.

Table 6.5. Age-specific Labour Force Participation Rates of Middlesbrough-born Population (Resident and Outgoing), 1881

Age	Male		Female	
	Resident	Outgoing	Resident	Outgoing
10–14	12.2	13.0	6.5	11.9
15–19	85.4	85.3	46.6	61.8
20–24	94.1	94.0	34.4	45.5
25–29	97.3	98.1	17.8	23.0
30–34	96.8	97.0	13.1	17.1
35–39	95.2	97.7	8.0	17.6
40–44	94.9	98.3	8.7	18.5
45–49	96.4	98.6	17.1	23.8
50–54	80.0	97.6	20.0	29.3
55–59	87.5	97.4	0.0	31.6
60–64	100.0	96.9	0.0	25.0
15–64	91.6	92.8	33.3	39.2

Sources: National Archives, Census Enumerators' Books, RG 11/4852.

Middlesbrough's historical trajectory was neither typical nor representative of Victorian cities. Yet careful generalization from the town's historical experience may yield worthwhile results. Its story has a significance for understanding late nineteenth-century urban centres more generally, because Middlesbrough's path encapsulated, in a condensed form and within a short period of time, the wider changes that were impacting upon Victorian communities. It would be a tragedy indeed should the vigour of Middlesbrough and its regional economy, with all that it contributed to Victorian prosperity, be lost. Historians cannot, nor should they, forecast the future, and no one can tell whether in future the town of Middlesbrough and its regional economy could revive and live on as a lasting reminder of Victorian industrialization and astonishing urban growth.

Appendices

Appendix 1 Land Sales by the Owners of the Middlesbrough Estate, 1848-91

Appendix 2 Wrought Iron Sales in the North of England, 1873-1917 (% by Weight)

Appendix 3 Wrought Iron Sales in the North of England, 1863-1917

Appendix 4 Infant Deaths in Middlesbrough, 1854-99

Appendix 5 Crimes by Migrants According to Duration of Stay in Middlesbrough, 1860s-1880s

Appendix 6 Crimes by Income Levels in Middlesbrough, 1863-85

Appendix 7 Crimes by Literacy Levels in Middlesbrough, 1861-89

Appendix 8 Crimes by Nationality in Middlesbrough, 1861-89

Appendix 1. Land Sales by the Owners of the Middlesbrough Estate, 1848-91

Year	No. of Sales	Total Area (square yards)	Total Value (£)
1848	4	2,408	1,053.3
1849	1	189	59.5
1851	1	354	118.6
1852	26	15,623	5,976.7
1853	13	57,531	9,886.7
1854	14	20,241	7,188.6
1855	33	34,622	13,078.9
1856	9	5,672	2,486.1
1857	16	28,681	8,544.2
1858	7	7,506	3,349.4
1859	14	19,788	7,506.2
1860	17	36,375	14,799.4
1861	7	10,622	5,133.7
1862	8	17,886	8,315.6
1863	17	32,624	15,324.2
1864	16	17,977	15,515.6
1865	33	65,430	32,117.9
1866	12	141,995	21,074.0
1867	6	10,532	2,765.7
1868	1	6,417	6,130.0
1869	4	6,698	4,558.0
1870	16	70,155	14,768.6
1871	28	60,516	27,960.4
1872	32	78,373	34,155.2
1873	19	185,996	41,896.4
1874	61	86,946	58,716.1
1875	18	29,136	24,169.5
1876	11	71,459	26,339.8
1877	5	14,257	7,583.4
1878	2	3,474	1,228.9
1880	1	6,365	1,750.1
1881	4	34,642	10,049.1
1882	8	6,808	3,599.2
1883	11	12,412	7,119.6
1884	8	15,160	7,017.8
1885	18	12,074	4,705.3
1886	18	16,257	5,575.8
1887	20	29,507	13,241.2
1888	10	8,617	4,412.3
1889	19	23,824	15,651.2
1890	17	11,611	7,188.9
1891	2	6,136	4,496.0

Source: Teesside Archives, U/OME(2) 5/1–5/4.

Appendix 2. Wrought Iron Sales in the North of England, 1873–1917 (% by Weight)

Year	Rails	Plates	Bars	Angles
1873	54.0	26.5	12.7	6.8
1874	45.3	30.6	15.6	8.5
1875	43.3	31.1	18.2	7.4
1876	25.4	41.1	21.1	12.5
1877	9.2	54.2	19.7	16.9
1878	5.1	55.5	18.6	20.8
1879	2.3	59.1	22.0	16.6
1880	5.3	62.2	14.7	17.7
1881	2.6	65.4	11.8	20.2
1882	0.9	68.6	9.9	20.6
1883	0.4	66.9	12.4	20.3
1884	0.8	63.0	19.2	17.0
1885	1.0	57.9	24.8	16.3
1886	1.0	58.8	26.1	14.1
1887	0.9	60.2	25.9	12.9
1888	0.5	61.7	24.3	13.5
1889	0.9	62.0	24.5	12.6
1890	1.4	53.6	31.1	13.8
1891	1.3	53.1	31.1	14.5
1892	2.2	45.4	34.8	17.5
1893	2.6	39.6	41.6	16.2
1894	2.5	40.7	41.8	15.0
1895	2.8	43.5	41.6	12.1
1896	1.9	37.9	46.9	13.3
1897	2.3	40.0	45.8	12.0
1898	2.5	37.0	47.3	13.1
1899	2.4	35.4	49.3	13.0
1900	3.3	31.0	50.2	15.5
1901	1.6	27.7	58.6	12.1
1902	1.4	16.1	67.5	15.0
1903	1.4	18.4	65.0	15.5
1904	0.6	17.9	71.1	10.5
1905	0.8	12.4	76.9	9.8
1906	1.1	11.7	77.3	10.2
1907	1.2	8.8	80.1	9.7
1908	1.8	8.0	82.6	7.6
1909	0.9	16.8	75.0	7.2
1910	0.8	18.7	72.9	7.6
1911	0.5	14.9	79.9	4.7
1912	0.5	12.4	84.4	2.8
1913	0.6	10.8	86.2	2.4
1914	0.3	18.3	79.3	2.2
1915	0.1	14.4	83.7	1.8
1916	0.0	11.0	85.3	3.7
1917	0.2	4.0	94.5	2.2

Source: Modern Records Centre, University of Warwick, Board of Arbitration and Conciliation for North of England Manufactured Iron Trade (MSS.365/BAG), Mr. Waterhouse's Returns (Sale of Manufactured Iron), 3 Vols, 1869–1919.

Appendix 3. Wrought Iron Sales in the North of England, 1863–1917

Year	Rails Sales (tons)	Price (£/ton)	Total Value (£)	Plates Sales (tons)	Price (£/ton)	Total Value (£)	Bars Sales (tons)	Price (£/ton)	Total Value (£)	Angles Sales (tons)	Price (£/ton)	Total Value (£)	Total Sales (tons)	Price (£/ton)	Total Value (£)
1863	19,543	6.2	121,167	30,538	9.4	287,057	13,016	6.6	85,906	13,628	7.1	96,759	76,725	7.7	590,783
1864	16,434	7.2	118,325	40,173	9.0	361,557	10,111	7.9	79,877	18,145	8.5	153,325	84,863	8.6	725,579
1865	62,045	7.1	440,520	45,476	8.8	400,189	19,253	8.0	154,024	11,442	7.5	85,815	138,216	7.8	1,071,174
1866	96,275	7.0	673,925	35,463	8.1	287,250	22,451	7.4	165,015	11,047	7.1	77,881	165,236	7.3	1,197,961
1867	155,275	6.3	970,406	44,886	7.5	334,401	35,387	6.7	237,093	11,204	6.7	74,507	246,742	6.6	1,616,160
1868	174,154	5.9	1,018,801	68,247	7.0	477,729	46,601	6.4	295,916	19,721	6.4	125,228	308,723	6.3	1,929,519
1869	90,613	6.1	548,209	31,839	7.2	227,649	18,237	6.3	113,981	8,652	6.3	54,075	149,341	6.6	978,184
1870														7.1	
1873	280,655	11.1	3,096,901	136,442	12.5	1,713,400	65,635	12.5	820,211	34,920	12.0	425,765	517,653	11.7	6,043,274
1874	265,020	9.8	2,593,338	178,273	11.3	2,004,310	91,053	10.8	965,783	49,500	10.6	524,585	583,847	10.5	6,087,969
1875	246,218	7.3	1,791,112	173,417	8.7	1,518,556	101,642	8.5	856,736	41,246	8.1	336,626	562,523	8.0	13,071,985
1876	102,833	6.4	660,270	172,374	7.5	1,287,762	88,304	7.3	639,392	52,664	7.0	367,628	420,175	7.1	2,976,981
1877	36,750	6.0	220,569	214,724	7.0	1,495,374	78,132	6.8	530,099	67,035	6.4	426,773	396,641	6.8	2,677,564
1878	21,646	5.4	119,026	233,964	6.3	1,474,354	77,783	6.2	481,438	87,652	5.6	491,513	421,045	6.1	2,566,298
1879	6,700	4.9	32,944	173,701	5.5	947,773	64,763	5.5	352,124	48,892	5.0	246,622	294,127	5.4	1,579,415
1880	31,825	6.2	200,616	380,764	6.3	2,415,613	89,560	6.4	572,899	109,326	5.7	620,111	611,473	6.2	3,820,569
1881	15,905	5.3	83,199	391,467	6.2	2,428,009	70,490	5.9	418,014	120,557	5.5	657,071	598,420	6.0	3,593,666
1882	5,610	6.0	33,202	433,217	6.4	2,779,435	62,570	6.5	407,022	129,647	5.9	764,340	631,043	6.3	3,975,685
1883	2,905	5.7	16,612	440,157	6.2	2,701,610	80,932	6.2	504,439	133,606	5.6	750,878	657,600	6.1	4,019,351
1884	3,516	5.1	17,942	270,912	5.2	1,431,968	81,577	5.6	455,756	72,282	4.9	351,292	428,286	5.2	2,257,407
1885	3,494	4.6	16,121	205,935	4.8	992,189	87,863	5.1	449,775	57,943	4.6	265,775	355,237	4.8	1,721,720
1886	2,740	4.3	11,795	167,284	4.5	752,759	74,234	5.0	367,484	39,932	4.4	177,154	284,188	6.9	1,309,376

Year	Rails			Plates			Bars			Angles			Year	Total		
	Sales (tons)	Price (£/ton)	Total Value (£)	Sales (tons)	Price (£/ton)	Total Value (£)	Sales (tons)	Price (£/ton)	Total Value (£)	Sales (tons)	Price (£/ton)	Total Value (£)		Sales (tons)	Price (£/ton)	Total Value (£)
1887	2,089	4.3	8,922	136,492	4.5	614,188	58,817	5	292,724	29,209	4.4	128,476	1887	226,607	4.6	1,046,930
1888	1,466	4.5	6,571	190,179	4.6	871,465	74,195	4.9	361,067	41,549	4.5	185,163	1888	307,389	4.7	1,455,927
1889	2,892	5.4	15,758	209,224	5.5	1,157,509	82,900	5.9	464,783	42,521	5.2	220,267	1889	337,536	5.5	1,856,841
1890	3,948	6.1	24,485	152,645	6.3	958,076	87,875	6.5	572,808	39,246	6.0	234,319	1890	283,711	6.3	1,789,625
1891	3,427	5.2	17,712	133,695	5.6	744,630	77,857	5.9	459,018	36,491	5.5	198,986	1891	251,472	5.6	1,415,980
1892	3,791	5.0	19,044	82,510	5.2	429,021	56,437	5.7	320,433	28,908	5.3	156,327	1892	171,645	5.4	920,849
1893	3,790	4.5	16,983	59,447	4.6	274,033	62,075	5.2	321,112	24,084	4.8	115,121	1893	149,405	4.9	726,215
1894	3,558	4.3	15,482	58,554	4.7	273,793	59,499	5.1	303,023	21,720	4.7	102,170	1894	143,333	4.9	695,136
1895	3,464	4.3	14,954	53,548	4.5	242,739	51,565	5.0	258,395	15,006	4.6	69,310	1895	123,585	4.7	585,749
1896	2,921	4.4	12,952	57,835	4.7	271,627	71,786	5.0	358,564	20,244	4.7	95,917	1896	152,788	4.8	740,459
1897	3,421	4.8	16,304	60,522	4.9	295,542	69,185	5.3	365,468	18,174	5.0	90,003	1897	151,302	5.1	767,577
1898	3,857	4.8	18,516	56,866	5.1	292,169	72,849	5.4	391,016	20,274	5.1	104,416	1898	153,845	5.2	804,790
1899	3,789	5.5	20,720	56,801	6.2	349,920	79,029	6.3	498,079	20,725	6.1	126,062	1899	160,346	6.2	996,979
1900	4,491	7.4	33,362	42,869	7.3	309,047	68,389	8.5	576,761	20,724	7.6	157,442	1900	112,448	7.9	1,075,873
1901	1,531	6.0	9,334	26,085	7.2	188,621	55,300	6.7	368,208	11,408	6.6	76,368	1901	94,326	6.8	642,702
1902	1,142	5.6	6,360	12,662	6.3	79,423	53,279	6.2	330,598	11,816	6.1	72,586	1902	78,897	6.2	489,064
1903	869	5.7	4,956	13,514	6.1	82,989	47,550	6.2	294,899	11,272	6.3	71,018	1903	73,204	6.2	453,796
1904	473	5.5	2,588	13,026	6.0	77,737	51,594	5.9	303,218	7,695	6.2	47,633	1904	59,209	5.9	431,554
1905	602	5.6	3,345	8,828	6.0	52,784	54,541	5.9	322,097	7,025	6.4	44,763	1905	70,994	5.9	421,695
1906	625	6.1	3,795	8,312	6.2	51,096	54,761	6.5	357,047	7,197	7.0	50,646	1906	70,897	6.5	462,168
1907	943	6.8	6,495	5,912	6.7	39,388	53,991	7.2	387,506	6,470	7.5	48,732	1907	67,315	7.2	481,437
1908	746	6.6	4,927	3,352	5.9	20,589	33,680	6.8	229,318	3,132	7.1	22,163	1908	40,910	6.8	276,884
1909	321	5.6	1,779	5,740	5.8	33,298	26,325	6.5	170,012	2,524	6.9	17,336	1909	34,907	6.4	222,244
1910	343	5.4	1,855	6,659	5.9	38,830	30,304	6.4	194,140	3,200	7.0	22,569	1910	41,636	6.3	263,584

Year												Year			
1911	263	5.6	1,491	8,032	6.1	49,187	42,847	6.3	268,474	2,492	6.9	17,324	1911	53,635	6.3	336,954
1912	324	5.6	1,848	8,689	6.3	54,344	55,521	6.8	378,479	1,860	7.1	13,209	1912	66,394	6.7	447,665
1913	370	6.3	2,340	6,854	6.6	44,252	51,311	7.5	386,309	1,429	7.6	10,865	1913	59,962	7.4	444,411
1914	134	6.5	855	9,651	6.7	65,122	41,801	6.8	285,679	1,131	7.3	8,174	1914	52,737	6.8	359,809
1915	35	7.7	258	7,288	8.1	57,534	41,142	8.4	344,896	914	8.6	8,154	1915	49,381	8.3	410,144
1916	5	11.5	55	5,349	11.4	60,074	41,192	12.2	502,989	1,804	11.6	20,534	1916	48,353	12.1	584,212
1917	21	16.3	341	1,311	13.7	17,739	39,015	13.5	528,043	925	13.9	12,673	1917	41,271	13.5	558,860

Source: Modern Records Centre, University of Warwick, Board of Arbitration and Conciliation for North of England Manufactured Iron Trade (MSS.365/BAG), Mr. Waterhouse's Returns (Sale of Manufactured Iron), 3 Vols., 1869–1919

Appendix 4. Infant Deaths in Middlesbrough, 1854–99

Year	No. of Early Neonatal Deaths	No. of Neonatal Deaths excl. Early Neonatal	Total No. of Neonatal Deaths	No. of Post Neonatal Deaths	No. of Infant Deaths	No. of Still Births	Unknown	Infant Deaths/ Neonatal Deaths	Neonatal/ Post Neonatal	Early Neonatal Deaths/ Infant Deaths
1854	5	5	10	35	45	2	0	4.5	28.5%	11.1%
1855	8	14	22	90	112	3	2	5.1	24.4	7.1
1856	19	15	34	75	109	0	0	3.2	45.3	17.4
1857	23	20	43	113	156	2	5	3.6	38.1	14.7
1858	22	14	36	107	143	0	0	4.0	33.6	15.4
1859	24	19	43	119	162	0	4	3.8	36.1	14.8
1860	21	16	37	100	137	0	4	3.7	37.0	15.3
1861	20	28	48	114	161	2	2	3.4	42.5	12.4
1862	31	13	44	107	151	0	3	3.4	41.1	20.5
1863	23	33	56	121	177	0	11	3.2	46.3	13.0
1864	37	23	60	146	206	0	5	3.4	41.1	18.0
1865	50	43	93	163	256	0	3	2.8	57.1	19.5
1866	50	54	104	192	296	0	4	2.8	54.1	16.9
1867	39	41	80	209	289	0	9	3.6	38.3	13.5
1868	36	40	76	166	242	0	6	3.2	45.8	14.9
1869	40 (38)	40 (39)	80 (77)	171 (167)	251 (244)	0 (0)	12 (12)	3.1 (3.2)	46.8 (46.1)	15.9 (15.6)
1870	43 (33)	36 (29)	79 (62)	196 (168)	275 (230)	0 (0)	4 (4)	3.5 (3.7)	40.3 (36.9)	15.6 (14.3)
1871	52 (40)	73 (58)	125 (98)	288 (247)	413 (345)	0 (0)	10 (7)	3.3 (3.5)	43.4 (39.7)	12.6 (11.6)
1872	81 (45)	44 (21)	125 (66)	255 (136)	380 (202)	0 (0)	8 (3)	3.0 (3.0)	49.0 (48.5)	21.3 (22.3)
1873	72 (23)	45 (10)	117 (33)	257 (81)	374 (114)	0 (0)	4 (4)	3.2 (3.5)	45.5 (40.7)	19.3 (20.2)
1874	84 (0)	61 (1)	145 (1)	299 (4)	444 (5)	0 (0)	2 (0)	3.1	48.5	18.9
1875	76 (1)	61 (0)	137 (1)	308 (0)	445 (1)	109 (0)	7 (0)	3.3	44.5	17.1
1876	73 (1)	44 (0)	117 (1)	205 (1)	322 (2)	114 (0)	3 (0)	2.8	57.1	22.7

Year										
1877	43 (0)	51 (0)	94 (0)	237 (1)	331 (1)	174 (0)	1 (0)	3.5	39.7	13.0
1878	46 (28)	44 (38)	90 (66)	261 (168)	351 (234)	163 (98)	1 (0)	3.9 (3.5)	34.5 (39.3)	13.1 (12.0)
1879	55	40	95	167	262	157	1	2.8	56.9	21.0
1880	52	53	105	274	379	143	0	3.6	38.3	13.7
1881	53	43	96	204	300	158	1	3.1	47.1	17.1
1882	74	59	133	336	469	179	2	3.5	39.6	15.8
1883	67	56	123	227	350	164	1	2.9	54.2	19.1
1884	57	50	107	244	351	174	2	3.3	43.9	16.2
1885	59	42	101	238	339	159	2	3.6	42.4	17.4
1886	52	48	100	279	379	156	5	3.8	35.8	13.7
1887	47	66	113	207	320	125	2	2.8	54.6	14.7
1888	73	45	118	265	383	153	0	3.3	44.5	19.1
1889	67	46	113	275	388	167	2	3.4	41.1	17.3
1890	56	58	114	303	417	172	2	3.7	37.6	13.4
1891	68	49	117	300	417	185	6	3.6	39.0	16.3
1892	74	64	138	305	443	150	5	3.2	45.2	16.7
1893	61	66	127	334	461	131	4	3.6	38.0	13.2
1894	66	51	117	219	336	122	4	2.9	53.4	19.6
1895	72	46	118	337	455	119	2	3.9	35.0	15.8
1896	55	54	109	289	398	132	2	3.6	37.7	13.8
1897	66	55	121	299	420	138	0	3.5	40.5	15.7
1898	74	47	121	343	464	138	2	3.8	35.3	15.9
1899	60	54	114	310	424	159	3	3.7	36.8	14.2

Notes: Figures in the parentheses between 1869 and 1878 are the burials in the Old Cemetery.

Source: Linthorpe Road Cemetery, Ayresome Gardens, Burial Registers, 4 Sep 1854–19 Dec. 1899, Teesside Archives, PR/ACK.

Appendix 5. Crimes by Migrants According to Duration of Stay in Middlesbrough, 1860s–1880s

Year	Native	Duration of Living 0 Years	0–0.5	0.5–1	1–2	2–3	3–4	4–5	5–6	6–7	7–8	8–9	9–10	10–	Total
1863	29	333	151	38	39	55	34	34	20	36	22	34	30	122	
1864	34	272	274	83	91	53	46	38	56	43	37	53	29	180	
1867	60	308	111	35	70	73	52	49	42	34	41	19	39	233	
1868	51	301	97	73	63	32	35	51	31	32	30	26	34	214	
1869	83	363	203	48	31	47	42	42	45	35	40	31	23	279	
Total	259	1,577	836	277	294	260	209	214	194	180	170	163	155	1,028	5,814
	4.4%	27.1%	14.4%	4.7%	5.1%	4.5%	3.6%	3.7%	3.3%	3.1%	2.9%	2.8%	2.7%	17.7%	100.0%
1870	71	272	187	70	43	45	41	34	37	43	54	31	25	264	
1871	67	398	181	63	75	63	40	36	49	32	38	28	21	273	
1872	103	409	265	84	82	58	51	31	35	29	30	31	16	122	
1873	125	431	175	107	86	58	33	39	31	37	21	19	39	204	
1876	70	142	53	31	31	32	34	37	25	27	19	11	10	153	
Total	436	1,652	861	355	317	256	199	177	177	168	162	120	111	1,016	6,007
	7.3%	27.5%	14.3%	5.9%	5.3%	4.3%	3.3%	3.0%	2.9%	2.8%	2.7%	2.0%	1.8%	16.9%	100.0%
1881	161	238	64	29	27	14	14	18	22	17	15	22	18	228	
1882	182	242	126	51	29	31	13	10	15	12	25	10	20	225	
1883	184	217	120	23	50	38	18	12	10	21	22	13	13	228	
1884	183	190	65	34	32	28	25	27	20	9	10	7	13	194	
1886	177	139	44	10	6	17	10	9	16	14	13	12	8	186	
1887	186	76	71	13	13	13	13	18	21	15	15	10	11	170	
1889	234	190	112	23	21	16	10	20	16	19	20	22	20	201	
Total	1,307	1,292	602	183	178	157	103	114	120	107	120	96	103	1,432	5,914
	22.1%	21.8%	10.2%	3.1%	3.0%	2.7%	1.8%	1.9%	2.0%	1.8%	2.0%	1.6%	1.8%	24.2%	100.00%

	Average No. of Custodies													
1860s	51.4	262.8	167.2	55.4	58.8	52	41.8	42.8	38.8	36	34	32.6	31	205.6
1870s	87.2	330.4	172.2	71	63.4	51.2	39.8	35.4	35.4	33.6	32.4	24	22.2	203.2
1880s	186.7	184.6	86	26.1	25.4	22.4	14.7	16.3	17.1	15.3	17.1	13.7	14.7	204.6

Notes: Number of cases in custody. Percentage of all custody cases during the period by the duration of stay in Middlesbrough.

Source: Teesside Archives, CB/M/C2/100, 101 & 102; CB/M/P, 23–24; CB/M/C, 39–60.

Appendix 6. Crimes by Income Levels in Middlesbrough, 1863–85

Average Weekly Income	1863	1864	1867	1868	1869	Total[a]	%
Out of Employment	124	226	505	260	362	1,477	28.9
0–15s.	88	30	44	28	91	281	5.5
15–20s.	276	368	167	194	274	1,279	25.0
20–25s.	222	274	236	232	184	1,148	22.4
25–30s.	87	144	138	117	147	633	12.4
30–35s.	22	32	24	8	16	102	2.0
35–40s.							
40s. ~							
On Their Own Account	26	44	52	37	37	196	3.8
Total	845	1,118	1,166	876	1,111	5,116	100.0
Average Weekly Income	1870	1871	1872	1873	1876	Total	%
Out of Employment	224	300	212	252	167	1,155	22.3
0–15s.	64	54	44	29	13	204	3.9
15–20s.	162	106	74	33	18	393	7.6
20–25s.	374	336	280	266	98	1,354	26.2
25–30s.	96	123	231	121	66	637	12.3
30–35s.	90	218	325	275	106	1,014	19.6
35–40s.				58	33	91	1.8
40s. ~				102	19	121	2.3
On Their Own Account	41	54	34	53	24	206	4.0
Total	1,051	1,191	1,200	1,189	544	5,175	100.0
Average Weekly Income	1881	1882	1883	1884	1885	Total	%
Out of Employment	280	292	239	307	394	1,512	42.8
0–15s.	20	42	33	33	31	159	4.5
15–20s.	56	83	54	59	48	300	8.5
20–25s.	117	112	146	84	84	543	15.4
25–30s.	63	70	78	62	39	312	8.8
30–35s.	80	116	103	62	27	388	11.0
35–40s.	12	26	24	14	4	80	2.3
40s. ~	11	27	33	2	13	86	2.4
On Their Own Account	34	46	30	20	22	152	4.3
Total	673	814	740	643	662	3,532	100.0

Note: Number of cases in custody. [a]Total number of cases in custody in the respective years.
Source: Teesside Archives, CB/M/C2/100, 101 & 102; CB/M/P, 23–24; CB/M/C, 39–60.

Appendix 7. Crimes by Literacy Levels in Middlesbrough, 1861–89

Literacy	1861	1863	1864	1867	1868	1869				Total	%
Neither read nor write	326	553	576	528	587	672				3,242	50.6
Only read & write imperfectly	250	266	439	409	430	563				2,357	36.8
Read only											
Read & write well	3	151	238	200	41	82				715	11.1
Received a superior education	4	17	36	29	12					98	1.5
Total	583	987	1,289	1,166	1,070	1,317				6,412	100.0

Literacy	1870	1871	1872	1873	1876					Total	%
Neither read nor write	578	618	637	617	312					2,762	46.1
Only read & write imperfectly	594	688	680	654	304					2,920	48.8
Read only				102	41					143	2.4
Read & write well	45	42	28	19	15					149	2.5
Received a superior education		4	1	3	3					11	0.2
Total	1,217	1,352	1,346	1,395	675					5,985	100.0

Literacy	1881	1882	1883	1884	1885	1886	1887	1889	Total	%
Neither read nor write	410	377	331	241	296	229	230	285	2,399	35.0
Only read & write imperfectly	439	545	571	538	520	410	428	669	4,120	60.1
Read only	31	51	59	54	23	17	27	19	281	4.1
Read & write well	6	15	7	2	5	5	4	4	48	0.7
Received a superior education	1	3	1	2			2	1	10	0.1
Total	887	991	969	837	844	661	691	978	6,858	100.0

Note: Number of cases in custody.

Source: Teesside Archives, CB/M/C2/100, 101 & 102; CB/M/P, 23–24; CB/ M/C, 39–60.

Appendix 8. Crimes by Nationality in Middlesbrough, 1861–89

Nationality	1861	1863	1864	1867	1868	1869			Total	%
English	293	405	506	546	469	650			2,869	44.8
Irish	221	447	623	486	477	497			2,751	42.9
Scottish	24	52	57	55	54	84			326	5.1
Welsh	29	46	74	53	39	45			286	4.5
Foreigners	16	32	29	26	31	41			175	2.7
Total	583	982	1,289	1,166	1,070	1,317			6,407	100.0

Nationality	1870	1871	1872	1873	1876				Total	%
English	591	658	666	810	331				3,056	51.1
Irish	490	527	491	407	272				2,187	36.6
Scottish	64	78	70	79	36				327	5.5
Welsh	40	53	62	63	27				245	4.1
Foreigners	32	36	57	36	6				167	2.8
Total	1,217	1,352	1,346	1,395	672				5,982	100.0

Nationality	1881	1882	1883	1884	1885	1886	1887	1889	Total	%
English	589	674	649	608	640	490	504	742	4,896	71.4
Irish	175	215	196	140	120	92	115	129	1,182	17.2
Scottish	63	54	66	52	50	38	39	49	411	6.0
Welsh	47	32	36	22	21	25	25	36	244	3.6
Foreigners	13	16	22	15	13	16	8	22	125	1.8
Total	887	991	969	837	844	661	691	978	6,858	100.0

Note: Number of cases in custody.

Source: Teesside Archives, CB/M/C2/100, 101 & 102; CB/M/P, 23–24; CB/M/C, 39–60.

Sources and Bibliography

I Manuscripts and Other Archival Sources

National Archives (Public Record Office)
HO 63/8, vols1 & 2, Annual Police Reports.
HO 107 /1256/1–6, Census Enumerators' Books, 1841.
HO 107 2383, Census Enumerators' Books, 1851.
RG 9 3685–9, Census Enumerators' Books,1861.
RG 10 4889–95, Census Enumerators' Books, 1871.
RG 11 4851, Census Enumerators' Books, 1881.
RAIL 667/1428, Stockton & Darlington, Wear Valley and Middlesbrough & Redcar Railway Pay Bill.
MH/113/4, Dr. Buchanan's Report on the Sanitary State of Middlesbrough-on-Tees, 1871.

Teesside Archives
Middlesbrough Borough Council
CB/M/T Abstract and Statement of Accounts and Funds of the Mayor, Aldermen, and Burgesses of the Borough of Middlesbrough for the Year Ending 30 June 1877.
CB/M/C 1/6 Local Board of Health, 1854.
CB/M/C 1/8 Local Board of Health and Burial Board, 1859.
CB/M/C 2/100, 101 & 102, Borough Clerk's Department, 2, Committee Minutes, Watch Committee Minute Books.
CB/M/C (2) 14/5b, Copy of Charter of Incorporation, 1853.
CB/M/C 1/1–2, Improvement Commission and Committees Minute Book.
CB/M/C (2) 9/57, CB/M/C 1/6, Map Showing Proposed Wards in Middlesbrough .
CB/M/C (2) 9/9, Plan of Ironmasters' District of Middlesbrough, 1866.
CB/M/E (5) 7/2, Plan of Middlesbrough, 1877.
CB/M/T, Poor Rate books 1846, 1849, 1856, 1858, 1861, 1862, 1871, 1872, 1876, 1880.
CB/M/P, 23–4, Middlesbrough Police Records, Reports from Chief Superintendents, later Chief Constables, to Watch Committees.
CB/M/C 39–60, Borough Clerk's Department, 1, Printed Minutes of Town Council.
CB/M/T, General District Revenue, etc., 1866–74.

CB/M/T, Statement and Account of Income and Expenditure, Commissioners under the Middlesbrough Improvement Act, 1854–5.

CB/M/T, Statement of Income and Expenditure, Town Council of the Borough of Middlesbrough, Acting in the Capacity of Commissioners under the Middlesbrough Improvement Act, 1841–53.

CB/M/H2, Annual Reports of the Medical Officer of Health and Chief Sanitary Inspector, 1898–1901.

CB/M/T, Statement and Account of Income and Expenditure of the Middlesbrough Improvement Act, 1841–50.

Owners of the Middlesbrough Estate
U/OME (2) 5/1–5/4, Land Sales Agreements.
U/OME 8/9, Map of Middlesbrough, 1845.
U/OME (2) 4/34, Middlesbrough Estate Valuation for 1844 and 1855.
U/OME (2) 4/15, Balance Sheets, 1845–55,.
U/OME (2) 5/87–100 etc., Title Deeds.

H/NOR 1/1, North Ormesby Hospital, Council Minute Book, 1867–1907.
H/NOR 10/1, North Ormesby Hospital, Case Book, 1861–70.
H/NOR 10/2, 3, North Ormesby Hospital, Case Books, 1883–8, 1885–1908.
H/MI 2/1/4, ff. 3–256, 1/5, ff. 1–348, North Riding Infirmary, House Committee, Minute Books.
U/BSC 1/1, Deed of Covenants amongst Proprietors of the Town of Middlesbrough in the County of York.
U/OD 1/1, Independent Order of Odd Fellows, Manchester Unity Friendly Society, 1a Minute Book, 1842–72, Rose of England Lodge.
PR/ACK, Linthorpe Road Cemetery, Ayresome Gardens, Burial Registers, 1854–99.
Middlesbrough-On-Tees Medical Charities, Hospital Sunday programme, 1872.

Modern Records Centre, University of Warwick
MSS 259/2/1/15, Amalgamated Society of Engineers, Monthly and Annual Reports, 1867.
MSS 259/4/14/1–107, Amalgamated Society of Engineers, Monthly Reports.
MSS 259/2/1/1, Amalgamated Society of Engineers, Annual Report of Middlesbrough Branch, 1876.
MSS 365/BAC, Board of Arbitration and Conciliation for North of England Manufactured Iron Trade, Minute Books, vol. 1, 1869–70.
MSS 365/BAC, Board of Arbitration and Conciliation for North of England Manufactured Iron Trade, Mr. Waterhouse's Returns (Sales of Manufactured Iron), Vols 1–3, 1869–1919.
MSS 365/BAC, Board of Arbitration and Conciliation for the North of England Manufactured Iron Trade, First Members, Origin and Objects, Rules, 1869.
MSS 365/CIA, Cleveland Ironmasters' Association, Minute Books, Vols 1 & 2, 1866–76, 1876–84.

MSS 365/NEI, North of England Iron Manufacturers' Association, Minute Books, 1865–80.
MSS 259, Rules of the Amalgamated Society of Engineers, Machinists, Mill-wrights, Smiths, and Pattern Makers, 1874.

Glamorgan Record Office
Dowlais Iron Company Collection
D/D G/C5/11/2, D/D G/C5/11/19, D/D G/C5/11/20.
D/D G/C5/15–16, On the Employment of Women and Children in the Iron Works of South Wales.

North Yorkshire County Record Office
QFR 1/49/16, 1/50/17, 1/51/10, 1/53/10, 1/54/10, 1/55/11, 1/56/10, 1/57/10, 1/58/10, 1/58/23, 1/43/18 (1865–1884), QFR 1/43/18 (1859), Assessment of County Rates for the North Riding of the County of York.

West Yorkshire Archive Service, Leeds
Leeds General Infirmary Admission and Discharge Register, 1815–17.

Guildhall Library, London
MS 14075/1, Ledgers of the Alliance, British and Foreign Fire and Life Insurance Company, from 231, 1830.

History Data Service, University of Essex
Census Enumerators' Books for Middlesbrough, 1881.

British Library of Political and Economic Science
Coll. Misc. 0003, Bell Brothers, Clarence Iron Works, Pay Books, Vol. 4, 1864–7.

Middlesbrough Central Library
MM 1942, Copy of the Diary of Joseph Pease,.
C669.14, Middlesbrough Chamber of Commerce Reports.
MMI 324 56361, *List of Persons intituled to vote in the Election of two Knights to serve as members of Parliament for North Riding of the County of York, in respect of Property situate within the Township of Middles-brough*... 1841.
MMI 352.17 73483, *Abstract and Statement of the Mayor, Aldermen and Burgesses of the Borough of Middlesbrough, under the Municipal Corpo-ration Acts: Middlesbrough Improvement Acts, 1845, 1856, 1866 and 1874.*
MMI 374/ MI 606, Rules of the Middlesbrough Mechanics' Institute and Library, 1844.

Durham Record Office
D/PS 5/2, Circulars concerning the extension of the Stockton and Darlington
    Railway to Middlesbrough, 1828.

II Printed Sources

British Parliamentary Papers
PP, 1831, XXXVII, Census enumeration abstract.
PP, 1851 [1691-I] LXXXVIII, Part I, Accounts and Papers: Population, Ages,
    Civil Condition, Occupations, etc.
PP, 1851–53 [1631] LXXXV, 1851 Census of Great Britain.
PP, 1862 [3056], L, 1861 Census, Population Tables, I, Numbers and Distri-
    bution of the People.
PP, 1867–8 [3980-I] XXXIX, Royal Commission on Trades Unions, Fifth
    Report.
PP, 1868–9 [4123-I] XXXI, Royal Commission on Trades Unions, Fifth
    Report.
PP, 1873 [872] LXXII, Census of England and Wales 1871, Pt. I, Vol. III.
PP, 1883 [3563], LXXIX, 1881 Census, II, Area, Houses, and Population.
PP, 1883 [3722] LXXX, Census of England and Wales 1881, Vol. III. Ages,
    Condition as to Marriage, Occupations, and Birth-Places of the People.

Newspapers
The Cambrian.
Middlesbrough Times.
Middlesbrough Weekly News and Cleveland Advertiser.
Stockton Gazette and Middlesbrough Times.
The Times.
Ironworkers Journal, 1869–72.

Statutes
Statutes at Large: 4 & 5 Vict., c. lxviii; 18 & 19 Vict., c. cxxv; 19 & 20 Vict.,
    c. lxxvii; 21 & 22 Vict., c. cxl; 29 & 30 Vict., c. cxliii; 37 & 38 Vict., c.
    cviii; 40 Vict., c. xxx; 51 & 52 Vict., c. xli.

Other
Annual Report of the Income and Expenditure of the Steam Engine Makers'
    Society, 1876.
Annual Reports, North Ormesby Hospital, Middlesbrough, 1859–1917.
Annual Reports of the State of the General Infirmary at Leeds, 1767–1870.
Forty-fourth Annual Report of the Registrar General of Births, Deaths, and
    Marriages in England (Abstracts of 1881), 1883.
Iron, Steel, and Allied Trades, Annual Reports to the Members of the British
    Iron Trade Association, 1878–81.

Supplement to the Forty-Fifth Annual Report of the Registrar General of Births, Deaths, and Marriages in England, 1885.
Transactions of the Iron and Steel Institute, Vols I & II, 1869 & 1870.
Transactions of the National Association for the Promotion of Social Science, Newcastle-Upon-Tyne, 1870, 1871.
Ward's *North of England Directory*, 1851.
Ordnance Survey 6", Yorks. VI, pub. 1857; 25", Yorks. VI, pub. 1895.

III Secondary Sources (Books and Articles)

Allen, R.C., 'Collective Invention', *Journal of Economic Behaviour and Organization*, 4(1) (1983), 1–24.

Andrews, R.B., 'Mechanics of the Urban Economic Base: Historical Development of the Base Concept', *Land Economics*, XXIX (2) (1953), 161–7.

Armstrong, W.G. *et al.*, (eds), *The Industrial Resources of the District of the Three Northern Rivers, The Tyne, Wear, and Tees including Reports on Local Manufacturers* (London, 1864).

Bade, K.J., 'Introduction: Population, Labour, Migration. Historical Studies and Issues of Current Debate', *Population, Labour and Migration in Nineteenth- and Twentieth-Century Germany*, ed. K.J. Bade (Hamburg, 1987), 1–14.

Banham, J., *Backhouses' Bank of Darlington 1774–1836*, Papers in North East History (Middlesbrough, 1999).

Banks, J.A., 'The Contagion of Numbers', *The Victorian City, Images and Realities*, I, ed. H.J. Dyos, and M. Wolff (London and Boston, 1973), 105–22.

Bell, C. and R. Bell, *City Fathers: the Early History of Town Planning in Britain* (Harmondsworth, 1972).

Bell, F., *At the Works: a Study of a Manufacturing Town (Middlesbrough)* (Newton Abbot, 1969 [1907]).

Bell, I.L., *Notes on the Progress of the Iron Trade of Cleveland on the North-East Coast of England* (Middlesbrough, 1878).

Bell, I.L., *Manufacture of Iron and Steel* (London, 1884).

Bell, I.L., *The Trade of the United Kingdom Compared with that of other Chief Iron-Making Nations* (London, 1886).

Berridge, V., 'Health and Medicine', *Cambridge Social History of Britain, 1750–1950*, 3, *Social Agencies and Institutions*, ed. F.M.L. Thompson (Cambridge, 1990), 171–242.

Birch, A., *The Economic History of the British Iron and Steel Industry, 1784–1879* (London, 1967).

Briggs, A., *Victorian Cities* (Harmondsworth, 1990).

Brody, D., *Steelworkers in America: the Non-union Era* (Cambridge, MA,1960).

Bullock, I., 'Spatial Adjustments in the Teesside Economy, 1851–81', unpublished PhD thesis, University of Newcastle upon Tyne (1970).

Bullock, I., 'The Origins of Economic Growth on Teesside, 1851–81', *Northern History*, IX (1974), 79–95.

Burnham, H. and G.O. Hoskins, *Iron and Steel in Britain 1870–1930: A Comparative Study of the Causes which Limited the Economic Development of the British Iron and Steel Industry between the years 1870 and 1930* (London, 1943).

Burton, J.J., 'Some Notes on the Early History of the Cleveland Iron Trade', *Monthly Journal of the Teesside Incorporated Chamber of Commerce*, 1(7) (1930), 104–11.

Butterworth, H., 'The Development of Technical Education in Middlesbrough, 1844–1903', *Durham Research Review*, 11 (1960), 27–34.

Carr, J.C. and W. Taplin, *History of the British Steel Industry* (Cambridge, MA, 1962).

Casson, M.C., 'An Economic Approach to Regional Business Networks', *Industrial Clusters and Regional Business Networks in England, 1750–1970*, ed. J.F. Wilson and A. Popp (Aldershot, 2003), 19–43.

Casson, M.C., *The World's First Railway System: Enterprise, Competition and Regulation on the Railway Network in Victorian Britain* (Oxford, 2009).

Chase, M., '"Dangerous People"? The Teesside Irish in the 19th Century', *North East Labour History Bulletin*, 28 (1994), 42–53.

Chase, M., *Early Trade Unionism: Fraternity, Skill and the Politics of Labour* (Aldershot, 2000).

Cherry, S., 'Beyond National Health Insurance. The Voluntary Hospitals and Hospital Contributory Schemes: a Regional Study', *Social History of Medicine*, 5(3) (1992), 455–82.

Cherry, S., *Medical Services and Hospitals in Britain, 1860–1939* (Cambridge, 1996).

Cherry, S. 'Before the National Health Service: Financing Voluntary Hospitals, 1900–39', *Economic History Review*, L(2) (1997), 305–26.

Cockcroft, J., 'The Great Strike in the Cleveland Iron Industry', *Cleveland and Teesside Local History Society Bulletin*, 25 (Oct. 1974), 1–10.

Cockerill, J. and J. Cockerill, 'Middlesbrough Pottery, 1854–87', *Cleveland and Teesside Local History Society Bulletin*, 62 (1992), 21–39.

Cookson, G., *The Townscape of Darlington* (Woodbridge, 2003).

Cookson, G., 'Quaker Families and Business Networks in Nineteenth Century Darlington', *Quaker Studies*, 8(2) (2004), 119–40.

Cookson, G. (ed.), *The Victoria History of the Counties of England, A History of the County of Durham, iv, Darlington* (Woodbridge, 2005).

Cookson, G., *Sunderland: Building a City* (Chichester, 2010).

'Correspondence', *Economic Journal*, XXIII (1913), 463–4.

Crafts, N., and A. Mulatu, 'What Explains the Location of Industry in Britain, 1871–1931?', *Journal of Economic Geography*, 5 (2005), 499–518.

Crew, D.F., *Town in the Ruhr: a Social History of Bochum, 1860–1914* (New York, 1979).

Croker, M., 'Early Hospital Provision in Middlesbrough, 1859–80', unpublished MA dissertation in Local History, Teesside Polytechnic (1986).

Crompton, H., *Industrial Conciliation* (London, 1876).

Daunton, M.J., *Coal Metropolis: Cardiff, 1870–1914* (Leicester, 1977).

Davies, K., 'Maternal Mismanagement or Environmental Factors? High Rates of Infant Mortality in Middlesbrough, 1890–1913', *Cleveland and Teesside Local History Society Bulletin*, 62 (1992), 40–60.

Day, A., 'A Spirit of Improvement: Improvement Commissioners, Boards of Health and Central-local Relations in Portsea', *Urban Governance: Britain and Beyond since 1750*, ed. R.J. Morris and R.H. Trainor (Aldershot, 2000), 101–14.

Doyle, B.M., 'The Changing Functions of Government: Councillors, Officials and Pressure Groups', *Cambridge Urban History of Britain*, III, 1840–1950, ed. M. Daunton (Cambridge, 2000), 287–313.

Doyle, B.M., 'Voluntary Hospitals in Edwardian Middlesbrough: A Preliminary Report', *North East History*, 34 (2001), 5–34.

Doyle, B.M., *A History of Hospitals in Middlesbrough* (Middlesbrough, 2002).

Doyle, B.M., 'Power and Accountability in the Voluntary Hospitals of Middlesbrough, 1900–48', *Medicine, Charity and Mutual Aid: the Consumption of Health and Welfare in Britain, c.1550–1950*, ed. A. Borsay and P. Shapley (Aldershot, 2007), 207–24.

Doyle, B.M., 'Competition and Cooperation in Hospital Provision in Middlesbrough, 1918–48', *Medical History*, 51 (2007), 337–56.

Doyle, B.M. and R. Nixon, 'Voluntary Hospital Finance in North-east England: the Case of North Ormesby Hospital, Middlesbrough, 1900–47', *Cleveland History*, 80 (2001), 5–19.

Drummond, D.K., *Crewe: Railway Town, Company and People, 1840–1914* (Aldershot, 1995).

Dupree, M., 'The Provision of Social Service', *Cambridge Urban History of Britain*, III, 1840–1950, ed. M. Daunton (Cambridge, 2000), 351–94.

Durkheim, É., *De la Division du Travail Social*, trans. G. Simpson (London, 1964 [1893]).

Ehmer, J., 'Tramping Artisans in Nineteenth-century Vienna', *Migration, Mobility and Modernization*, ed. D.J. Siddle (Liverpool, 2000), 164–85.

Ehmer, J., *Bevölkerungsgeschichte und historische Demographie, 1800–2000* (München, 2004).

Evans, N., 'Two Paths to Economic Development: Wales and the North-east of England', *Regions and Industries: a Perspective on the Industrial Revolution in Britain,* ed. P. Hudson (Cambridge, 1989), 201–27.

Fitzgerald, R., *British Labour Management and Industrial Welfare, 1846–1939* (London, 1988).

Friedlander, D. and R.J. Roshier, 'A Study of Internal Migration in England and Wales, Part I: Geographical Patterns of Internal Migration, 1851–1951', *Population Studies*, XIX(3) (1969), 239–79.

Gilzean-Reid, Sir H. (ed.), *Middlesbrough and its Jubilee: a History of the Iron and Steel Industries with Biographies of Pioneers* (Middlesbrough, 1881).

Gjers, J., 'Description of the Ayresome Ironworks, Middlesbrough, with Remarks upon the Gradual Increase in Size of the Cleveland Blast Furnaces', *Journal of the Iron and Steel Institute*, 3 (1871), 202–17.

Gjers, J., 'President's Address', *Proc. Cleveland Institution of Engineers* (1878), 30–54.

Glass, R., *The Social Background of a Plan: a Study of Middlesbrough* (London, 1948).

Goldsmith, M. and J. Garrard, 'Urban Governance: some Reflections', *Urban Governance: Britain and Beyond since 1750*, ed. R.J. Morris and R.H. Trainor (Aldershot, 2000), 15–27.

Gott, R., *Henry Bolckow: Founder of Teesside* (Middlesbrough, 1968).

Green, E.M., 'Royal Exchange: Marketing and Its Management in the Cleveland Pig Iron Trade, 1864–73', unpublished MA dissertation in Local History, Teesside Polytechnic (1989).

Griffiths, S., *Griffiths' Guide to the Iron Trade of Great Britain* (London, 1873).

Gwynne, T. and M. Sill, 'Welsh Immigration into Middlesbrough in the Mid-Nineteenth Century', *Cleveland and Teesside Local History Society Bulletin*, 31 (1976), 19–22.

Gwynne, T. and M. Sill, 'Census Enumeration Books: a Study of Mid-Nineteenth Century Immigration', *Local Historian*, 12 (1976), 74–9.

Habakkuk, H.J., *American and British Technology in the Nineteenth Century; the Search for Labour-saving Inventions* (Cambridge, 1967).

Hall, A.A., 'Wages, Earnings and Real Earnings in Teesside: a Reassessment of the Ameliorist Interpretation of Living Standards in Britain, 1870–1914', *International Review of Social History*, XXVI (1981), 202–19.

Harris, J., 'Did British Workers Want the Welfare State? G.D.H. Cole's Survey of 1942', *The Working Class in Modern British History*, ed. J. Winter (Cambridge, 1983), 200–14.

Harrison, B.J.P., 'Ironmasters and Ironworkers', *Cleveland Iron and Steel: Background and Nineteenth-century History*, ed. C.A. Hempstead (Redcar, 1979), 231–53.

Harrison, J.K., 'The Development of a Distinctive Cleveland Blast Furnace Practice, 1866–1875', *Cleveland Iron and Steel: Background and Nineteenth-century History*, ed. C.A. Hempstead (Redcar, 1979), 81–115.

Harrison, J.K., *John Gjers, Ironmaster: Ayresome Ironworks, Middlesbrough* (Lelielaan, 1982).

Herson, J., 'Irish Migration and Settlement in Victorian Britain: a Small-town Perspective', *The Irish in Britain, 1815–1939*, ed. R. Swift and S. Gilley (London, 1989), 84–103.

Hicks, J.R., 'The Early History of Industrial Conciliation in England', *Economica*, 10 (1930), 25–39.

Higgs, E., *Making Sense of the Census: the Manuscript Returns for England and Wales, 1801–1901* (London, 1989).

Hobsbawm, E.J., *Labouring Men: Studies in the History of Labour* (London, 1986).

Hochstadt, S., *Mobility and Modernity: Migration in Germany, 1820–1989* (Ann Arbor, MI, 1999).

Hoover, E.M., *The Location of Economic Activity* (New York, 1948).

Howard, N.P., 'The Strikes and Lockouts in the Iron Industry and the Formation of the Ironworkers' Unions, 1862–9', *International Review of Social History*, 18 (1973), 396–427.

Hubbard, W.H., 'Aspects of Social Mobility in Graz, 1857–80', *Historical Social Research*, 14 (1980), 3–26.

Hudson, P., *The Genesis of Industrial Capital: a Study of the West Riding Wool Textile Industry, c.1750–1850* (Cambridge, 1986).

Hudson, P., 'The Regional Perspective', *Regions and Industries: a Perspective on the Industrial Revolution in Britain*, ed. P. Hudson (Cambridge, 1989), 5–40.

Hudson, P., *The Industrial Revolution* (London, 1992).

Hudson, P., 'Industrial Organization and Structure', *Cambridge Economic History of Modern Britain*, 1, *Industrialisation, 1700–1860*, ed. R. Floud and P. Johnson (Cambridge, 2004), 28–56.

Hudson, R., 'Institutional Change, Cultural Transformation, and Economic Regeneration: Myths and Realities from Europe's Old Industrial Areas', *Globalization, Institutions and Regional Development in Europe*, ed. A. Amin and N. Thrift (Oxford, 1994), 196–216.

Isard, W., 'Some Locational Factors in the Iron and Steel Industry since the Early Nineteenth Century', *Journal of Political Economy*, 56 (3) (1948), 203–17.

Isard, W., 'The General Theory of Location and Space-Economy', *Quarterly Journal of Economics*, 63 (4) (1949), 476–506.

Jackson, J.H., Jr, *Migration and Urbanization in the Ruhr Valley, 1821–1914* (Boston, MA, 1997).

Jackson, J.H., Jr, 'Migration in Duisburg, 1821–1914', *People in Transit: German Migrations in Comparative Perspective, 1820–1930*, ed. D. Hoerder and J. Nagler (Cambridge, 1995), 147–75.

Jackson, J. H., Jr and L.P. Moch, 'Migration and the Social History of Modern Europe', *Historical Methods*, 22(1) (1989), 27–36.

Jeans, J.S., *Notes on Northern Industries: written for the Iron and Steel Institute of Great Britain* (London, 1878).

Johnson, P., 'Risk, Redistribution and Social Welfare in Britain from the Poor Law to Beveridge', *Charity, Self-interest and Welfare in the English Past*, ed. M.J. Daunton (London, 1996), 225–48.

Jones, E.L., *The European Miracle: Environments, Economies, and Geopolitics in the History of Europe and Asia* (Cambridge, 1987).

Kirby, M.W., *Men of Business and Politics: the Rise and Fall of the Quaker Pease Dynasty of North-East England, 1700–1943* (London, 1984).

Kirby, M.W., *The Origin of Railway Enterprise: the Stockton and Darlington Railway, 1821–1863* (Cambridge, 1993).

Klessmann, C., 'Long-distance Migration, Integration and Segregation of an Ethnic Minority in Industrial Germany: the Case of the Ruhr Poles', *Population, Labour and Migration in Nineteenth- and Twentieth-century Germany*, ed. K.J. Bade (Hamburg, 1987), 101–14.

Landes, D.S, *The Unbound Prometheus: Technological Change and Industrial Development in Western Europe from 1750 to the Present* (Cambridge, 1969).

Langewiesche, D. and F. Lenger, 'Internal Migration: Persistence and Mobility', *Population, Labour and Migration in Nineteenth- and Twentieth-century Germany*, ed. K.J. Bade (Hamburg, 1987), 87–100.

Laslett, P., 'Family and Household as Work Group and Kin Group: Areas of Traditional Europe Compared', *Family Forms in Historic Europe*, ed. R. Wall, J. Robin and P. Laslett (Cambridge, 1983), 513–64.

Lawton, R., 'Mobility in Nineteenth-century British Cities', *Geographical Journal*, 145(2) (1979), 206–24.

Lee, B. and R. Reinders, 'The Loss of Innocence, 1880–1914', *Introduction to American Studies*, ed. M. Bradbury and H. Temperley (London and New York, 1987), 176–94.

Lee, E.S., 'A Theory of Migration', *Migration*, ed. J.A. Jackson (Cambridge, 1969), 282–97.

Leonard, J.W., 'Urban Development and Population Growth in Middlesbrough, 1831–71', unpublished DPhil thesis, University of York (1975).

Lewis, R., Robina Nixon and B.M. Doyle, *Health Services in Middlesbrough: North Ormesby Hospital, 1900–48* (Middlesbrough, 1999).

Lillie, W., *The History of Middlesbrough: an Illustration of the Evolution of English Industry* (Middlesbrough, 1968).

Lind, H., 'Internal Migration in Britain', *Migration*, ed. J.A. Jackson (Cambridge, 1969), 74–98.

Lock, Max (ed.), *The County Borough of Middlesbrough: Survey and Plan* (Middlesbrough, 1946).

MacRaild, D.M. (ed.), *The Great Famine and Beyond: Irish Migrants in Britain in the Nineteenth and Twentieth Centuries* (Dublin, 2000).

Marshall, A., *Principles of Economics*, Vol. I, 9th ed. (London, 1961).

Matthew, H.C.G., *Gladstone, 1809–1874* (Oxford, 1986).

McCord, N. and Rowe, D.J., 'Industrialisation and Urban Growth in North-East England', *International Review of Social History*, 22 (1977), 30–64.

Meyer, S., 'In-Migration and Out-Migration in an Area of Heavy Industry: the Case of Georgsmarienhütte, 1856–70', *People in Transit: German Migrations in Comparative Perspective, 1820–1930*, ed. D. Hoerder and J. Nagler (Cambridge, 1995), 177–99.

Milne, G.J., *North-East England, 1850–1914: the Dynamics of a Maritime-Industrial Region* (Woodbridge, 2006).

Mooney, G., 'Stillbirths and the Measurement of Urban Infant Mortality Rates, *c.* 1890–1930', *Local Population Studies*, 53 (1994), 42–52.

Morris, R.J., 'Clubs, Societies and Associations', *Cambridge Social History of Britain, 1750–1950*, Vol. III, *Social Agencies and Institutions*, ed. F.M.L. Thompson (Cambridge, 1990), 395–443.

Moser, C.A. and W. Scott, *British Towns: a Statistical Study of their Social and Economic Differences*, Centre for Urban Studies: Report No. 2 (Edinburgh and London, 1961).

Musgrave, P.W., *Technical Change, the Labour Force and Education: a Study of the British and German Iron and Steel Industries, 1860–1964* (Oxford, 1967).

North, D.C., 'Location Theory and Regional Economic Growth', *Journal of Political Economy*, 63(3) (1955), 243–58.

North, D.C., *Institutions, Institutional Change and Economic Performance* (Cambridge, 1990).

Nossiter, T.J., *Influence, Opinion and Political Idioms in Reformed England: Case Studies from the North-east, 1832–74* (Brighton, 1975).

Odber, A.J., 'The Origins of Industrial Peace: The Manufactured Iron Trade of the North of England', *Oxford Economic Papers*, N.S. 3(2) (1951), 202–20.

Orde, A., *Religion, Business and Society in North-East England: the Pease Family of Darlington in the Nineteenth Century* (Stamford, 2000).

Pickstone, J.V., *Medicine and Society: a History of Hospital Development in Manchester and its Region, 1752–1946* (Manchester, 1985).

Pinker, R., *English Hospital Statistics, 1861–1938* (London, 1964).

Piore, M.J. and Charles F. Sabel, *The Second Industrial Divide: Possibilities for Prosperity* (New York, 1984).

Pollard, S., 'Town Planning in the Nineteenth Century: the Beginnings of Modern Barrow-In-Furness', *Transactions of the Lancashire and Cheshire Antiquarian Society*, LXII (1952–3), 87–116.

Pollard, S., 'Labour in Great Britain', *The Industrial Economies: Capital, Labour, and Enterprise*, ed. P. Mathias and M. M. Postan, *Cambridge Economic History*, 7(I) (1978), 97–179.

Pollard, S., *Peaceful Conquest: the Industrialization of Europe, 1760–1970* (Oxford, 1982).

Pooley, C.G., 'Welsh Migration to England in the Mid-nineteenth Century', *Journal of Historical Geography*, 9(3) (1983), 287–306.

Pooley, C.G., 'The Longitudinal Study of Migration: Welsh Migration to English Towns in the Nineteenth Century', *Migrants, Emigrants and Immigrants: A Social History of Migration*, ed. C.G. Pooley and I.D. Whyte (1991), 143–73.

Pooley C.G. and J. Turnbull, *Migration and Mobility in Britain since the Eighteenth Century* (London, 1998).

Pooley, C.G. and J. Turnbull, 'Migration and Urbanization in North-West England: A Reassessment of the Role of Towns in the Migration Process', *Migration, Mobility and Modernization*, ed. D.J. Siddle (Liverpool, 2000), 186–214.

Porter, J.H., 'Wage Bargaining under Conciliation Agreements, 1860–1914', *Economic History Review*, 2nd ser., XXIII (3) (1970), 460–75.

Porter, J.H., 'David Dale and Conciliation in the Northern Manufactured Iron Trade, 1869–1914', *Northern History*, 5 (1970), 157–71.

Porter, M.E., *On Competition* (Boston, 1998).

Praed, L., *History of the Rise and Progress of Middlesbrough* (Newcastle upon Tyne, 1863).

Pressat, R., *The Dictionary of Demography* (Oxford, 1985).

Pressnell, L.S., *Country Banking in the Industrial Revolution* (Oxford, 1956).

Ranger, W., *Report to the General Board of Health on a Preliminary Inquiry into the Sewerage, Drainage, and Supply of Water, and the Sanitary Condition of the Inhabitants of the Borough of Middlesbrough, in the North Riding of the County of York* (London, 1854).

Ravenstein, E.G., 'The Laws of Migration', *Journal of the Royal Statistical Society*, 48(2) (1885), 167–235.

Redford, A., *Labour Migration in England, 1800–1850* (Manchester, 1964).

Reeder, D. and R. Rodger, 'Industrialisation and the City Economy', *Cambridge Urban History of Britain*, Vol. III, 1840–1950, ed. M. Daunton (Cambridge, 2000), 553–92.

Richmond, A.H., 'Sociology of Migration in Industrial and Post-Industrial Societies', *Migration,* ed. J.A. Jackson (Cambridge, 1969), 238–81.

Rosés, J.R., 'Why Isn't the Whole of Spain Industrialized? New Economic Geography and Early Industrialization, 1797–1910', *Journal of Economic. History*, 63 (2003), 995–1022.

Rössler, H., 'Travelling Workers and the German Labour Movement', *People in Transit: German Migration in Comparative Perspective, 1820–1930*, ed. D. Hoerder and J. Nagler (Cambridge, 1995), 127–45.

Sabel C. and J. Zeitlin, 'Historical Alternatives to Mass Production: Politics, Markets and Technology in Nineteenth-Century Industrialization', *Past & Present*, 108 (1985), 133–76.

Schooling, Sir W., *Alliance Assurance, 1824–1924* (London, 1924).

Seth-Smith, M., *200 Years of Richard Johnson and Nephew* (Manchester, 1973).

Sharlin, A., 'Natural Decrease in Early-modern Cities: a Reconsideration', *Past & Present*, 79 (1978), 126–38.

Sigsworth, E.M., 'Gateways to Death? Medicine, Hospitals and Mortality, 1700–1850', *Science and Society, 1600–1900*, ed. P. Mathias (Cambridge,1972), 97–110.

Smith, H. Llewellyn, 'Influx of Population (East London)', *Life and Labour of the People in London*, ed. C. Booth, III (London, 1892), 58–148.

Smith, M.T., *Human Biology and History* (London, 2003).

Southall, H.R., 'The Tramping Artisan Revisits: Labour Mobility and Economic Distress in Early-Victorian England', *Economic History Review*, XLIV (2) (1991), 272–96.

Southall, H.R., 'Mobility, the Artisan Community and Popular Politics in Early Nineteenth-century England', *Urbanizing Britain: Class and Community in the Nineteenth Century*, ed. G. Kearn, and W.J. Withers (Cambridge, 1991), 103–30.

Staber, U.H., 'The Social Embeddedness of Industrial District Networks', *Business Networks: Prospects for Regional Development*, ed. U.H. Staber, N.V. Schaefer and B. Sharma (Berlin and New York, 1996), 148–70.

Stout, G., 'The 1888 Pneumonia in Middlesbrough', *Journal of the Royal Society of Medicine,* 73(9) (1980), 664–8.

Stout, G., *History of North Ormesby Hospital* (Redcar, 1989).

Szreter, S., *Health and Wealth: Studies in History and Policy* (New York, 2005).

Taylor, D., *Policing the Victorian Town: the Development of the Police in Middlesbrough, c.1840–1914* (Basingstoke, 2002).

Taylor, D., 'The Infant Hercules and the Augean Stables: a Century of Economic and Social Development in Middlesbrough, c.1840–1939', *Middlesbrough: Town and Community, 1830–1950*, ed. A.J. Pollard (Stroud, 1996), 53–80.

Temperley, H. and M. Bradbury, 'Introduction', *Introduction to American Studies*, ed. M. Bradbury and H. Temperley (London and New York, 1987), 1–21.

Thane, P., 'Government and Society in England and Wales, 1750–1914', *Cambridge Social History of Britain, 1750–1950*, Vol. III, *Social Agencies and Institutions*, ed. F.M.L. Thompson (Cambridge, 1990), 1–61.

Thernstrom, S., *The Other Bostonians: Poverty and Progress in the American Metropolis, 1880–1970* (Cambridge, MA, 1973).

Tholfsen, T.R., *Working Class Radicalism in Mid-Victorian England* (London, 1976).

Tilley, P. and C. French, 'Record Linkage for Nineteenth-century Census Returns: Automatic or Computer-aided?', *History and Computing*, 9 (1997), 122–33.

Tirado, D.A., E. Paluzie, and J. Pons, 'Economic Integration and Industrial Location: the Case of Spain before World War I', *Journal of Economic Geography*, 2 (2002), 343–63.

Tocqueville, A. de, *De la Démocratie en Amérique*, trans. A. Goldhammer (New York, 2004 [1835]).

Tomlin, D.M. and M. Williams, *Who Was Who in Nineteenth-century Cleveland* (Redcar, 1987).

Tomlinson, W.W., *The North Eastern Railway, Its Rise and Development* (London, 1914).

Turner, F.J., *The Frontier in American History* (Malabar, FL, 1985 [1920]).

Turner, J.J., 'The Frontier Revisited: Thrift and Fellowship in the New Industrial Town, *c*.1840–1914', *Middlesbrough: Town and Community, 1830–1950*, ed. A.J. Pollard (Stroud, 1996), 81–102.

Warren, K., *Consett Iron, 1840 to 1980: A Study in Industrial Location* (Oxford, 1990).

Webb, S. and B. Webb, *English Local Government, 4: Statutory Authorities for Special Purposes with a Summary of the Development of Local Government Structure* (London, 1963 [1922]).

Weindling, P., 'Linking Self Help and Medical Science: the Social History of Occupational Health', *The Social History of Occupational Health*, ed. P. Weindling (1985), 2–31.

Welton, T.A., 'On the Distribution of Population in England and Wales and its Progress in the Period of Ninety Years from 1801 to 1891', *Journal of the Royal Statistical Society*, LXIII (1900), 527–89.

Williams, M., *The Pottery that Began Middlesbrough* (Redcar, 1985).

Wilson, J.F. and A. Popp (eds), *Industrial Clusters and Regional Business Networks in England, 1750–1970* (Aldershot, 2003).

Woods, R., *The Demography of Victorian England and Wales* (Cambridge, 2000).

Woods, R., *Death before Birth: Fetal Health and Mortality in Historical Perspective* (Oxford, 2009).

Woollard, M., *The classification of occupations in the 1881 census of England and Wales,* Historical Censuses and Social Survey Research Group Occasional Paper, No.1, Department of History, University of Essex (1999).

Yasumoto, M., *Industrialisation, Urbanisation and Demographic Change in England* (Nagoya, 1994).

Yasumoto, M., 'Migrants in Middlesbrough in the Nineteenth Century: A Possibility to Study a Longitudinal Migration Profile and Others', *The Economic Review of Komazawa Univ*ersity, 31(3) (1999), 1–36.

Yasumoto, M., 'Medical Care for Industrial Accidents in a Late-nineteenth Century British Voluntary Hospital: Self-help, Patronage, or Contributory Insurance?', *Michael* (Publications of the Norwegian Medical Soc.), 3(3) (2006), 135–56.

Index

Acts of Parliament, Local and Personal   6,
    17–21, 63, 187
Adamson, George   6
Addison, R.   21
agriculture   7, 92–3, 118
Alexander, James   139, 141–2, 146
Alliance, British and Foreign Fire and Life
    Insurance Co.   3, 4
apprenticeship   152–4
arbitration *see* industrial arbitration

Baare, Louis   36
Backhouse family 4
Baring, Francis, of Baring Brothers   3
Barrow-in-Furness   2
Bell, Sir Isaac Lowthian   35, 52–3, 192
Benson, G.H.   52–3
Birkbeck, Henry   3–4, 6
Blenkinsop, William   17
Bochumer Verein   36, 191
Bolckow, Henry F.W.   14, 17, 19, 26, 46, 51,
    153, 179
Brick-making   4, 5
Briggs, Asa   1, 177
Britain, Joseph   181
Budd, J. Palmer 52
building societies *see* mutual societies and
    self-help

cartels 44–5, 192
Chapman, George   17
charity *see* religious institutions; mutual soci-
    eties and self-help
Chilton, William   3
Cleveland Main Seam *see* ironstone mining
Cleveland Warrant Stores   27, 29–31, 43,
    45, 47, 48–51
coal transportation   1–2, 6
Connal, William   49
Consett, Warcop   3
construction industry   7–9
Craster, Dr   181
crime   105–8, 208–12
Crompton, Henry   189–90
Cubitt and Donkin   5, 6

Dale, David   189
Darlington   6, 18, 101–3, 194
De L'isle and Dudley, Lord   181
demography   61–109; age structure   63–5;
    birth rates 67; causes of death 70–1, 164;
    death rates 70–1, 82, 164–5; dependency
    ratio 196–8; family structure 84–7, 131–4;
    illegitimacy 68–9 ; infant mortality (IMR)
    68–9; 195, 206–7; marriage rates 68–71,
    74, 85–7, 120–2; morbidity rates 158–65;
    mortality 67 ; population growth 7–8,
    62–8; record linkage methodology 71–5,
    110; sex ratio 65–7, 105–6; stillbirth rates
    (SBR) 68, 195–6; suicide rates 68–9; *see*
    migration
Dixon, John   14
docks *see* Middlesbrough, port of
Dowlais Iron Co.   111, 114, 119, 122, 175
Durkheim, Émile   106, 177

education 43, 51, 152–4; *see* Middlesbrough
    institutions
employers' associations   110, 154–5; Cleve-
    land Ironmasters' Association 27, 43–5,
    49, 154–5, 188; North of England Iron
    Manufacturers' Association 27, 43–4,
    154–5, 173–4, 188, 189
engineering   10, 137–46; Acklam Pipe
    Foundry 58; Anderston Foundry 58;
    Cleveland Bolt and Nut Works 58;
    Cochrane Grove and Co. 58; Crewdson,
    Hardy, and Co. 58; Gilkes, Wilson 180;
    Hill and Ward 58; Jones Brothers 58; Joy
    and Co. 58
epidemics   182–3, 196–7; *see* hospitals;
    medical services
Essex, University of, History Data
    Service 126
Evans, William   14
export base   18–19, 33, 39–40, 46, 51, 117

Fairbridge, William   17
Fallows, William   17, 46, 51
Feversham, Lord   181

Garvey, John   173
gasworks   4, 5, 20
Georgs-Marien Mining and Foundry Co. 92–3
German Steel Works Association 44
Germany: Aachen 75–6; Berlin 75–6; Bochum in the Ruhr 13, 76, 80, 89, 91, 93, 94, 95, 137, 152; Dortmund 95; Duisburg 67, 72, 91, 93, 95; Düsseldorf 75–6, 81, 94; Essen 95; Frankfurt 94; Georgsmarien-hütte 92–3; Karlsruhe 73; Köln 75–6 ; Krefeld 89; Lower Rhine 95; Magde-burg 75–6 ; Münster 75–6; Quedlinburg 75–6; Ruhr valley 95; see iron and steel industry; Migration
Gibson, Francis   3
Gilkes, Edward   179
Gillot, Thomas   53
Gjers, John   35
Glasgow Exchange   47
governance   25–6, 178–80, 186–7;   see Middlesbrough local government
Graves, Ann   4
Graz (Austria)   80, 81, 90, 93, 96, 131, 135
Gribbin, John   18
Guisborough   102
Gurney family   3–5

Heckscher–Ohlin model   42
Holmes, John Gilbert   18
hospitals: Broomlands Children's 183; Cleveland Asylum 183; Coatham Convalescent Home 182; funding 158, 165–78, 180–7; Glasgow Maternity 196; Hemlington Smallpox 183; Leeds General Infirmary 164, 167–8, 185; Middlesbrough Workhouse Infirmary 183; North Ormesby (Middlesbrough Cottage Hospital) 157–78, 179, 181–2, 184–7; North Riding Infirmary 178–87; Royal Maternity Charity, London 196; West Lane Isolation   182–3
housing: company-sponsored 12–14; house-building 7–15; houses with shops 12–15; lodgers 15, 84, 132; owner-occu-pied 12–13
Howson, Mr   52
Hughes, Thomas   190

industrial accidents and injuries 157–9, 161–5, 169–70, 173; see hospitals; medical services
industrial arbitration 27, 44, 154–5, 188–90, 198; Board of Arbitration and Conciliation for the Hosiery Trade 189; Board of Arbi-tration and Conciliation for the Lace Trade 189; Board of Arbitration and Conciliation for the North of England Manufactured Iron Trade 27, 43, 57, 154–5, 188–90
industrial clustering and agglomera-tion 28–60, 183, 188, 190
industrial innovation and diffusion 34–5, 43–5, 51–4, 191–5, 198; collective invention 44–5, 53–4; see iron and steel industry, Cleveland Practice
industrial location 41–4, 193–4
industrial structure 110–15, 177, 192–5, 198
iron and steel industry 9–11, 18–19, 21–2, 28–60, 110–15, 188–95; calcination 34; blast furnaces 34–6, 54, 113; Cleveland Practice 34–6; Gilchrist-Thomas Process 115, 153–4, 191; markets 36–41, 191–3, 202–5; transport 38–40
iron and steel industry, in England 29–32, 190; Scotland 31–2; Wales 32, 111, 114–15, 119–20; Germany, 32–3, 36–8, 44–5, 191–2; Europe 32–3, 36–8, 55; United States of America 32–3, 35–8, 191–2; Japan 36–8
iron- and steel-works; Bell Brothers 14, 56, 172, 173, 174, 181, 192; Bolckow, Vaughan and Co. 4, 14, 23, 43, 56, 57, 114, 115, 119, 170, 175, 181, 185; Clay Lane and South Bank Iron Works 168; Cochrane and Co. 14, 168–9, 170; Consett Iron Co. 189; Fox, Head and Co. 56; Gilkes, Wilson 43, 56, 180; Gjers, Mills, and Co. 168; Hopkins, Gilkes and Co. 57; Port Clarence Ironworks see Bell Brothers; Samuelson and Co. 170; Snowden and Hopkins 168, 169, 170; Witton Park Mill 175; and see Bochumer Verein; Dowlais Iron Co.
iron workers 35–6, 92, 101, 111–15, 146–56; see trade unions
ironmasters 26, 47, 179, 180, 181, 195; district 34, 56; see employers' associations
ironstone mining 2, 28–9, 114, 115; imports 191
Irving, John   3

Kane, John   152, 189
Kettle, R.   190
Kingston University, Centre for Local History Studies   72, 75

labour market 110–56, 175; participation rates 198–9; recruitment 115; subcon-tracted labour 111–14
Laws, William   18

Manchester Royal Exchange 48
Marshall, Alfred 41, 58, 152, 193–4
Martin, Simon 3, 5
Mary, Sister, of Anglican Christ Church Sisterhood 169
medical services 157–87, 198; Medical Office of Health 183; National Health Service 187; *and see* hospitals
Menelaus, William 52–3, 111, 175
Merthyr Tydfil 119, 122
Middlesbrough industries and businesses: *see* agriculture; brick-making; construction; engineering; gasworks; iron and steel; potteries; railways; ship-building
Middlesbrough institutions and public buildings: Chamber of Commerce 27, 43, 45–6; Cleveland Club 48; Cleveland Institution of Engineers 44–5, 52–3; Department of Science and Art 153; Iron and Steel Institute 44–5, 52–3; Iron Works Building Society 14; Literary and Philosophical Society 46; Mechanics' Institute 44, 51, 152–3, 179; Royal Exchange 27, 43, 45–8; School of Science 153; town halls 20, 23, 27, 47; workhouse 183; and *see* hospitals
Middlesbrough local government 15–27, 178–87, 195; Board of Guardians 183; Borough Council 18–27; common council 16; finance 11–12, 19–26; Improvement Commissions 17–21; Justices of the Peace 19; Local Board of Health 19, 26–7; policing 22–3, 105; town surveyors 16; *see* governance
Middlesbrough places: Albert Park 179, 187; Eston 18; Linthorpe 7, 19, 62–3; Marton 19; Monkland 3; Normanby 19; Ormesby 19; South Bank 19
Middlesbrough, port of 1–6, 18–19, 43; Middlesbrough Dock Co. 5, 6
migration: age-specific 77–81, 87–9; inward 1, 9–10, 65–6, 75–9, 116–28, 146–56; internal in Germany 61, 67, 72–4, 80, 81, 87–98, 103, 137, 138, 139; internal in USA 62–3, 76, 87–9, 93, 103, 137; Irish 9–10, 65–6, 90, 99–101, 120–37, 175; outward 73, 76, 79–85, 126–8, 130–1, 135, 198; persistence 87–98, 131–2, 134–5; profile 75–87; Scottish 9–10, 65–6, 90, 99–101, 122–3; skill-specific 9–10, 91–5, 116–28, 137–56; stepwise 99–104; Welsh 65–6, 90, 99–101, 119–22; *see* demography
Mordue, Charles 144–6

Mundella, A.J. 189–90
mutual societies and self-help 14, 107–8, 158, 165–78, 198; building societies 14; cooperative societies 184; friendly societies 184; Independent Order of Oddfellows 185; Roman Catholic Fund 172; sick clubs 172

National Provincial Bank 181, 185

occupations 7–10, 92, 136–7
Otley, Richard 9, 18
Owners of the Middlesbrough Estate 2–8, 16–17, 18, 21, 25–6, 47, 201

Palmer, C.M. 53
parliamentary representation 19
Pease, Edward 3
Pease family 1, 4, 6, 180–1
Pease, Joseph 1, 3–6, 8, 9, 18, 21, 47, 181
police *see* Middlesbrough local government
Poor Law Board of Guardians 183
population *see* demography; migration
potteries 9; Middlesbrough Pottery Co. 4, 5, 9

Quakers (Society of Friends) 3–6

railways 1–7; railway towns, 2; *and see* Stockton and Darlington Railway Co.
Ramsey, Robert 18
religious institutions: Anglican Christ Church Sisterhood 169; Anglican Order of Holyrood 178–9; Roman Catholic Church 180
Richards, E. Windsor 119
Richardson, Overend and Co. 4
Richardson, Thomas 3–4, 6, 21
Rothschild, Nathan Meyer 3

Samuelson, Sir Bernhard 153
Schofield, Richard 139–41, 143, 146
Scottish Pig Iron Association 49
self-help *see* mutual societies
Sharp, Isaac 18
ship-building: Raylton, Dixon and Co. 58
shops and shopkeepers 12–13, 15, 26, 27, 91, 195
Sidney, Henry 18
Smith, J.T. 52
Stockton 19, 101–3
Stockton and Darlington Railway Co. 2–7, 17–18, 43, 49, 50, 180
Stokesley 102

strikes and lockouts   44, 114, 186, 188–9
Sunderland   101–3

Taylor, William   179
technological innovation and diffusion *see*
     industrial innovation
Tees, River: Conservancy Commission   43;
     Tees navigation 43
Teignmouth, Lord   181
town planning   3–27, 195
trade unions   27, 44, 110, 137–46, 152,
     155–6; Amalgamated Society of Engineers
     138–46, 174, 176; National Amalgamated
     Association of Malleable and Other Iron-
     workers 152, 189; National Association of
     Puddlers, Shinglers, Rollers, Millmen and
     Others 189; Steam Engine Makers Society
     174, 176
Trotter, Peter   181

United States of America: Atlanta 89, 137;
     Boston 76, 89, 91, 93, 137; Massachusetts
     76; Northampton 76, 89; Philadelphia 76;
     Poughkeepsie 76, 89, 137; Rochester 89;
     Waltham 76
urban growth   1–27, 63, 104–5, 195–9, 201

Vaughan, John   14, 51, 119, 153

wage rates   113–15, 146–7, 155, 175–7, 190–1
welfare provision   157–87; *see* hospitals;
     medical services; charities
Whitby   102
Whitwell, T.   53
Williams, Edward   52, 119
Wilson, Isaac   179, 180

Young, Dr   173
Zetland, Earl of   181

Regions and Regionalism in History

Volumes already published

I: *The Durham Liber Vitae and its Context*, edited by David Rollason, A. J. Piper, Margaret Harvey and Lynda Rollason, 2004

II: *Captain Cook: Explorations and Reassessments*, edited by Glyndwr Williams, 2004

III: *North-East England in the Later Middle Ages*, edited by Christian D. Liddy and Richard H. Britnell, 2005

IV: *North-East England, 1850–1914: The Dynamics of a Maritime-Industrial Region*, Graeme J. Milne, 2006

V: *North-East England, 1569–1625: Governance, Culture and Identity*, Diana Newton, 2006

VI: *Lay Religious Life in Late Medieval Durham*, Margaret Harvey, 2006

VII: *Peasants and Production in the Medieval North-East: The Evidence from Tithes, 1270–1536*, Ben Dodds, 2007

VIII: *The Church of England and the Durham Coalfield, 1810–1926: Clergymen, Capitalists and Colliers*, Robert Lee, 2007

IX: *Regional Identities in North-East England, 1300–2000*, edited by Adrian Green and A. J. Pollard, 2007

X: *Liberties and Identities in the Medieval British Isles*, edited by Michael Prestwich, 2008

XI: *The Bishopric of Durham in the Late Middle Ages: Lordship, Community and the Cult of St Cuthbert*, Christian D. Liddy, 2008

XII: *Northern Landscapes: Representations and Realities of North-East England*, edited by Thomas Faulkner, Helen Berry and Jeremy Gregory, 2010

XIII: *The Keelmen of Tyneside: Labour Organisation and Conflict in the North-East Coal Industry, 1600–1830*, Joseph Fewster, 2011

XIV: *The Rise of an Early Modern Shipping Industry: Whitby's Golden Fleet, 1600–1750*, Rosalin Barker, 2011

Printed and bound by CPI Group (UK) Ltd, Croydon, CR0 4YY

23/04/2025

14661041-0002